Just Wanna ® Copyright
FOR MAKERS

A Legal Roadmap for Creatives

Sidne K. Gard and Elizabeth Townsend Gard

C&T PUBLISHING
Another Maker Inspired!

PUBLISHER: Amy Barrett-Daffin

CREATIVE DIRECTOR: Gailen Runge

SENIOR EDITOR: Roxane Cerda

ASSOCIATE EDITOR: Karly Wallace

COVER DESIGNER: April Mostek

BOOK DESIGNERS: April Mostek and Sidne K. Gard

PRODUCTION COORDINATOR: Zinnia Heinzmann

ILLUSTRATOR: Sidne K. Gard

PHOTOGRAPHY COORDINATOR: Rachel Ackley

INDEXER: Johnna VanHoose Dinse

Published by C&T Publishing, Inc., P.O. Box 1456, Lafayette, CA 94549

Library of Congress Cataloging-in-Publication Data

Names: Gard, Sidne K., 2003- author. | Townsend Gard, Elizabeth, 1967- author.

Title: Just wanna copyright for makers : a legal roadmap for creatives / Sidne K. Gard and Elizabeth Townsend Gard.

Description: Lafayette, CA : C&T Publishing, 2024. | Includes index. | Summary: "Learn all the legal ins and outs of creating and repurposing creative work. Find out how to enforce your copyrights and understand how to use public domain content and sell your works legally. Get the scoop on copyright as it applies to various disciplines from quilting to body art"-- Provided by publisher.

Identifiers: LCCN 2024023622 | ISBN 9781644034347 (trade paperback) | ISBN 9781644034354 (ebook)

Subjects: LCSH: Copyright--United States--Popular works. | Fair use (Copyright)--United States--Popular works. | Copyright infringement--United States--Popular works. | Trademarks--Law and legislation--United States--Popular works. | Plagiarism--United States--Popular works. | BISAC: BUSINESS & ECONOMICS / Small Business | LAW / Intellectual Property / Copyright

Classification: LCC KF2995 .T69 2024 | DDC 346.7304/82--dc23/eng/20240528

LC record available at https://lccn.loc.gov/2024023622

Printed in China

10 9 8 7 6 5 4 3 2 1

Dedication

To Ron Gard, who makes everything seem possible and fun, and who makes Team Gard who we are. We love you, and appreciate everything you do, and especially what you did to help us get this book out. Your encouragement and thoughtfulness are appreciated beyond words.

And to Kit Montgomery, who everyday exemplifies what it means to be a maker and an artist, whether it's sewing a hundred felt rats or making comics about vampires that happen to be silly little guys. Thank you for being Sid's partner in crime at art school and for being exactly who you are.

Acknowledgments

To Roxane Cerda for her amazing editing, kindness, and eye for detail, who magically transforms our manuscripts and Karly Wallace, April Mostek, Gailen Runge, Sophia Scardaci, Zinnia Heinzmann, and Johnna VanHoose Dinse. And again, to Nancy Jewell, who got this book series all started. Thanks to Amy Barrett-Daffin, for believing in the *Just Wanna®* series. We are so proud to be part of the C&T family.

To those who taught us writing. To Sid's teachers at the New Orleans Center for Creative Arts: Anya Groner, Tia Clark, Andy Young, Anne Gisleson, and Lara Naughton, who shaped who they are as a writers, and of course, to Yvette Cuccia, the woman who always cheers on our little community of teenaged artists. To Kirin Wachter-Grene, Sophie Goalson, Leila Wilson, and Beth Hetland, who have helped navigate the next stages of writing, art, and life. And to Sid's fifth grade English teacher, Kimberly Lichetenberger, thank you for making writing a constant presence in life. For Elizabeth, it was Robert Wohl (1937–2023), her dissertation chair, and especially Sarita Seinberg Townsend (1940–2008), who read everything Elizabeth wrote many times over, and Robert Joel Townsend (1937–2019), who was so much in so many ways.

The last seven years have been a big journey, and we've made friends along the way. This book could not have been written without tremendous support and insight. To our more than 400 Just Wanna Quilt podcast guests and over 4,000-strong Quilting Army on Facebook, who shared their stories with us, we are so very grateful. The Quilting Army lived this book during COVID-19. We wrote the first version just as lockdown happened, and we had weekly Zoom sessions for months. You formed how we thought about copyright and makers from start to finish, and we love you for that. What quilters do, the world does. And it is reflected in this book. We love the quilting community, and we thank you. And to Scott Fortunoff, Mary Fons, Janice Sayas, and Pam Weeks, who go the extra mile and answer so many ridiculous questions. You are heroic.

To our found family: to Ina Gard, who gives her support to us every day, as a grandmother, mother-in-law, and friend; to Mary Yetta for always being there to eat curry and talk through all the problems; and to Skyler Yetta, an honorary Gard who always makes his own road in life in the best and weirdest ways. To Remy and Patrick, who contribute in their own cat way, and never missed a Zoom meeting. And finally to Rocky and Abigail, who in their own dachshund way, really did try to contribute this time, even if they thought copyright was some kind of yummy treat.

CONTENTS

Introduction   8

How to Use This Book   10

Icons Used in This Book   10

Additional Resources   10

Summing Up   11

Ready? Let's Dive In!   11

Part I: Creating   12

Copyright Basics   13

What is Copyright?   13

Key Copyright Concepts   15

Copyright Law is a Federal System   16

You and the U.S. Copyright Office   18

U.S. Copyright Sits in a Global World   18

A Little Bit of Copyright History and AI Too   20

Economics and Attribution   21

Theories of Creating   22

We All Wear Two Hats   24

What's Your Idea?   25

Fixation   25

Tangible Medium of Expression   25

When an Idea Turns into Expression   26

Idea Contracts   26

Protecting Your Idea   27

The Idea is Just the Starting Point   28

Creating a Copyrightable Work   29

Making an Original Work   29

Making Derivative Works   32

The Copyright is Distinct from the Object   33

What Goes into Your Copyrightable Work?   33

Identifying Non-Protectable Elements 34

What is a Non-Protectable Element? 34
Not Copyrightable Subject Matter 35
Facts Versus Fictional Facts 38
Let's Talk About Shapes, Baby 40
Letters, Words, Titles, and Short Phrases 41
Logos 42
Dance Moves 42
Book Designs 43
Typeface and Fonts 43
Nature 43
Colorization 44
Fabric 45
Jewelry 45
Common Characters, Tropes, and Scenes 45
Games, Toys, Stuffed Animals, and Puppets 46
Putting it All Together 46

Who is the Author? 47

Categories of Author 47
Work for Hire 50
Who Can Be an Author? 54

Creating Photographs 55

The Photographer is the Author 55
Documenting Copyright for Other Kinds of Works 55
Photographs as Fine Art 55
Photographs Don't Extend Copyright 55
Photographs out in the World 56
Using Photographs in Art 56
Photographs on Covers or for Commercial Use 58
Photographs and Videos of Events 58
Registering Photographs at the U.S. Copyright Office 58

Part II: Borrowing 60

An Introduction to Permissible and Impermissible Uses 61

Permissible Uses 61
Not Cool: Infringement 64

Identifying the Public Domain 65

Very Old Published Things? In the Public Domain! 65
Off Limits: Always Under Copyright 68
It Depends: January 1928-March 1989 68
Table for U.S. Works Published Before 1978 69
Unpublished Works Before 1978 70
Foreign Works 70
Pre-1972 Sound Recordings 71
The Strange Case of Artwork 72
The Realist View on Copyright 74
Layers of Copyright, or the MUD System 75
What Can You Do With Public Domain Works? 76
Use Public Domain Works 76

Fair Use Basics 77

What is Fair Use? 77
Fair Use and Comment, Criticism, and Parody 80
Examples of Fair Use 83
Not Fair Use 84

Art and Fair Use 86

Don't Be a Market Replacement 86
Collage Art is Better 86
Using Others' Art in a Commercial Setting 87
First Sale Doctrine and Art 87
Using Images Online for Your Website 87
Another Angle: Code of Best Practices for Visual Arts 88

Using Trademarks   90
What is a Trademark?   *90*
Key Trademark Terms   *91*
The **Rogers** *Test: Determining Source Identifier or Expressive Content*   *92*
Copyright Versus Trademark   *95*
Other Permissible Uses of a Trademark   *95*

No 10% Change Rule ...
But Maybe 90%?   97
How Did This Myth Get Started?   *97*
What If Something is Changed by 90%?   *99*

Studying Commercial Versus
Non-commercial Uses via Fanworks   101
What is a Fandom?   *101*
Why Fans Create Things   *102*
Fan Writing Versus Fan Art When it Comes to Intellectual Property   *103*
Fan Conventions aka the Rise of Cons   *105*
Beware of Section 103(a)   *105*
The Grey Area of Borrowing   *105*

The Copyright Life Cycle Worksheet   106
The Life Cycle Lesson   *106*
Download the Form   *106*
The Five Stages of a Copyrighted Work   *106*
Words of Advice   *107*

Part III: Protecting   110

How Long Does Your Copyright Last?   111
The Term is Based on the Type of Author   *111*
A Little Thing Called Termination Rights   *112*
What Happens to Your Copyrighted Works When You Die?   *112*
Underlying Works   *113*
Terms in Other Countries   *113*

Copyright Notice   114
Diving into Copyright Notice   *114*
What If There is No Notice?   *117*
The Advantages of Copyright Notice   *117*

Copyright Rights Statements   118
The Rights Themselves   *118*
Rights Statements   *119*
What is a Creative Commons License?   *119*

Registering Your Creative Work   121
Why Register at the U.S. Copyright Office?   *121*
Some Basic Questions   *122*
Application Overview   *122*
Before You Start   *123*
Types of Works   *123*
Many Types, Many Opportunities   *125*
Which Application?   *125*
Basic Information for the Registration Application   *126*

Moral Rights   127
Best Practices: Give Credit Where Credit is Due   *128*
The Visual Artists Rights Act (VARA): Copyright Law and Moral Rights   *128*
Integrity of Copyright Management Information   *134*

Licensing and Transferring Your
Copyright   135
Selling Works: Things to Think About   *135*
Copyright Agreements   *135*
Copyright Transfer for Other Reasons   *136*

Part IV: Enforcing 138

When Things Go Wrong   139
  Mechanisms for Addressing Infringement   139
  Going Down the Enforcer Path   140
  Notice and Takedown   140
  Cease and Desist Letters   142
  Social Pressure   143
  In the End, What Do You Get?   143
  Copyright Claims Board: A New Alternative   144
  A Note on Innocent Infringers   144

Copyright Infringement   145
  Right of Reproduction   145
  Additional Defenses to Copying   146
  Substantial Similarity Test   149
  A Fabric and Pattern Designer Sues   154
  Making Exact Copies: Some Common Scenarios   155
  Other Rights and Infringement   157
  Criminal Liability   159

What About Plagiarism?   160
  What is Plagiarism?   160
  Call-Out Videos: YouTube, Social Enforcement, and Plagiarism   161

Copyright Claims Board   162
  Background   162
  Basic Information   162
  Timing and Statute of Limitations   164
  How Much Does it Cost?   165
  What If You Get a CCB Claim Notice as a Respondent?   165
  What About the Smaller Claims Option   165
  What We Know So Far   165

How Far Can You Go? A Different Perspective on Enforcement   166
  Pretty Far   167
  Don't Raise a lot of Money and Compete with the Copyright Holder   170
  Don't Commercialize Your Cool Website   171
  Don't Mess with Dr. Seuss   172
  Don't Use Others' Work Without Permission As a Commercial   173
  Just Get Permission and License, but Fanworks Are Often Okay   173
  A Word of Warning: Copyright Claims Board and Photographers   174
  Respect the Little Guy   175
  Large Lessons from Crochet and Knitting   177
  The Reality of Copyright Today   179

Conclusion   180

Resources   181
  Copyright Office Main Page   181
  Compendium III   181
  Circulars   181
  Fair Use Index   181
  Registering Your Copyright   181
  U.S. Copyright Law   181

Index   188

About the Authors   192

Introduction

Just Wanna Copyright for Makers is a legal resource for the busy, creative entrepreneur.

Copyright happens every day. You take a photo. You create a painting. You write an email. You take months to make a quilt. You take days to create digital fan art. Each of these are creative works that potentially have a copyright.

This book makes copyright more accessible to those who are immersed in creating: artists, quilters, makers, crafters, and other creatives. Many creatives are not aware or do not know anything about copyright law. And what they do know is often murky, or sometimes confusing. We believe that having a strong command of copyright increases creativity and confidence, and on the whole, makes for a better community of making.

Copyright does a lot of heavy lifting, but because of the structure of the system, copyright law is not as straightforward or obvious as studying for a driving test. It is more nuanced and complicated, and it often includes a risk assessment of how likely someone is to sue or react badly to an unauthorized or even a legal use.

We all interact with copyright every day, and yet, most of us will never be involved in a copyright scuffle, even if we technically (whether accidentally or on purpose) commit copyright infringement daily.

Copyright law governs many things, including:

- The creative works of our world—paintings, literature, films, quilts, street graffiti, woodworking, software, and music, to name just a few.

- Our everyday activities—posting photos on Instagram, Pinterest, Facebook, and other social media outlets, writing emails, and doing homework.

- The ability to do Internet searches, record TV shows to watch later, and make copies of software onto your computer.

Photo © Willow Olson

Elizabeth Townsend Gard and Sidne K. Gard are a team: a law professor and an artist/crafter/writer. Together, they tackle the questions surrounding entrepreneurship for start-ups and businesses, as well as the legal issues arising for artists, makers, and creatives.

Elizabeth Townsend Gard (she/her) is a law professor at Tulane University Law School, specializing in copyrights, trademarks, and intellectual property issues (and she loves to quilt). She is also the host of the *Just Wanna Quilt* podcast, which explores the culture and legal side of the quilting and craft industry.

Sidne K. Gard (they/them) is an artist, writer, and crafter. Currently, they're an undergraduate Distinguished Scholar at the School of the Art Institute of Chicago and the managing editor of *F Newsmagazine*.

Together, we set out on a journey to understand and communicate the key legal elements of business to creatives who are also entrepreneurs. *Just Wanna Copyright for Makers* is the result of that work. We explain and translate key terms for you and walk you through the process.

Over the last five years, Elizabeth has interviewed more than 400 people about their relationship to sewing, crafts, and intellectual property for the podcast *Just Wanna Quilt*. Industry leaders, regular quilters, celebrities, lawyers, law professors, artists, and many entrepreneurs have come to talk to her about their experiences. This project began as an exploration of the business of quilting, but it quickly expanded to the craft and art industries and those who love to make. Some were entrepreneurs. Others were hobbyists. And as we learned from them, we saw that their questions and experiences were the same, whether they were knitters selling on Etsy or someone starting a tech company. That's how this book series, *Just Wanna for Makers* began.

This is combined with Sid's expertise as a professional and scholarly artist with their pulse on social media. The book would not be the same without insight, conversations, and discussions between us. Together, we set out to understand what people actually do, and how the law impacts, reflects, or contradicts those creative endeavors.

One of the key ares that people often need information about is copyright law. Copyright is at the core of artists' creations, lives, and businesses. But for many, really understanding copyright law seems out of reach. We are meeting you where you are, hoping to provide a resource that will let you take control of the choices in your artistic and/or entrepreneurial development.

Teddie Bernard (they/he) is a comic artist who is on this copyright journey with us. Teddie's comic *Bad Parable* tells the story of a set of anthropomorphic characters confronting the difficulties of the times we live in. He has graciously agreed to have his characters go on this *Just Wanna Copyright for Makers* journey with us. We have a feeling that what Teddie and his band of characters think about the world of copyright may reflect your own thoughts, and so we welcome them to the narrative. To see more of *Bad Parable* and Teddie's other comics, go to teddiebernard.net.

BEV
the beaver

BEV IS A CHILL GUY WHO LOVES MAKING CRAFTS WITH FRIENDS.

YELLO
the mouse

YELLO IS A CROCHETER WHO ENJOYS THE BEACH.

KAT
the cat

KAT IS A WRITER AND AN ASPIRING ZINESTER.

WINNIE
the Pooh

WINNE (the) POOH IS A FICTIONAL CHARACTER IN THE PUBLIC DOMAIN.

TEDDIE
the cartoonist

TEDDIE WRITES THE COMIC STRIP "BAD PARABLE."

How to Use This Book

This book walks you through the basics of copyright with a maker's view in mind. We encourage you to read through from start to finish to understand the system. If you are having a particular problem, feel free to go directly to that section.

We know that you have likely had experience with copyright—and some of the related common terms such as fair use, but we are not presuming any knowledge. This book has been written for both the beginner and the expert. We hope to help you place copyright into a larger legal context that helps you think through where law intersects with your own making and artistic practice.

PART I: CREATING takes you through the basics of creating works, from what makes a protectable, copyrightable work to who is viewed as the author. By the end of Part 1, you should feel confident in legally making creative works.

PART II: BORROWING looks at the nuts and bolts of what materials you borrow from others' works, and how borrowing occurs.

PART III: PROTECTING begins with discussing how long your copyright lasts. It then looks at how you can increase the protection of your work, including registering your copyright with the U.S. Copyright Office.

PART IV: ENFORCING teaches you different methods for enforcing your copyright when someone tries to infringe on your work and dives into how far you can go in terms of borrowing others' works.

Icons Used in This Book

A few helpful icons are designed to make it easier for you to use this book. When you see these symbols, you'll know what to do.

 Lawyer time icon alerts you that the question or issue at hand may be more complicated than a DIY solution. You are not required to hire an attorney when you encounter something sticky, but we tell you when it may be a wise decision.

 Online resources icon lets you know when additional resources on the Web may be helpful in understanding a particular topic.

Additional Resources

Finally, we want to introduce you to the Copyright Life Cycle Worksheet (page 106) and the weblinks document. Every creative work goes through a process to be made and then, sometimes, put out into the world. This worksheet helps track that cycle from inspiration to creation to publication and then to that work you made becoming inspiration for you or others. It's a cycle! The Copyright Life Cycle Worksheet allows you to feel confident in understanding how the process of making and the systems of copyright work in tandem. You can write down your influences, ideas, resources (creating a legal record), and also recognize what others might use of your work once it is out in the world.

Weblinks are sometimes long and difficult to type accurately. To make it easier for you to quickly find the page you need we've provided a list of links found in *Just Wanna Copyright for Makers*.

To access the document through the tiny url, type the web address provided into your browser window. To access the document through the QR code, open the camera app on your phone, aim the camera at the QR code, and click the link that pops up on the screen.

tinyurl.com/11566-documents-download

Before you begin working your way through the book, open up this document and keep it handy on your computer. When you find a webpage that you want to visit, scroll down and find the corresponding chapter title. Under each chapter title, you'll find a listing of the direct weblinks for each site discussed in the book. Simply click on the link and avoid lots of extra typing.

Web addresses can also change from time to time. We will update the web addresses in this document when notified of a change to any website addresses found in *Just Wanna Copyright for Makers*.

Summing Up

In short, upon reading this book, we hope that:

- You will have a strong understanding of copyright and how to tackle various issues and scenarios that arise.

- You will know the basics of how copyright interacts with your own creative process.

- You will learn how to protect your copyrighted works, and alternatively how to make them more accessible for others to build upon and use your works.

- You will have a toolbox for addressing copyright infringement, both if you find yourself being accused of it, or if someone else infringes on your work.

- You will be able to address various uses, including knowing the different way copyright works when it comes to works you'll sell versus works that are for personal use.

- You can help educate others in understanding the relationship of the law to the creative process and selling creative works in the marketplace.

Ready? Let's Dive In!

We're going to take you through the messy but fun world of copyright, so pour yourself a cup of tea, grab a cookie, and let's do this!

PART I
Creating

Why do we create? What legal elements should we know that will enhance our creative process? How does creating in a commercial setting potentially change what we do?

In this part you will learn:

1 **Copyright basics.** Gain a vocabulary about copyright, learn how it is different from other areas of intellectual property law (and what intellectual property law is), and get ready for your copyright journey.

2 **Ideas.** Find out when an idea becomes a protectable, copyrighted work, and when ideas can be protected by contract law.

3 **Non-protectable elements.** Learn about the building blocks that are not protected by copyright that everyone uses in their creative works. These are the elements of culture that we are all free to use, without getting permission—squares, circles, and so much much more beyond just simple shapes.

4 **Authorship.** Understand who, for legal purposes, is the author. This chapter takes you through the concepts of work for hire, employees, and being an independent contractor.

5 **Taking photographs.** Discover the many legal questions that can arise when taking and using photographs.

Copyright **Basics**

This book is a step-by-step guide through copyright from having an idea to fixing that idea by putting pen to paper (or needle to fabric) and creating a work to protecting and enforcing your copyright to that work.

This book sets out to accomplish two tasks: to help you think about copyright law as you are creating, and if you care about enforcement, to help you protect and understand enforcement choices. Not everything you make or do is protected by copyright, or rises to needing additional protection; or you may actually want to encourage people to use your work and share. We will help you think through that part of the equation as well.

You'll likely need a couple of evenings to read through the book, but then you will have a strong knowledge of copyright, be more proficient at making decisions on the resources you use, and know whether you want to aggressively enforce your copyright or want to share it with the world. You also will have an understanding of what to do if someone thinks you have infringed their work, or if you think someone has infringed yours. And, you will be ready to apply for registration with the U.S. Copyright Office, should you need that level of legal protection for what you are creating.

> *This book sets out to accomplish two tasks: to help you think about copyright law as you are creating, and if you care about enforcement, to help you protect and understand enforcement choices.*

What is Copyright?

Copyrighted works are all around us; from a poster on a wall, a song being played on the radio, a gallery full of fine art, a new building constructed downtown, to the software used in our car. Copyright law is what protects those works, and allows the copyright holder the control to sell, distribute, and make new works. Copyright is about protecting art, photography, architecture, software, music, books, dances, and anything else that is creative.

What's special about copyright is that the moment you create something a **copyright exists**, for more on this concept jump to Common Questions (page 14). It's magical. When you create a work, copyright adheres instantly. You sketch a design for a sculpture. That sketch has a copyright, then when you make the sculpture, that now has a copyright, too.

You can also take several steps to strengthen the protection of your creations. The protection you have on a given work gets stronger if you put a **copyright notice**, that © with the name of the copyright holder and the date, on it, which we'll dive into in Copyright Notice (page 114). A copyright notice lets the world know you are **enforcing** your copyright, which we'll cover in Part IV: Enforcing (page 138). If you then successfully register your copyright with the U.S. Copyright Office you are presumed to be the copyright holder, and you could go to court or use the new Copyright Claims Board, should someone infringe your work. (See Registering Your Creative Work, page 121.) Each step makes your copyright stronger, but you can also decide *not to enforce*, or even share your work.

Copyright can also be thought of in other ways, beyond the mere act of creating. Copyright is:

- **An economic system.** I create, therefore I have the exclusive right to sell my creations and keep others from selling similar creations without my permission. (See Utilitarianism, page 22.)

- **A moral system.** I create, therefore I should be credited with making my creation. (See The Visual Artists Rights Act (VARA): Copyright Law and Moral Rights, page 128.)

- **A trade system.** I create in the United States, and because of treaties, my creations are automatically protected all over the world. (See Copyright Treaties, page 18.)

- **A federal government grant.** I create, therefore the federal government grants me a limited right to control my creation, with exceptions, for a limited time. (See Copyright Law is a Federal System, page 16.)

- **Regulation between creators.** I create but others do too, so I need to know what resources I can use for my creation that don't infringe on others' creations. (See Copyright is About Relationships, page 16.)

- **Complex.** I create but I have no idea if what I do is legal or not, or what to do. Can I sell this work, even if I used a character from a famous comic? How different does my work have to be from the work that inspired my idea? Should I be afraid of the "copyright police"? (That's not really a thing).

We're going to help with all of these scenarios and especially that last one through this book. We will help you sort out what you used for inspiration, how you created your work, how to protect your work, and what happens if someone infringes or claims you infringed on their work.

Common Questions

Before we dive into the nitty-gritty of copyright, let's address a couple of questions we get all the time.

Do I have to do anything to get a copyright? Nope! It just happens when you make a creative thing, but you can take more steps to gain stronger protection.

What do I get with copyright? You have the exclusive right to make copies, distribute, share, and sell your work along with many other rights. We'll explore this more in Copyright Rights Statements (page 118). Though these rights are exclusive to the copyright holder, it doesn't mean others can't use your work and, or elements from your work. Also, your exclusive rights last a long time but not forever, which we'll discuss in How Long Does Your Copyright Last? (page 111).

If you are feeling hesitant, that's okay. We've worked with a lot of creatives over the years, and we get it.

Key Copyright Concepts

Ideas Aren't Protectable

You start with an idea, but ideas themselves are usually not protectable. In What's Your Idea? (page 25) we'll discuss how you might protect an idea using a contract, but in general, until you convert your idea into an actual creation, don't share it!

Some Elements of Creating Aren't Protectable

Non-protectable elements are the building blocks of our culture that everyone can use to create with. This includes things such as shapes and the alphabet, to name two. We'll take you through all of the types of non-protectable elements so that you feel comfortable in your choices in your artistic practice in Identifying Non-Protectable Elements (page 34).

Using Others' Creative Works

You want to use a Vincent van Gogh painting, make fan art of *Oppenheimer*, or option a novel to make into a big-time movie. You want to use existing creative works to create or build upon. This book terms that *borrowing*. There are a number of kinds of legal and illegal borrowing and we'll review these in Part II: Borrowing (page 60).

Public Domain Works

A poem, a painting, a film, for all creative works, their copyright lasts a limited (albeit a long) time. Once the copyright term has expired, then the work comes into the public domain, free for anyone to use in any way they want. This is an important part of how the system works. A work gets copyright protection for a while, then the work is free for anyone in the world to use without asking permission. We'll teach you when that occurs, see Identifying the Public Domain (page 65).

Permissions

Another way to build upon an existing work is to ask permission from the copyright holder, which we'll cover in Permission (page 61). Copyright holders control certain exclusive rights.

Fair Use

You can use a copyrighted work without permission from the copyright holder under certain situations, such as commenting on or criticizing someone else's work. (See Fair Use Basics, page 77.)

Grey Areas of Borrowing

If your uses don't fit into the previous categories, they may or may not be legal borrowing. We'll explore this topic in Part II: Borrowing (page 60) and How Far Can You Go? A Different Perspective on Enforcement (page 166).

Doctrine of Functionality

Copyright does not protect functional things. Functional things include techniques, methods, math, and steps. *However*, the expression of the technique is protectable, for example a manual describing a technique is likely under copyright. This includes a recorded class (for example, YouTube videos). But, the techniques being demonstrated are not protected even if the video itself is, which we'll dive into in Identifying Non-Protectable Elements (page 34).

Aesthetic Separability

What if you have a functional lamp, but the lamp is also a sculpture? If you can separate out the aesthetic part from the functional, then you have a copyrightable work. (See Not Copyrightable Subject Matter, page 35).

Copyright Infringement

You create something, post it online, then find that someone has swiped your creation and they are claiming it as their own. There are mechanisms to deal with this that we'll explain in Copyright Infringement (page 145). The rights in copyright are not absolute. We'll learn about those rights, and the limitations to them in Copyright Rights Statements (page 118), Part I: Creating (page 12), and Part II: Borrowing (page 60).

Copyright is About Relationships

One strange, yet interesting aspect of copyright law is that relationships matter.

- Your relationship with the materials you are using. For example, you used your camera to take a photograph of the elephant at the zoo. (See Creating Photographs, page 55.)

- Your relationship with what you are doing with the work you are creating. For example you are selling photographs of the elephant to the zoo. (See Selling Works: Things to Think About, page 135.)

- Your relationship to how the work was created. For example, you are employed by the zoo to take photographs. (See Who is the Author?, page 47.)

Not Every Finished Work Gains Copyright

Let's say that you purchase a paint-by-number kit. No one expects that somehow a new copyright arises from completing that kit. We will also see that for copyright, you have to have a modicum of creativity (a legal term) in order to gain copyright protection. We will teach you how to evaluate whether you have made it over that bar in Modicum of Creativity (page 29).

Sid and Elizabeth's attempt at a paint by number kit, *All the Flowers*, by Kittie McCall (Gailson, 2022)
Photo © Sidne K. Gard

Bundle of Rights

If your work qualifies for copyright protection, you gain a bundle of rights: the right to make copies, distribute them, publicly display them, publicly perform them, and make derivative works (making something new based on the original work), see The Rights Themselves (page 118).

Copyright Law is a Federal System

In the United States, copyright law is created by the United States Congress, and is a federal law. The current law is the Copyright Act of 1976, which has been updated and added to for the last fifty years. All of copyright law goes back to the Intellectual Property clause in the U.S. Constitution, which allows Congress to pass laws "to promote the progress of science ... by securing for limited times, to authors ... the exclusive right to their respective writings ... " We will be learning the laws that are instilled in this clause. But for now, the key concepts are that copyright lasts "limited times," is given by the government to "authors" who are granted "exclusive rights" to their "writings," see Copyright Basics (page 13).

This is important. Your copyright in a work only exists because a federal law says it does. There is no natural right that what you create is yours. Copyright law gives you that property right. If we didn't have copyright law, you could make up a song, and then everyone could sing it, record it, and do whatever they wanted with it. The Copyright Act of 1976 prevents that, at least in theory. (See Part III: Protecting, page 110.)

Courts interpret the law. Some copyright cases are really important, especially those decided by the U.S. Supreme Court. We will stop and discuss key cases along the way, like *Feist v. Rural Telephone Company* and

Andy Warhol Foundation for the Visual Arts, Inc. v. Goldsmith. When you see these, they are usually italicized to let you know that it is the case, rather than a person that is being discussed. There are other cases from the Federal District Courts (the first step in the legal system) and Appellate Courts (the second step and the step before a case might be accepted by the U.S. Supreme Court). These can be important too, and we will include the relevant cases.

Understanding Case Citations

We will be referring to specific cases at times. These could be district court cases, appellate court cases, or U.S. Supreme court cases. We will include the case name in italics, followed by some numbers, followed by the year.

All copyright cases are federal cases and decisions issued by federal courts are published in printed books called reporters. If you have the name of the case and citation, you can look it up on the Internet. You will find summaries and even the full case. So, let's understand what the citation means. The cases are published in a report, and the reporter is published in volumes, with new volumes being released on a regular basis. Citations are listed in the following manner.

Case name: These are the parties to the case and are presented in italics. *Andy Warhol Foundation for the Visual Arts, Inc. v. Goldsmith*

Location in the federal reporter: 382 (volume number) F. Supp.3d (reporter) 312 (page case begins)

Court and the year: In this case, the Second District of New York (S.D.N.Y 2018)

U.S. District Courts: There are 94 federal district courts in the United States. These are the trial courts, the first step in a copyright case. So, for the Andy Warhol case, the first case is: *Andy Warhol Foundation for the Visual Arts, Inc. v. Goldsmith* 382 F.supp.3d 312 (S.D.N.Y 2018). Broken down, this citation is: *Andy Warhol Foundation for the Visual Arts, Inc. v. Goldsmith* (name) 382 (volume number) F.supp.3d (reporter) 312 (page case begins) S.D.N.Y 2018 the court and the year.

U.S. Appellate Courts: There are thirteen appellate courts. For copyright cases, we often see cases from the Second Circuit Court (which includes New York) and the Ninth Circuit Court (which includes Los Angeles). In the *Andy Warhol* case, the case was appealed to the Second Circuit Court. The citation for that case is *Andy Warhol Foundation for the Visual Arts, Inc. v. Goldsmith* 992 F.3d 99, (2nd Cir. 2021). In this instance, there was a second rehearing at the appellate court level (which happens sometimes), and that citation is *Andy Warhol Foundation for the Visual Arts, Inc. v. Goldsmith* 11 F.4th 26 (2nd Cir. 2021). Broken down, this citation is: *Andy Warhol Foundation for the Visual Arts, Inc. v. Goldsmith* (name) 11 (volume number) F.4th (reporter) 26 (page case begins) (2nd Cir. 2021)—the court and the year.

U.S. Supreme Court: This the highest court in the land. The citations are always: [volume number] U.S. [page number] Date. The *Andy Warhol* case went all the way up to the U.S. Supreme Court. Here is the citation. *Andy Warhol Foundation for the Visual Arts, Inc. v. Goldsmith* 598 U.S. 508 (2023). Broken down, this citation is: *Andy Warhol Foundation for the Visual Arts, Inc.v. Goldsmith* (name) 598 (volume number) U.S. (reporter) 508 (page) (2023)—the year.

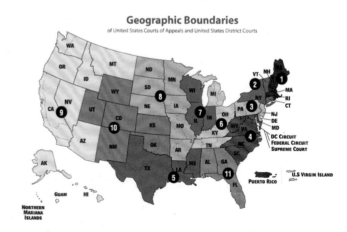

Geographic Boundaries
of United States Courts of Appeals and United States District Courts

The Circuit jurisdictions in the U.S.

You and the U.S. Copyright Office

The U.S. Copyright Office, a branch of the Library of Congress, is the government agency that oversees copyright, including the registration system. (See Registering Your Creative Work, page 121.) The U.S. Copyright Office is a great resource for understanding copyright.

The Library of Congress • *Photo by Shawn Miller/Library of Congress*

EXPLORE THE U.S. COPYRIGHT OFFICE WEBSITE

The U.S. Copyright Office's website is full of helpful information! Go explore at copyright.gov. One of the best resources is their circulars, which explain different key concepts of U.S. Copyright law. You can find these at copyright.gov/circs

FREE ASSISTANCE

There are groups, including the Volunteer Accountants and Lawyers for the Arts, that will help creatives and makers with copyright issues. For more information related to assistance, see vlaa.org/get-help/other-vlas.

Compendium III at the U.S. Copyright Office

Throughout this book you'll see references to the *Compendium of U.S. Copyright Office Practices*. This is a resource created by the U.S. Copyright Office to help their staff determine whether a work qualifies for copyright. Within the compendium, they have compiled all kinds of information from their process along with cases. It is an invaluable source of information and can be used to understand all kinds of issues. For more information, go to copyright.gov/comp3.

U.S. Copyright Sits in a Global World

It is also important to understand one more key issue. Each country enacts their own copyright laws, which governs what happens in their country. Copyright is based on the concept of *territoriality*, or in other words, the laws of a particular country, and in this case, not where the work was created, but where the accused harm is happening. This means that when a situation arises, you need to look at the country where the potential infringement occurred. If you are an Australian author and you are upset about infringement occurring in the United States, you sue *in the United States*. Anyone doing business or making their works accessible to the United States needs to know the laws in the United States.

Copyright Treaties

Early in the history of copyright, the world had a problem. England was only protecting English works, and France was only protecting French works. They had to make agreements so that England would also protect French works, and France would protect English works (called *bilateral treaties*). But then, it quickly got complicated. Where does Spain fit in?, for example, and so multinational copyright treaties were adopted. There have been many, but the foundational one is called the Berne Convention. It governs how copyright works are treated around the world. The best part of the **Berne Convention** is that when you create a work in the United States, that work is automatically protected in most countries in the world! There are approximately seven countries that are not part of the Berne Convention.

THE WORLD INTELLECTUAL PROPERTY ORGANIZATION

To learn more about copyright around the world and the treaties that govern copyright between countries, including more on the Berne Convention, go to the World Intellectual Property Organization, wipo.int.

U.S. TREATY RELATIONS

Want to understand more about the United States's relationship with other countries? Go to Circular 38A, International Copyright Relations at the U.S. Copyright Office copyright.gov/circs/circ38a.pdf.

Types of Intellectual Property

Copyright sits within a legal field called *intellectual property* that includes not only copyrights but also trademarks, patents, trade secrets, and rights of publicity. Each category has its own requirements and potentially protects different aspects of your business.

Here is a breakdown of these categories, their legal basis, protections, and how you would acquire each type of intellectual property.

	Trademark/ Trade Dress	Patents	Copyrights	Trade Secrets	Rights of Publicity
What it Protects	Source identifiers of products, services, and packaging	Inventions, design patents	Creative works, including photographs, books, films, art, and software	Business information deliberately kept secret	Persona of individuals for privacy and for commercial exploitation
Legal Basis	Federal, state, and local protection	Federal	Federal	Federal and state	State (laws vary state to state)
How to Acquire These Rights	Federal: apply at the United States Patent and Trademark Office (USPTO) State: apply to the state Local: common law use only	Apply at the USPTO	Rights arise automatically upon fixation*, but you can apply for registration at the U.S. Copyright Office for stronger protection	Protected, as long as it's kept secret	Varies depending on the state, but usually they just exist

*Fixation is a technical term of copyright, which means that you have fixed your creative work in a tangible medium of expression—a book, film, photograph, digital art, and so forth. You'll learn more about fixation in Fixation (page 25)?

A product or service can potentially be covered by more than one area of intellectual property. Think of an iPhone.

The iPhone encompasses a lot of different types of intellectual property:

- The iPhone logo and name are protected by federal trademarks.
- The hardware has patents on it.
- The software is protected by copyright and patent law.
- Apple definitely has trade secrets about the manufacturing process and other business issues.
- Steve Jobs's right of publicity, even after his death, continues legally for a long time.

As recently as October 2022, the USPTO granted Apple 2,285 new patents including the animation used in the Touch ID setup. Apple also has many trademarks related to the iPhone.

This is all to say that one object can include many components of intellectual property protection.

Another good example is labels. These could be copyrighted. The name and the logo on the label may be trademarks and the look and feel of the label may be trade dress. Even the glue could potentially be patented! There's a lot of overlap between different types of intellectual property.

A Little Bit of Copyright History and AI Too

Copyright is about the right to copy. Get it? It's in the name.

Technology and copyright have gone together from the beginning. Copyright only became a legal concept after the invention of the printing press, because it was only then that copies could be easily and economically made. So, laws developed to decide who could print a book and when that right expired.

As new things could be created by technology, copyright had to adjust to protect them. The nineteenth and twentieth centuries are full of examples. Think about the invention of photography, and then film, but we also had the player piano, radio, televisions, sound recordings, and film strips.

At the end of the twentieth century, technology began to create new mechanisms of transmitting and reproducing creative works. First, we had the photocopier, which allowed people to make copies in ways that previously had only been available to publishers (see Making Exact Copies: Some Common Scenarios, page 155). So too, with the tape recorder. And then came the Internet and digital copies—perfect copies. And with the Internet, new mechanisms for creating works—apps and software that made it easier for us to create our own patterns, films, self-published books, and then distribute them through YouTube, Facebook, Amazon, and other platforms. Technology made copies, but it also created new forms of art: photographs, films, sound recordings, digital art, and 3-D printing are examples, and these can also be easily duplicated and disseminated. And then the Internet changed the game again.

Before the age of the Internet, copyright really only mattered to the big players: the publishers, the movie industry, and the recording industry. We purchased books, we went to see movies, we listened to the radio. Now, we make and disseminate our own movies, photographs, novels, art, music, and pretty much anything else. The dividing line between creating and publishing has become much more murky.

Copyright law takes time to catch up to technology, but it always does. That's why we have many amendments to the Copyright Act of 1976. In some ways, the federal copyright law is a living document, always echoing technology's evolution. At the moment, the issue is Artificial Intelligence, but we were worried about technology many times before. We have had to ask questions. Do photographs gain copyright protection? (Yes.) What about piano rolls? (Yep.) Can people upload perfect copies of songs from compact discs? (Nope.) Can Google make thumbnail images of photographs for searching? (Yes.) And now, we are facing generative AI.

Artificial Intelligence and Copyright

We are in a new era of copyright history in the making. Artificial intelligence has arrived and is taking the world by storm. On the one hand, makers and artists want to use AI to create works. On the other hand, they fear that people will use AI to create works.

The problems raised by new technology are not new to copyright. We saw this with photography. (Will photographers replace painters?) Every time there is a new technology, there is new fear, and also excitement about using that technology to create and replicate. This area is moving fast. Check the U.S. Copyright Office for more updates, copyright.gov.ai

Economics and Attribution

People care about copyright violations in two spheres: economics and attribution.

Economics

When people earn their living from copyrighted works they often care a great deal when someone uses their work without permission. A copyright attorney from a major Hollywood studio once said that every time someone pirates a copy of a movie, they are hurting the families of those who depend on the income from that pirated work—including janitors, scriptwriters, prop masters, and drivers, that those are the people getting hurt. We hear this frequently from pattern makers as well. Their livelihood depends on people purchasing their patterns, and when people copy them, that limits their ability to pay for their rent, mortgage, kid's tuition, vet bills, and so on. There is a sense that it is wrong to take something, that it hurts them personally, and that it is unfair economically.

Attributing Work to the Creator

People also care when someone else takes credit for their work, sometimes even more than the economic injustice. This is called the *right of attribution*, and is part of a larger bundle of rights called *moral rights*. The right to be named, along with a host of other moral rights, is important. Until fairly recently, copyright law in the United States has not been as interested in moral rights, and lawmakers only grudgingly allowed certain visual artworks moral rights protection, and only for a certain period of time. (See The Visual Artists Rights Act (VARA): Copyright Law and Moral Rights, page 128). But as a community and as a society, we care a great deal about moral rights, even if copyright law does not. Not taking credit for something that is not yours, and naming the author is really really important for many. And state laws come in to fill the gap where copyright law lacks, see Moral Rights (page 127).

Commercial Versus Noncommercial Uses

There is a divide in our world between commercial and noncommercial use. Making a crochet pattern you found on Ravelry as a baby gift? Your use is noncommercial, and it is just what the creator of the pattern hopes you do with it. That same designer may feel very differently when you sell the baby blankets in mass quantities using that pattern or sell the pattern as your own. These would be commercial uses. We'll discuss this more in How Far Can You Go? A Different Perspective on Enforcement (page 166). But for now, we turn to theories of why we create.

Theories of Creating

There are three theories that influence our thinking about copyright, and help us to understand all of these scenarios a bit better.

Utilitarianism

Copyright, from the beginning, was recognized as a government-created *bargain*. The United States government gives you an exclusive right to your creative work for a specific time (see Copyright Rights Statements, page 118 and How Long Does Your Copyright Last?, page 111). By giving copyright and control of a work to an author, society benefits (see Who is the Author?, page 47). How? You work hard to make something and make it available to the public, or you work hard to get the creation into museums so we can view it, or you publish a book with your new technique or creation. In all three scenarios, the public benefits from your hard work. This is called *utilitarianism*, and it comes from Jeremy Bentham (1748–1832). This idea of a *utilitarian economic system* is important. Society benefits from your private control. When you think of it as economics, a lot of things start to make sense. Later, society benefits from the relinquishment of that control, with the work coming into the public domain, allowing others to build upon your work (see Use Public Domain Works, page 76).

> *The United States government gives you an exclusive right to your creative work for a specific time.*

Lockean Labor Theory

John Locke (1632–1704) examined how property is created. We start with a world where no personal property exists. Then, someone comes along and picks an apple off of a tree. Locke asserts that by mixing one's labor in picking the apple with the object itself, you create ownership. So, how does this translate into artistic and craft works? Most makers fall into the Lockean Labor Theory. You mix your creativity with resources and create a soft sculpture. It is yours, and you may not have any incentive to sell it. You may give it away or keep it, but you have the right to let the world know it's yours. You mixed a part of yourself into the resources with your creative labor. The basic idea of Lockean Labor theory is this: mix creative labor with things and get something.

Soft sculpture by Kit Montgomery depicting a larger than life blood-soaked rosary modeled after the rosaries given to children. This piece explores childhood religious trauma. Kit mixed a part of their identity with creative labor to produce this piece, ergo Lockean labor theory. • *Photo and artwork © Kit Montgomery*

Personhood Theory

The basic premise here is that people develop their identity when interacting with property. Your wedding ring, a favorite toy, the house that has been in your family for 100 years—these are all things that may define who you are, and you put a value on these things that is beyond how much they cost or the replacement value. They mean more to you than what money can offer.

From left to right, Scruffy, Pinky, and Mimzy, beloved toys in the Gard home. These stuffed animals are so loved they're irreplaceable. • *Photo © Sidne K. Gard*

Think of the tapestry you spent 100 hours making. Not all crafters and artists are creating in a capitalist, get-it-done-as-fast-as-possible way. Some prefer to take time to create something imbued with their own personhood, labor, and creativity. The work has more value than what someone would pay for it.

To look at this another way, consider charity knitting. If you wanted to be most efficient with providing hats to those in need, having a Facebook group spend a year creating 100 hats would not be the first idea. But by doing so, those hats would be imbued with something more, a message to people in need that they matter. That idea that someone the person in need didn't know took the time to make something is meaningful. Crafters engage in these activities all of the time.

Conflicting Theories of Creating

One thing we have seen in copyright since the advent of the Internet is conflict between those creating on a utilitarian model (think record companies, publishers, and movie studios) and the fans and consumers that create out of love of the thing. It took a while for content owners to understand that in the Internet age, fans of their content were going to create, post, and sell things celebrating that content. Some still don't. For the most part though, they seem to have created a balance between protecting their copyright and understanding spaces for creativity for fans. There are also now mechanisms to help with the balance between copyright holders and their fans (see Studying Commercial Versus Non-commercial Uses via Fanworks, page 101).

What is different sometimes in the maker and craft space is the relationship between those making and those learning to make. Commercial content creators are *creating tangible items* for others to use to create tangible items. Unlike going to see the latest Marvel movie and dressing as one of the characters (cosplay), quilters go to their local quilt shop, buy fabric and maybe a pattern, and then they make the quilt themselves. Some fabrics and patterns have warnings not to use them for commercial use, or only for personal use (one we saw read "for personal consumption only"). But what is interesting is that the crafting world is a whole industry that is making things for others to use to make things, which results in interesting boundaries.

El Torres cosplaying as Spider-Gwen from the *Spiderverse* franchise.
Photo © Annissa Mu

We All Wear Two Hats

In many ways, copyright has two hats, and we, as creators, wear them both simultaneously.

- **Creator Hat:** We are all creators of culture. Every one of us takes photos, writes emails, and much more.

- **User Hat:** We are also all users and borrowers of culture. No one creates in a vacuum. We are inspired by art, nature, and our fellow artists and crafters. We build on those that come before us, and those that come after us will build upon what we do.

When you think about copyright, think with both hats—you are a creator who is potentially protective of your works, but to create that work you are a user, relying on others' works, techniques, things in the public domain, and ideas. We are going to work through each of these concepts and more to better understand how copyright works. And of course, the hats matter more if you are using work in a commercial setting. Everything gets more intense.

Our philosophy is simple. Understand how copyright works, make choices, and decide how much you want to protect your work. You are in control. We're here to help, so keep turning these pages.

What's Your *Idea*?

Having an idea for a new creative work is awesome! But you have to do more than just think of something to gain copyright. Ideas themselves, no matter how brilliant, are not inherently protectable by copyright. However, the expression of an idea is potentially eligible for copyright protection.

> *Copyright begins when you **fix an idea** in a **tangible medium of expression**.*

The idea becomes an expression of an idea, and that is potentially a copyrightable work. (See Creating a Copyrightable Work, page 29.) Let's look at these concepts further.

Fixation

When you sew those quilt pieces together and make that quilt top, you have fixed the idea of making a quilt top. It is potentially protected by copyright. Everything fixed is potentially protected by copyright. Your fixed work doesn't need to be finished: a sketch, a recording, a small sample all count. Any fixation works.

Why do you need fixation? Think of a judge deciding whether your sculpture of a giant turtle has infringed someone else's giant turtle sculpture. The law demands fixation in order to gain copyright protection, in part because if there is a dispute between one creator and another, their works can be compared (see Copyright Infringement, page 145).

Tangible Medium of Expression

The tangible part can be any form: paper, fabric, a digital file, a photograph, it just has to be *fixed in a tangible medium of expression*. That's the legal phrase. Tangible can be physical or digital. The full phrase in the Copyright Act of 1976 is: "fixed in any tangible medium of expression, now known or later developed, from which they can be perceived, reproduced, or otherwise communicated, either directly or with the aid of a machine or device." Section 102(a) of the Copyright Act of 1976 (Resources, page 181).

When an Idea Turns into Expression

Ideas are not protected. Only the expression of the idea is. Your version of an idea is protected once you express it in a fixed form. The question becomes where is the boundary between an idea and the expression of that idea. That is sometimes what gets litigated, which we'll discuss in depth in Copyright Infringement (page 145). The court must determine if one party borrowed just the idea or transgressed and borrowed the expression. This is often referred to as the Levels of Abstractions, which is used in copyright infringement cases (see Substantial Similarity Test, page 149). At what point is an abstract idea a protectable expression? We will explore this more later, but for now, know, "Nobody has ever been able to fix that boundary, and nobody ever can," wrote the famous Judge Learned Hand. It's not a precise science.

Idea Contracts

Though ideas are not usually protected, and they are not protected by copyright law, some industries have idea contracts, which do protect ideas under contract law. These are contracts where companies agree to pay you to use your ideas. In these cases, there is a contract that declares that if a company signs the contract to use your idea, you will be compensated for it. If you don't have that kind of contract, no one has to pay for your ideas. You can have an express contract (in writing) or an implied contract (people agree, but it is not in writing), but you have to have a contract if you want to enforce getting paid for your idea.

Don't Blurt out Your Idea and Expect to Get Paid for It

The 2004 case *Keane v. Fox Television Stations, Inc.*, 297 F. Supp. 2d 921 (S.D. Tex. 2004) gives us the concept of the blurting out doctrine. Harry Keane had a great idea for a talent show that he called *American Idol*. He told everyone—in mass mailings, to potential financiers, and to production companies. He even posted the idea on the Internet. Fox Television developed the idea and even called it *American Idol*. The Court decided there was no implied contract. He blurted out his idea everywhere. There was no obligation to pay him. Lesson? Don't blurt.

Pitching Ideas

Some industries have an informal system, where you pitch an idea, like a book proposal, and if the company likes it, you sign a contract. However, there's no contract in place that keeps the company from using your idea with a different author.

Types of Pitching

There are a number of ways we see ideas discussed in the overlap between the legal and creative worlds.

UNSOLICITED IDEAS

Without any request to do so, you pitch your idea. No one asked you for the idea, but you still gave the idea. There is no relationship, expectation of payment, or that you will be involved if someone goes forward with using the idea without you. But they may put a contract in place with you.

IDEAS ENCOURAGED

In this scenario, there is something like a suggestion box where you are offered the opportunity to share your ideas. That's it. There's no expectation that you get to keep the idea that you have put in the box. You have given that idea to them. You should not expect compensation.

SOLICITED IDEAS

You are asked to submit an idea, for example, a book proposal. There is an expectation or an implicit contract that a relationship will arise should they choose your idea.

❖

Protecting Your Idea

What if you want to protect your idea before you have gotten around to expressing it?

- **Don't blurt.** The blurting out doctrine says that if you go around telling people or posting about it online, you can't get too upset when someone else uses it without including or asking you. You gave it away to the world.

- **Contract.** In some fields, you sign a contract that if they use the idea, they will pay you.

- **NDA.** Requesting a signed non-disclosure agreement when pitching something to a company is common, but is beyond the scope of this book.

- **Make it.** Get it fixed in a tangible medium of expression, then share it.

- **Document Your Idea.** Write down your ideas! Then, if later someone thinks or claims that

you copied their work, you can show that you documented your process. When brainstorming and expressing your ideas on the page, here are some things to think about including, from a legal standpoint: the date, where your idea came from, what is influencing your idea, sketches, links, screenshots, and the like.

NAVIGATING CONTRACTS

Think you need a contract and/or have a problem with a promise related to an idea? You may want to hire an attorney to help you.

The Idea is Just the Starting Point

As artists, makers, crafters, and creatives, we all know that ideas are just the beginning. Ideas exist to evolve, and as we fix our ideas into something tangible, they often begin to mean something more to us. We also can go in different directions with the same idea, and that's kind of fun.

Ideas as Artistic Challenges

Drawfee: Starting with a Prompt

A great example of how very different pieces of art can come out of one idea is from the YouTube channel, Drawfee who are four professional artists based out of New York where they challenge each other to do various silly art prompts.

Drawfee videos always start with an idea, and by the end of the video, you'll usually have seen three to four unique pieces of art born out of that idea. In their video, "Making FOUR Different Drawings out of ONE Pose" they commentate their artmaking processes over time-lapse videos of each of them doing their drawings. Though they each started with the idea of the same pose, they each go in very different directions.

Watch any Drawfee video on Youtube at youtube/@drawfee to see how different the creations can be from one prompt. That's idea/expression in action.

Project QUILTING: Ready for the Next Season?

As crafters and artists, we love challenges. Drawfee is just one example, another is Project QUILTING, which has been going on for over a decade and a half. For a few short weeks each year, Kim Lapacek puts out challenges, and quilters have to make a quilt within the given time period. The quilts are posted, and a random winner is chosen. Ideas and prompts have included things such as "Primary Colors", "Flying Geese", "Florals", and others. What happens is amazing work. Each year Kim hosts a twelve-week season with six prompts. For more, see kimlapacek.com/project-quilting.

Ideas are a playspace for us makers. And we all want to be able to play.

Creating a *Copyrightable* Work

Making an Original Work

You create a work, but how do you know that it has copyright protection? Works must meet the qualification of being creative enough to gain copyright protection. You will soon see that not all works that are created are protected by copyright. A work is either protected by copyright or it's in the public domain. Those are the only two choices.

Copyrighted works. A work is protected by copyright if it meets the standard of **originality** which requires a **modicum of creativity** plus **independent human creation**.

Public domain works. Public domain means that a work no longer or never did have copyright protection. (See Identifying the Public Domain, page 65.) The public domain is an important part of the whole copyright ecosystem. Once a work is in the public domain, we all can use the work any way we want.

Originality Standard

Works must be **created** by an **author**. It's in the U.S. Constitution, and it's in the Copyright Act of 1976. Copyright protects original works of authorship. This is called the *originality standard*.

The originality standard has two parts: a modicum of creativity and independent human creation.

Modicum of Creativity

Is your work *creative enough* to gain copyright? Not everything we create qualifies for copyright. You need to have a modicum of creativity to gain

Then they all crowded round her once more, while the Dodo solemnly presented the thimble, saying "We beg your acceptance of this elegant thimble;" and, when it had finished this short speech, they all cheered.

Alice thought the whole thing very absurd, but they all looked so grave that she did not dare to laugh; and, as she could not think of anything to say, she simply bowed, and took the thimble, looking as solemn as she could.

The next thing was to eat the comfits: this caused some noise and confusion, as the large birds complained that they could not taste theirs, and the small ones choked and

Here you can see an original illustration from the first edition of *Alice in Wonderland*. Because *Alice* and the illustrations were published in 1865, it is in the public domain.

copyright. Don't panic. There are good reasons for this that we all want, and it is not based on how clever or how beautiful your work is.

There are three U.S. Supreme Court copyright cases that can help us understand how much creativity is enough creativity:

Burrow-Giles Lithographic Co. v. Sarony, 111 U.S. 53 (1884),

Bleistein v. Donaldson Lithographing Co., 188 U.S. 239 (1903), and

Feist Publications, Inc. v. Rural Telephone Service Co., 499 U.S. 340 (1991).

Creativity is about choices. *Burrows-Giles* tells us that you can be creative, even when using equipment, like cameras. In this case, a photographer took a picture of Oscar Wilde, and the court wrote that the act of deciding the lighting, background, pose of Wilde, and the like qualified as enough creativity to be protected by copyright. That is still true today. When you take a photograph, your choices are enough *creativity* to gain copyright. Photographs have a very low bar of creativity. Other works have a bit more challenge. But the idea is that the choices you make create the copyrighted work.

One of the photographs at issue in the Oscar Wilde photography case.

Copyright doesn't judge for artistic value. *Bleistein* tells us that creativity can come in many forms, and it doesn't have to be "high art" or "fine art." Courts do not judge how good a work is. That's called **aesthetic non-discrimination.** This case was about circus posters, and circus posters in 1903 qualified for copyright, even if people thought they were merely advertisements and not respectable artwork.

From childhood scribbles to masterpiece paintings, the skill or merit of a work doesn't matter when it comes to copyright.

The circus poster in *Bleistein* that gave us the concept that copyright is not based on an aesthetic judgment.

Copyright requires a creative spark. Finally, *Feist* tells us that the requirement of creativity is low. It says that most works can easily reach that requirement, "as they possess **some creative spark** 'no matter how crude, humble, or obvious' it might be. Originality does not signify novelty; a work may be original even though it closely resembles other works so long as the similarity is fortuitous, not the result of copying [...]."

Feist concerned phonebooks, and whether alphabetizing by last name was creative enough to gain copyright protection. The court determined that it was not.

So, what is it in your field that is similar to alphabetizing? Something that if someone did that, it wouldn't be protectable because it wouldn't have enough creativity. Would it be a standard pattern or typical way of doing things? Ask yourself, is what I am considering protecting like the alphabetizing in the *Feist* phonebook case?

You have to have creative labor. Just because you worked hard on something or spent a lot of money on something doesn't mean copyright will reward you. We call that *sweat of the brow,* and no copyright is rewarded in the United States for non-creative labor. (This is not necessarily true in the United Kingdom, or in other parts of the world.)

Copyright is about creativity, and so the labor that is protected is creative. The 1863 *Jane Stickle* quilt is a great example. There's a quilt made in the 1860s that is complicated, takes a long time to make, and became really popular. People try to make it exactly as the original author. Sometimes they change colors, but even though it is difficult, the sweat of making it does not allow for a new copyright.

Andi Barney decided to make a Dear Jane quilt during COVID-19, and by 2024, she had completed her version. She made a lot of choices on which fabric to use, which color to use in which block, and how to quilt it. But none of that was enough to gain a new copyright. The labor she did was sweat of the brow. And the creative labor just didn't provide a new copyright on the work. Recolorization isn't enough. See Colorization, page 44.

Sampler Quilt, Jane A. Stickle, 1863, used with permission from The Bennington Museum.

Quilt top by Andi Barney • *Photo by Andi Barney*

Let's sum up modicum of creativity. Putting things together in a creative way, regardless of how they "look," is how you get to a modicum of creativity.

Independent Creation Requirement

The creative work must be done by a human. That's what's meant by independent creation. There must be a human author, for more on authorship, see Who is the Author? (page 47). This also means that facts and things that already exist are not authored, and therefore cannot gain protection, which we'll review in Identifying Non-Protectable Elements (page 34).

Let's consider facts versus a compilation of facts.
Feist also addresses one more key element: facts are not authored, and therefore do not gain protection under copyright. The word "facts," in *Feist*, stands for many kinds of non-protectable elements, which we'll explore in Identifying Non-Protectable Elements (page 34). A fact is not protectable by copyright because it is not independently authored. This includes a circle, things found in nature, and the date you were born. Facts are really quite a broad category: they are things discovered, not made by humans, or data, for example. Common objects are included as well.

However, if you put a bunch of facts together, that may be eligible for copyright. That is called a **compilation of facts**. A compilation is the **selection, arrangement, and coordination** of pre-existing materials. That is its legal definition. This can include copyrighted and non-copyrightable elements. As long as the selection, arrangement, and coordination have a modicum of creativity, the work gains copyright protection. When we choose blocks, fabric, and how we will quilt the top, we are creating a compilation.

Our compilations are protectable because of our selection, arrangement, and coordination. This is a way to think about the creative process. Everything we do as creatives in some way requires a thoughtful selection, arrangement, and coordination. Even taking an impromptu photograph. Why did you paint that vase blue? Why put these beads next to each other? It's a part of the creative process.

A subset of compilations is collective works. A collective work is a group of copyrighted works put together, such as in anthologies or books where different authors contribute independently protectable works, like short stories. For a work to be considered a collective work (as opposed to the larger category of compilation), each contribution must be copyrightable on its own (either still under copyright or in the public domain). Being included in the collection doesn't change the original copyright. The collection itself gets copyright protection for its selection, arrangement, and coordination.

Making Derivative Works

When you make something, you are usually making an original work. But sometimes you are building on an original work to create something new, what is called a *derivative work*.

A derivative work is a work based upon one or more pre-existing works. You start with an already existing work, then make something new, "such as a translation, musical arrangement, dramatization, fictionalization, motion picture version, sound recording, art reproduction, abridgment, condensation, or any other form ..." 17 U.S.C. Section 103.

Originality Standard for Derivative Works

The derivative work must be "recast, transformed or adapted" in such a way as to be distinct and identifiably different from the original.The recasting, transforming, or adapting is how you meet the originality standard for a derivative work.

The Exclusive Right to Make Derivative Works

The copyright holder of the original work has the exclusive right to create derivative works (see Copyright Rights Statements, page 118). You need permission (implied or explicit) to create derivative works of another's copyrighted piece. In creating a derivative work (with permission), you gain certain rights to the new creation, but the underlying work still belongs to the copyright holder. The takeaway is that a derivative **must recast, transform, or adapt** *an original work into something distinct and different.*

Quilt artist Lyric Kinard created a quilt using images from the New York Public Library. She took a photograph and then collaged it into a quilt. The photograph was an image that was old enough to be in the public domain (See Use Public Domain Works, page 76.) She then collaged it into a quilt, using other resources and her creativity. She created a derivative work.

Quilt by Lyric Kinard • *Photo by Elizabeth Townsend Gard*

Exceptions

Derivative works are made from existing works. Sometimes these are authorized by the copyright holder and sometimes they aren't. Think fanart (see Studying Commercial Versus Non-commercial Uses via Fanworks, page 101). And sometimes, even though they are not authorized by the copyright holder, the law allows it—this is, in part, what fair use allows. If you meet certain qualifications under Section 107 of the Copyright Act of 1976 (fair use), then you can make a derivative work using someone else's original work without permission, which we'll unpack in Fair Use Basics (page 77). These blurry exceptions can get complicated in our world, but legally unauthorized derivative works that are not based on public domain works and do not qualify for fair use are not protected by copyright. It becomes up to the copyright holder what to do. (See How Far Can You Go? A Different Perspective on Enforcement, page 166.)

The Copyright is Distinct from the Object

If you create a painting and sell it, unless stated otherwise, you are selling the physical copy. Copyright does not automatically transfer with the purchase of the object. If you want copyright to transfer, you have to create a contract *signed and in writing* (see Licensing and Transferring Your Copyright, page 35).

What Goes into Your Copyrightable Work?

You have your idea. Awesome! But creative works are made up of more than just an idea. We have identified a variety of types of resources that creatives use, besides, of course, your skill, imagination, and ideas. The next chapter starts to think about the resources available to all makers, and then Part II: Borrowing (page 60), looks at all of the ways artists borrow from existing works.

Identifying *Non-Protectable* Elements

> *You can use non-protectable elements to your heart's content! What you have to be careful of is moving in on someone's protectable expression of those works.*

What is a Non-Protectable Element?

Non-protectable elements are key to building any copyrighted work. You don't want to lock basic building blocks up because we all have to use them. And that's the role of copyright: to be the gatekeeper between expression, ideas, and non-protectable elements. Creativity is built upon non-protectable elements that we all can use such as the alphabet, words, circles, and colors. There are more, and this chapter looks at the building blocks we use to create works.

There's a big list of common elements everyone can use, and there are different reasons for each item on the list. On this list, you'll find common elements that every art or craft uses, including shapes, stock characters or elements of the craft, artistic styles, basic tropes often seen in the art or craft, scenes, and plot points. This chapter goes into depth into many building blocks—those that are non-protectable, and also those that may or may not be, depending on a number of factors.

NON-PROTECTABLE ELEMENTS IN THE COMPENDIUM

The U.S. Copyright Office's compendium defines all of the elements and more that we are going to go through. Want a more in depth explanation? You can find the compendium online by going to copyright.gov/comp3.

CIRCULAR 33: WORKS NOT PROTECTED BY COPYRIGHT

The U.S. Copyright Office has prepared a short pamphlet on the general topic of works not protected by copyright. See copyright.gov/circs/circ33.pdf.

In many ways, a copyrightable work is something that starts with an idea and then combines non-protectable elements with your own creativity (even a modicum) in a particular selection, arrangement, and coordination to create an original work. See how much you already know about copyright? (For a refresher, see Copyright Basics, page 13.) In this chapter, you'll learn to identify non-protectable elements. You use these in a number of ways. For example, maybe you want to use a fleur de lis, which is not protectable as a shape on its own. Use it! Knowing the list will help you feel more confident in your choices.

On the flip side, someone might like the idea they found in your work, where you use fleur de lis. Unless their use has crossed over to copying your expression, they can also take that idea and use it, which we covered in What's Your Idea? (page 25) and we'll cover in more depth in Copyright Infringement (page 145).

You may also be making patterns, directions, or developing techniques. This chapter will help you recognize when what you are doing is covered by copyright, and when it is free for everyone to use.

Not Copyrightable Subject Matter

Copyright covers **creative works**, but not the techniques or tools used to make those creative works, which we discussed more in Doctrine of Functionality (page 15).

Copyright does not protect:

- **Techniques and procedures.** The techniques you develop, or learn from a YouTube video, are not protectable by copyright. Nor is the technique you follow from a craft book. (The YouTube video or the book itself, of course, is protected, in its expression). You can use the techniques, teach them to others, and profit from them.

- **Math.** A knitted plushie may be protected by copyright, but the directions—the math is not. Same goes for the ingredients for the recipe for cookies or the ratio for dyes.

- **A mere listing of ingredients or contents.** This means that a recipe is not protectable. An explanation in a cookbook, crafts book, or manual can be copyrightable in the selection, arrangement, and coordination, as well as the text, photos, and drawings. But the functional ingredients or directions themselves are not protectable.

- **Things protected by patents.** If you have a patent on it, it's likely not also protectable by copyright. The product Bloc Loc is a ruler system that locks a seam so that when cutting, a pieced seam doesn't move. Block Loc has a patent on the technology, and a trademark on the name. They created a pattern book, which is protected by copyright. But the rulers themselves do not have a copyright on them because they are not protectable under copyright.

With this, let's look at more specific things that have been identified by the Copyright Office as not protectable by copyyight.

Patterns, Stencils, How-to, and Templates

Patterns, stencils, how-to, and templates often have functional elements. But the expression of how to use or make the pattern, template, and so on. is likely protectable. You write a book, you make a YouTube video. That's your expression.

Protectible examples could be:

- **Pattern books.** The book itself is protectable.

- **Drawings, photographs, and text.** These elements in a pattern book are protectable as long as they have sufficient originality. (See Originality Standard, page 29.) This includes introductions, photographs, technical diagrams that demonstrate cutting, stitching, weaving, or other techniques required by the pattern, as well as illustrations of the completed items.

Non-protectable elements include:

- **The technique or steps being demonstrated.** Registration does not extend to the method, techniques, or tools. Copyright does not mean that it protects the thing itself being demonstrated.

- **The individual pieces of the pattern that creates a useful article.** Registration does not extend to the individual pattern pieces that are used to create a useful article. For example, the parts of a dress such as the sleeve, pocket, or the like are not protected by copyright.

Clothing and Sewing Patterns

Clothing is not protectable under copyright because it is seen as functional, which we covered in Doctrine of Functionality (page 15). We buy dress patterns because they are helpful and convenient, not because we can't make the dress unless we pay its author. Although the pattern itself, the photo, directions, and packaging, with sufficient selection, arrangement, and coordination is likely protectable, the shapes making up the pattern and the math of the pattern are not protectable.

Merger Doctrine and the Blank Forms Rule

There are two more functional elements. If the only way to say what needs to be said is one way, then the **merger doctrine** applies and the idea and the expression merge into one. This means that others can use it too. You can't be the only one to be able to express: "Cut 2 of these and sew them with a ¼″ seam." That's not a protectable expression.

Related to this is the **Blank Forms Rule**. Blank forms are not registrable when they are designed solely to convey information. Examples of blank forms include time cards, graph paper, account books, diaries, bank checks, scorecards, address books, report forms, order forms, and vouchers.

The Concept of Conceptual Separability

The functional aspects of works are not protectable, but if there are aesthetic elements that can be distinct from the functional elements, those can be protectable. The decorations on a blank form may be protectable. For example, checks decorated with illustrated puppies. The illustration of the puppies is protectable but the check form itself is not.

In contrast, our Big Trademark Application List from *Just Wanna Trademark for Makers* is not a blank form, as there is selection, arrangement, and coordination—choices and art that make it different from a blank form. But the idea of the trademark list is not protectable, and the practical aspects are separable from the aesthetics of the list.

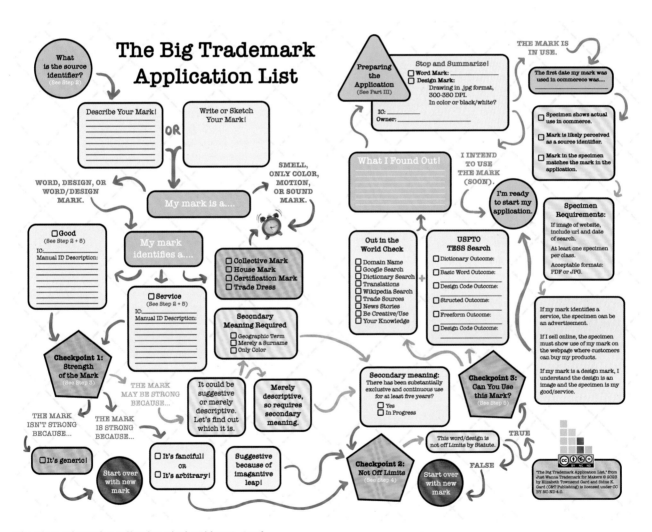

The Big Trademark Application List by Sidne K. Gard

Facts Versus Fictional Facts

Facts are not created, and therefore are not protected by copyright law, which we discussed in Originality Standard (page 29). That seems simple enough, but copyright, of course, has to complicate it. What counts as facts? Math. Dates. Historical information. No one owns these elements. Note: math is seen as both functional and a fact.

Fictional Facts

What about fictional facts treated as facts? For example, imagine you are obsessed with *Gilmore Girls*, and know all of the plot points of the show. Those are *not* facts. The fact that Lorelai and Rory live in Stars Hollow is not considered a fact because fictional stories are not facts, they were *created* (see Originality Standard, page 29).

There is a case where a quiz book about the television series *Seinfeld* was found infringing because the authors of the quiz book did not ask permission of the copyright holder to use the facts of the show. The plot and character details of *Seinfeld* were made by humans, and so they are protectable. They met the originality standard.

Reality Check: Though people shouldn't be able to create things with fictional facts, they do. Of course they do. We live in a world filled with fan culture and of people selling fan made works. It's totally breaking copyright law, but often the owners of the intellectual property only start to enforce it when there are large commercial interests at play. We'll be talking more about selling fan works in Studying Commercial Versus Non-commercial Uses via Fanworks (page 101) and How Far Can You Go? A Different Perspective on Enforcement (page 166). When someone makes a list of all of the books Rory Gilmore read on *Gilmore Girls*, and then sells that list as a coloring book on Etsy, yes, that is infringing. But as we will see later, the threshold for the copyright holder caring leaves a lot of room.

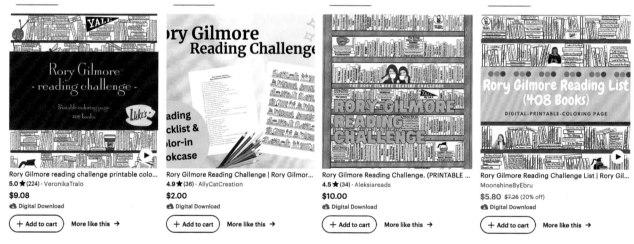

A small selection of the available Rory Gilmore reading lists on Etsy.

Facts in Government and Medical Documents

Government documents are also not protectable, which is exciting (you can use them to create things) and also means that you can't keep others from using them (they are in the public domain). So, what can you do with government documents? You can use the information in them, of course. You can also use the documents themselves and create art with them. You may run into privacy questions, though, which is beyond the scope of this book. It is also important to note that medical records have their own set of legal issues, including those under the laws of the Health Insurance Portability and Accountability Act (HIPAA).

But census records and other federal government documents? Use them! They are public documents and public facts.

HIPAA LAWS

For more on patient privacy and medical records, you can go to Department of Health and Human Services website, hhs.gov/hipaa.

An image of the U.S. Census. You can find this at Ancestry.com, but their access doesn't impact on the copyright status. The U.S. Census records are in the public domain.

X-Rays, Medical Imaging, and Non-Medical Echo Sonography

Usually, these are not protectable because they are facts. They are functional, with no creative input, so says the law. However, if they are part of a literary work such as a medical textbook, they may be part of a compilation, which itself may be protected.

An artist can take medical imaging and create art with it. The art itself will be protected, but that does not change the underlying status of the medical images used. What if the X-ray images are used to make creative expressions? Then there may be the modicum of creativity necessary. The use changes the possibility of copyrightability.

Let's Talk About Shapes, Baby

Copyright does not protect common geometric shapes, either in two-dimensional or three-dimensional form. That doesn't mean you can't build a business based on shapes!

The company Paper Pieces recognized that they have no copyright or property right in the shapes that they make for English Paper Piecing. They have a property right in the convenience of making hundreds of specifically-shaped heavy paper hexagons or diamonds. We order the shapes on paper because it is convenient, the company does the math, and we trust the brand (trademark). But their business is not based on the idea that they hold a copyright in the hexagon. In addition, the patterns made by those basic shapes are the selection, arrangement, and coordination of basic shapes which could be protectable. Some of the patterns, however, are in the public domain, because like the phone book in *Feist*, they just don't reach the level of creativity required (see Modicum of Creativity, page 29).

How Much Expression Turns Shapes into a Copyrightable Work?

Shapes on their own are not protectable. When do you know the shapes that you are using have enough creativity to move to copyrightable? The U.S. Copyright Office actually provides an example that is very quilty. A purple rectangle with six evenly-spaced dots (that looks like a domino) is *not protectable*. One simple geometric shape, or eight of them, is not seen as creative enough.

But an image with lots of shapes is protectable. In contrast, the U.S. Copyright Office gives the following example, as protectable.

We also see a denial for Croc charms (called Jibbitz), because they are common symbols and designs.

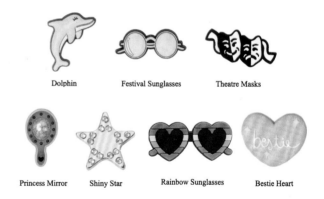

Dolphin   Festival Sunglasses   Theatre Masks

Princess Mirror   Shiny Star   Rainbow Sunglasses   Bestie Heart

Granny Square as the Ultimate Building Block

Crocheters actually give us one of the best examples of a building block in the form of granny squares. They are made by working out from the center of the block in rounds. They're a super common motif in crocheting, and you can make them at many different scales. Sometimes they're hexagonal, but traditionally they're square. From corner-to-corner granny squares to mosaic granny squares to countless others, there are a lot of different stitch patterns you can do to make different designs. None of these stitch patterns are copyrightable, they're all common blocks. Every crocheter gets the chance to try out whatever granny squares they want.

So what is protectable?

What most people do with granny squares is make 10s and 100s of them and then put them together to create a larger blanket, sweater, bag, vest, placemats, and anything else they can imagine. It is this selection, arrangement, and coordination that becomes potentially copyrightable.

Photo by Sidne K. Gard

Only by putting the building blocks (in this case, the granny squares) together to create something unique is there the possibility for copyright. They have a chance at protection as a whole, but not as individual blocks.

Letters, Words, Titles, and Short Phrases

These are not copyrightable. You cannot copyright individual numbers, letters, or individual words.

This includes:

- Title of a book or name of a company
- Domain name or URL
- Name of a character
- A catchphrase
- Mottos, slogans, or other short expressions
- Made up words

When you see adorable phrases and want to use them, you can. Elizabeth's favorite: "A day without quilting is like a day … just kidding. I have no idea what a day without quilting is like." It is important to know that although they cannot be protected by copyright, these short phrases may be protected by trademark. For more on how to research trademarks, turn to our first book, *Just Wanna Trademark for Makers* (by C&T Publishing).

Logos

Logos may be protected by copyright, but we see with registration refusals that to gain copyright protection on a logo you have to have quite a bit more than merely a word, color, and shape. Logos are one of the categories where refusal is the highest. If you are using words or short phrases in commerce to identify a company, product, or service, that's considered a trademark. Under copyright, the registration of logos suffer from the problem that lettering, short words, and basic shapes are not protectable by copyright. Here are a few examples of mere words or slogans that were denied registration at the U.S. Copyright Office.

Dance Moves

Choreography is protected by copyright, as long as it is fixed in a tangible medium of expression (for example, recorded on a video). Individual steps are not protected, nor are short combinations of steps. Yoga poses are not protected (yes, there are legal cases related to yoga). You can, however, create a copyrighted dance, and even register ballets and other pieces of dance. The question, of course, is how far do you have to go to create a copyrightable work from non-protectable dance elements? That's not completely clear.

Also, social dances (like the Foxtrot) are not protectable, they are seen as *functional*, and something that everyone in society should be able to do (see Doctrine of Functionality, page 15).

While that seems simple enough, it may be more complicated. There was a dance from a television series, *The Marvelous Mrs. Maisel*, which then became a TikTok craze. Does this turn it into a social dance? Is it still protectable? And, there is a current case where a video game developer took a series of dances off of social media and copied them directly into their game without permission. Is that okay? See how quickly non-protectable and protectable gets muddy? The video game case ended in a settlement with the celebrity choreographer.

A still from the *Marvelous Mrs. Maisel*

A still found on TikTok from one of the many virtual versions of the dance

Book Designs

The U.S. Copyright Office will not allow registration solely on the overall design of a book, its cover, design, or layout. You can't lock up for decades where to place the numbers on a page. But the selection, arrangement, and coordination of the specific book cover or layout is protectable. What is not protected includes the choice and size of fonts, the placement of numbers, and the arrangement and layout of the page including placement of illustrations with text.

Why is this the case? Graphic artists and publishers in the 1970s sought to make sure that under the new Copyright Act of 1976 that the U.S. Copyright Office would not lock up templates and basic designs with copyright registration.

Typeface and Fonts

Are typefaces or fonts protected by copyright? The Compendium says "As a general rule, typeface, type font, lettering, calligraphy, and typographic ornamentation are not registrable." These are seen as building blocks of expression, and therefore are more like facts. This is super interesting because Google puts out fonts that they say you can use without restrictions while other companies claim copyright on fonts. Note, however, that this is the United States Law; in the United Kingdom and elsewhere fonts are protectable under copyright.

The good news for those that want copyrightable fonts is that if you put bunnies or flowers into the alphabet, you are golden. Basically, add something to make it more than just letters. But a blue texture effect (for example, weathered-and-worn or chalk) is not protectable. You can see why. We don't want the weathered-and-worn or chalk alphabet locked up with a property right.

Nature

Found it in nature? Well, that's nature's, not yours. And if you purified it, that is potentially protected by a patent. However if you find things in nature and then make them into art, that is potentially protected. See the difference? And if you draw your version of nature, that is totally protectable.

This illustration of a chicken is protectible by copyright. A chicken itself is not. • *Hen at High Noon © Sorin Sukumaran*

Colorization

Changing the color of something is just not enough. When you choose the yarn color to create a pattern, you do not necessarily get a copyright in *your version* of the pattern. Merely changing the color does not create a new copyrighted work, it has to be something more. If you combine creative authorship with colorization, the U.S. Copyright Office recognizes that this is copyrightable.

William Donaldson Clark's original 1858 photograph of Princes Street in Edinburgh

Sid took a public domain photograph and recolored it in Photoshop. They also added illustration in the sky, including stars, bats, and a crescent moon. This likely has enough creativity to move beyond mere "colorization." • *Old Cityscape with Bats © Sidne K. Gard*

Fabric

Most times fabric designs are protected but other times not. Common fabric patterns are not protectable, including:

- Solids
- Chevrons
- Plaids
- Basic polka dots
- Stripes
- Gingham
- Houndstooth

You can probably think of others. The U.S. Copyright Office also will not register textures.

Here are some recent refusals of fabrics.

Jewelry

Jewelry gets rejected for registration a lot at the U.S. Copyright Office. First, the usefulness is separated out, like the clasp, but there is also the problem of common shapes and motifs that everyone should be able to make.

THINKING OF REGISTERING JEWELRY?

If you are planning to register jewelry with the U.S. Copyright Office, you might want to speak with a lawyer. Jewelry is challenging to successfully register.

Common Characters, Tropes, and Scenes

Common (called stock) characters are not protectable. Think of the manic pixie dream girl, or the wise old wizard who gives the young hero a quest.Nor are common settings, events, scenes, or other general tropes. These can also include elements that are basic to a historic story.

There is also a concept called *scène à faire,* which is a scene in a book or film which is almost obligatory for a book or film in that genre. For example, if you're animating a story about zombies, it is perfectly reasonable for you to include the normal tropes of zombies: eating brains, killing them by hurting their brains, being turned into a zombie if you are bitten by one. But, this also means you can't stop others from using those same tropes. What are the stock characters and scènes à faire in your artmaking discipline ? Can you identify patterns or other elements that are so common that they would not be protectable?

Another example is a masked magician dressed in magical garb, who reveals the tricks. The Ninth Circuit Court of Appeals in 1988 found this not to be distinctive enough to gain copyright protection.

The Case of Sunbonnet Sue

In 1902, *The Sunbonnet Babies Book* was published. It was written by Eulalie Osgood Grover and illustrated by Bertha L. Corbett, who was called the mother of the Sunbonnet Babies. The character of Sunbonnet Sue was based on British artist Catherine "Kate" Greenaway's children's illustrations. Now, works published before 1924 are in the public domain, but it wasn't because the Sunbonnet Babies copyright had expired that Sunbonnet Sue became a stock character. That happened long before the copyright expired. Over a million copies of the *Sunbonnet Babies Primer* were sold. Another artist, Bernhardt Wall, also created bonneted children. The idea of bonneted children whose faces you couldn't see became widespread.

Between 1900 and 1930, Sunbonnet Sue quilts became popular as people created adaptations from adaptations, and newspapers and magazines spread the Sunbonnet Sue craze with their own quilt versions.

The key stock elements are the oversized hat turned to the side, an A-line dress, and one arm and foot showing. She is usually engaged in an activity like cleaning, gardening, or baking. What makes her a stock character is that everyone treats her as such. You can now find adaptations of Zombie Sunbonnet Sue, Dead Sunbonnet Sue, Sex Worker Sunbonnet Sue, and other parodies. There again, the idea of all these different Sues are not protected, but the expressions of these Sues are.

A.
B.
C.

A. Belle Brunner's Sunbonnet Sue quilt made by her Grandma Anna in 1975.

B. Quilt blocks Stacy Harding received from her mother-in-law who got them from her mother-in-law!

C. A quilt in the New England Quilt Museum's Collection.

Games, Toys, Stuffed Animals, and Puppets

These are seen usually as artistic, creative, protectable works. But they all have non-protectable elements: eyes, basic game pieces, and stuffing. It is important to note that the idea of the game is not protected, nor is any system, method, or device related to the game. Others can make their own version of the game, as long as they are not using the expression of the original game.

Putting it All Together

So, are you beginning to see the pattern? Things we want everyone to be able to use are *not protectable*, and the list of what that includes is long. But when you put the non-protectable elements together, and add a modicum of creativity, bam! Copyright!

Who is the *Author*?

When you think of the author, you think of the person that created the painting or wrote the novel. But legally, that is not always true. For instance, when Spike Lee wrote the film, *Malcolm X*, he was not the legal author, even though the credits for the film are "Written by Spike Lee." Warner Brothers was the legal author.

Copyright law presumes that the creator of a work, any type of creative work, is the author of that work. The author controls the exclusive rights of copyright including when to give permission, and when to sell and license the work (see Licensing, page 136. Equally important, the copyright term is based on the author's death, or if there are joint authors, the last surviving author's death (see How Long Does Your Copyright Last?, page 111). And then, as with the Lee example, a work can be owned by an employer or someone else, even from the beginning. So, we have to now dive into who is the legal author, and categories of authorship.

> *Copyright law presumes that the creator of a work is the author of that work.*

Categories of Author

We have a number of categories: individual authors, joint authors, anonymous, and pseudonymous authors. These are the people creating the works. But there is also a category of works where the employer is considered the legal author, and that's its own whole kettle of fish.

Individual Author

This is the default category. You created something, you are the author! You control all of the things that go with copyright like when the work is distributed, who makes authorized derivative works, and the like. The current term lasts for your lifetime plus 70 years.

You don't need to do anything more than create your work to have a copyright in your work, but there are steps to make the copyright stronger. See Part III: Protecting (page 110). You will have to get used to the idea that sometimes people may use your work, and in many instances that it is okay, which we'll discuss in more depth in Part II: Borrowing (page 60), and Part IV: Enforcing (page 138).

Anyone can be an author—from a two-year-old painting to a great novelist. You can create art, music, audiovisual works, anything! If the author is a minor, the parents or guardians may need to sign contracts or other legal documents related to the copyrighted work.

Joint Authorship

You and someone else (or a number of people) created a work together. To be a joint author, there are a few requirements. First, here is the definition from the U.S. Copyright Office. "A 'joint work' is a work prepared by two or more authors with the **intention** that their contributions be **merged into inseparable** or **interdependent parts of a unitary whole**." This is how the Copyright Law defines a joint author.

There are a few important points.

1. You must, as joint authors, believe you are joint authors **at the time** of creation. You cannot **after the fact** decide to be joint authors. If you feel that you contributed a great deal but didn't get credit, after creation is not the time to claim joint authorship. It is something that is decided *jointly* at the time of creation. Who is named matters. Registering with the U.S. Copyright Office matters, as it provides a record of who is the author.

2. Each author also **must contribute creative work**, and not merely financially or sweat of the brow. See Creating a Copyrightable Work, page 29).

3. You don't have to do equal shares, but each author's contribution must be substantial enough to stand on its own as a copyrightable expression.

4. The ownership is considered a *tenants in common*, meaning that each joint author can exercise the non exclusive rights without the permission of the other authors, but there is a duty to account for the shares of the profits from any use or license. However, joint authors must all agree to exclusive licenses, transfers, and assignments of rights in writing (see Licensing, page 136).

5. Each author must **intend to integrate** their creative work. Intention matters. The parts are meant to merge into one.

Sid and Elizabeth are joint authors of the book *Just Wanna Trademark for Makers*. They wrote and merged their parts into an inseparable or interdependent unitary whole. They intended to be joint authors at the time of creation and intended to integrate their creative work. It doesn't matter how much Sid or Elizabeth does individually (for example, it doesn't have to be 50/50). What matters is that both contributed creatively. It can't just be having the idea or providing a computer, they both had to contribute creative labor (Modicum of Creativity, page 29).

Joint Versus Collective Versus Derivative Works

Joint authorship is different from a collective work, where each author(s) contributes separate and independent works to create a collection, which may qualify for copyright protection based on the selection, arrangement, and coordination (see Originality Standard, page 29). It is also different from a derivative work where there is an original work, and then a new creative part is added (see Making Derivative Works, page 32).

Rent

In *Thomson v. Larson*, 147 F.3d 195 (2d Cir. 1998), the Second Circuit court addressed the question of who counts as an author. This is not the first time it was addressed, but it has become a key case in understanding legal authorship. Jonathan Larson wrote the Broadway musical, *Rent*. He had an early co-author, Billy Aronson, who was credited, "original concept and additional lyrics by Billy Aronson," but Larson was the main author.

Over the next few years, Larson developed the rock opera. As part of the process, he hired Lynn Thomson to work on the script, and she was paid $2,000 and given the credit "Dramaturg." The contract did not discuss ownership or writing credits beyond that. Larson died suddenly after the final dress rehearsal for the Off-Broadway opening. When the show moved to Broadway, Thomson was hired again for $10,000 plus $50 a week for her dramaturgical services. She wrote to the Larson heirs asking for a small percentage of the royalties, and they obliged with one percent of the author's royalties. Nevertheless, negotiations broke down, and Thomson sued, alleging she should be co-author of the work, and receive sixteen percent of the royalties. The district court found that Thomson was not a co-author, and she appealed. The Second Circuit Court agreed that Larson was the sole author, and not Thomson. Let's see their reasoning.

The question is, did Lynn Thomson's work meet the statutory definition of a joint authorship? Since Larson was deceased, they looked to a number of elements including:

- Decision-making authority over changes and what is included in a work. Larson had final and sole approval of all changes.

- Billing and credit. Every script listed Jonathan Larson as the author, including the biography for Playbill.

- Written agreements with third parties. In this case, these were in Larson's name.

- Additional evidence from witnesses. This included conversations and discussions related to authorship at the time.

Work for Hire

Work for hire is a legal term, and also a legal category of authors. You may be hired to create something and you call it a "work for hire," but the law means something very specific. You are either an employee doing work in the course of your employment or an independent contractor. An employee creates work made for hire; an independent contractor does not. This is really important. If you are an employee, your employer owns your work. If you are an independent contractor, you own your work. You can give a license or assign the full copyright as part of a contract, but the person who hired you doesn't legally automatically own the copyright. They likely have a non-exclusive license to use the work, but they don't have other rights unless you agree to grant them (see Licensing, page 136).

Of all of the legal concepts in this chapter, understanding whether you are an employee or an independent contractor is really important for any maker, so we'll take a bit of time to understand this. There is a third category, commissioned works which again is a legal term and very limited, and we will discuss that subsequently.

Let's dive into further defining an employee within the course of their employment and an independent contractor.

The Difference Between "Employee Within the Course of Their Employment" and "Independent Contractor"

The 1989 U.S. Supreme Court case, *Community for Creative Non-Violence (CCNV) v. Reid*, 490 U.S. 730 (1989) is the U.S. Supreme Court case that helps us determine whether, under the meaning of the law, someone is an employee or an independent contractor. Even better, this case involves art!

In this case, a sculptor, James Earl Reid, was hired to create a sculpture for a non-profit organization. He was given an idea—to create a statue in the form of a homeless man, woman, and child that harkened back to Mary, Joseph, and Baby Jesus. But the parties did not indicate who was the author. Reid made the statue and it was a hit. The non-profit wanted it to go on tour; the artist thought it too fragile to tour and the lawsuit ensued. The question at the heart of this case was who *owned* the statue?

CCNV v. Reid helps us understand the test to use to determine if the work you are doing is within the course of your employment (employer owns the work) or if you are an independent contractor (you own the work). It all comes down to the concept of **the party's right to control the manner and means by which the work is accomplished**.

There are the eleven factors, and you weigh them to see where the creation most likely falls. It usually is pretty clear, but sometimes it is uncertain. The balance is usually tipped in favor of which tax form is used, a W-2 for employees; a W-9 for independent contractors.

Factor	Employee	Independent Contractor	*CCNV v. Reid*
1. Skills required *Are these specialized skills (for example, putting in a stylized custom iron fence) or are they general skills?*	General skills	Specialized skills	Reid was hired because of his specialized skill as a sculptor.
2. Source of the instrumentalities and tools *Does the employer or the crafter/maker supply the tools?*	Employer supplies the tools	Independent contractor supplies the tools	Reid supplied his own tools.
3. Location of the work *Is the work physically done as part of the company's business or are you hiring someone to do the work in their studio?*	Works at the company's business	Works at their own space, or comes into to do a localized, specific task at the company's business (think plumber)	Reid created the sculpture in his studio.
4. Duration of the relationship between parties	Long-term relationship	Only the specific hired job	Reid was hired to create the sculpture, nothing more.
5. Whether the hiring party has the right to assign additional projects to the hired party	Yes, has the right to assign additional projects	No, only if agreed	Reid had only agreed to create this one sculpture.
6. The extent of the hired party's discretion over when and how long to work	Employers usually set hours and requirements for the job (such as clocking in), work laptop, and so on.	Independent contractor has discretion over when and how long to work	Reid worked when he wanted to on the statue, there was no clocking in.
7. The method of payment	Ongoing paycheck	Payment for the specific services	Reid got paid an advance and a final sum once it was completed.
8. The hired party's role in hiring and paying assistants, and whether the work is part of the regular business of the hiring party	The company provides assistants to help with the regular work of the employee.	It is up to the IC whether to hire; it may be included in the contract	Reid had control over whether he had assistants.
9. Whether the hiring part is in business	The business of the company is the thing.	The business of the independent contractor is the thing.	Reid was a sculptor, CCNV was a non-profit homeless charity.
10. The provision of employee benefits	If there are health, retirement, and other benefits, more likely to be seen as an employee	No benefits? Likely an independent contractor.	Reid was not given any employee benefits while making the sculpture.
11. The tax treatment of the hired party	Are you given a W-2? Likely, the IRS and your employer consider you an employee.	Did you fill out an I-9 and had to pay your own taxes? The IRS considers you an independent contractor.	Reid was likely given an I-9.

The court found that the sculptor was an independent contractor and, thus, the copyright holder. Here is their reasoning. Reid had special skills, had his own tools, worked at his own studio, and the relationship only lasted as long as it took to create the sculpture. The hiring party could not assign additional tasks, direct when and how long to work, and it wasn't the business of the non-profit to make sculptures. The sculptor received no employee benefits, and he was taxed as an independent contractor. Reid held the copyright; CCNV had a non-exclusive license to the sculpture (see Licensing, page 136).

Are you an Independent Contractor?

- Do you supply your own instruments?

- Can you be assigned other tasks?

- Do you use your own space to create?

- Is your business is based on the work being done, and not the specialty of the client?

- Do you receive benefits?

- Do you pay your own taxes or are they paid by the hiring party?

- Do you have assistants chosen by you and not your client?

If you are an independent contractor, you hold the copyright unless you assign it in writing signed by both parties. Unless there is an agreement to the contrary, you retain the copyright in the work, even though a third party paid you to make/create the work. They receive a non-exclusive license to use the work. But unless there is a contract in place, no assignment or exclusive license has been created by the act of creating the work for someone else or even getting paid. You still hold the copyright (see Licensing, page 136).

This is interesting, yes? You quilt someone's quilt. No copyright agreement is in place. If you created your own copyrighted design on a client's quilt, you hold the copyright to the quilting (not the quilt itself), not the person who owns the quilt. Do you see how this could be powerful? You can use that

design elsewhere. It is important to note that there is an implied non-exclusive license for the client to do all the things people normally do with a quilt. But there is no implied non-exclusive license to publish it, make directions for the quilting itself, or exercise other rights. You retain the copyright on that portion (see Licensing, page 136).

Commissioned Works

So, we now know there are two categories for work: work for hire and independent contractors. Unfortunately, there is one more we must learn, and its title is confusing: commissioned works. This is a legal category, and not what we normally think of as "commissioned work."

A commissioned work is a specific legal thing—and has to fit within the definition. Most creative works do not fit within the legal definition of a *commissioned* work. The person who commissions the work is the legal author. But just because you order a "commissioned" work doesn't mean it is legally a commissioned work; it is likely a work done by an independent contractor. You gotta love copyright at this point. There are three requirements to meet the work-for-hire definition of a commissioned work.

1. Commissioned: The work must have been ordered to have been made in exchange for some sort of payment. You can't make something and then see if someone wants to purchase it. It has to be commissioned by a hiring party.

2. Category: It has to be used in one of the following nine categories. This is a *closed list*, which means that it has to fit within one of these specific uses:

- A contribution to a collective work, (see Independent Creation Requirement, page 32)

- As a part of a motion picture or other audiovisual work

- As a translation

- As a supplementary work, which includes works in a published work like introductions, conclusions, illustrations, explanations, revisions, commentary, forewords, afterward, maps, charts, tables, editorial notes, afterword, editorial notes, musical arrangements, answer material for tests, bibliographies, appendices, and indexes

- As a compilation

- As an instructional text

- As a test

- As an answer material for a test

- As an atlas

That's it. For most makers, our works do not fall into this category, and so you can't use this part of the law to determine authorship. Artwork is not included as a specific category. Note: we've been using compiilation as a concetp of selection, arrangement, and coordination, but here compilation is more like the phonebook or an anthology.

3. **Contract:** If your work fits into one of these categories, there has to be an **express, signed agreement** in place as well. Even commissioned and falling into one of the specific categories, you still have to have it in writing.

Remember Spike Lee and *Malcolm X*? He likely fell under work for hire under this category, as part of a motion picture or other audiovisual work. Warner Bros. Entertainment Inc. is the legal author, even though Lee is considered the "author" to most viewers.

A Different Kind of "Commissioned"

Interestingly, many artists, especially digital artists, use the word commissioned when under copyright law they really mean *independent contractor*. Artists often think of commissions as artwork that someone has specifically requested and paid them to make. If you scroll on the artsy side of Instagram or Tumblr, you'll often see artists posting about their commission prices or that their commissions are open. Under copyright law, they are creating works whose copyright does not automatically transfer to the person buying the art, and the artist can make derivative works or copies because they still hold the copyright. If desired by both parties, there could also be a written contract with a signature, transferring the copyright.

"Commissioned" art by Spencer Creighton, which is in fact a work done as an independent contractor. Someone else created lore about the dog, and then Spencer was commissioned by wolf_studios683 to create the character design. • *Artwork © Spencer Creighton*

Anonymous and Pseudonymous Works

There is one more category: anonymous and pseudonymous works, meaning that the identity of the author(s) is unknown, either because we do not know the author (anonymous) or because the author doesn't want to be known (pseudonymous). These can be individual, joint, or work for hire. They can be original works, derivative works, or compilations (including collective works). If the identity of the author(s) is revealed, they are no longer anonymous or pseudonymous, and they are categorized in the appropriate category. This may impact on who controls the work and the length of the copyright term (see How Long Does Your Copyright Last?, page 111).

Who Can Be an Author?

Copyright law has a strict policy: only humans are capable of being an author for the purposes of gaining federal copyright protection. Not the divine, not animals, and not AI (see also Independent Creation Requirement, page 32). So, when someone claimed that a monkey took a selfie, and then became upset when *Wikipedia* didn't pay them a licensing fee for posting the image, *Wikipedia* (rightly) responded, no copyright, no license fee. The monkey was not human, and therefore, the work that it created was in the public domain and not protected by copyright. (It became a whole litigated thing).

And now, we are facing the question of whether AI-generated art (where artificial intelligence creates a work either on its own or through prompts) is protected by copyright. The U.S. Copyright Office is conducting a study, but for now, the answer is no. If it is created by AI, it is not protected by copyright. This is an ever-changing aspect of the law, so be on the lookout as litigation continues.

> **INTERESTED IN LEARNING MORE ABOUT AI AND COPYRIGHT?**
> The U.S. Copyright Office has some great resources on this. Check out copyright.gov/ai.

The reported photograph taken by a monkey, and therefore no copyright, or in this case, credit. See en.wikipedia.org/wiki/Monkey_selfie_copyright_dispute

Creating *Photographs*

Photographs come into play within copyright law in a number of ways, from being the subject of protection as works of art themselves to documenting things that are not protectable, like sports games. There are so many intellectual property elements related to photographs, they deserve their own chapter, so we gave them one!

Earlier you learned that the selection, arrangement, and coordination of taking the photograph is *creative enough* to qualify for copyright protection. (See Originality Standard, page 29). Let's learn a bit more!

The Photographer is the Author

Generally, the person who takes a photograph is the legal author (barring our discussion in Who Can Be an Author?, page 54). So, when a tourist asks you to take a photograph of them, you hold the copyright. Weird, right?

Documenting Copyright for Other Kinds of Works

Want to register a painting, a quilt, or other kinds of art? You will likely take a photograph of it. You are capturing the underlying work.

Photographs as Fine Art

In the United States, all photographs that meet the requisite originality requirement are automatically protected by copyright (see Originality Standard, page 29). The originality requirement for photographs is rather low. Did you take the photo? You're good! When photographs fit into the category of fine art, they are also protected by a thing known as moral rights (see The Visual Artists Rights Act (VARA): Copyright Law and Moral Rights, page 128). But this is only a small category of works.

Photographs Don't Extend Copyright

If you take a photograph of an eighth-century sculpture, it doesn't create a new copyright for the sculpture. The photograph is a *slavish copy*, meaning a copy with no originality. This means that you also don't have much of a copyright on that image. There is even a weird case that says that you don't obtain a copyright on a photograph of an old work. Museums even sometimes resort to asking for an access fee to get a high resolution image.

The Three Graces, sculpture by Antonio Canova, 1814–1817, Italy
Photo by Sidne K. Gard

Photographs out in the World

If you are on a public street, you do not need permission to photograph people, events, and/or buildings that are visible from the street. There is no expectation of privacy.

Now, you also have to consider the right of publicity: the economic right to exploit one's name, likeness, and other aspects of what makes you who you are. Someone can't use your image commercially (if the use doesn't qualify for fair use) without your permission.

So, can you take photographs of crowds? Yes. Can you use that without permission? Yes, but you can't use someone's image on your label without permission. You are using their right of publicity to sell your product.

Using Photographs in Art

There are many ways photographs are used in art. So, there is not only one answer. But you knew that already, didn't you? Photographs can be used as references for drawing. They can be used as part of a collage. They can also be manipulated in software to become something very different.

Take Your Own Photographs

When you can, take your own photographs. You just have more control over what you can do with them.

Using Model Releases

While beyond the scope of this book, if you are using individuals in photographs that you are taking, ideally, you would have them sign a model release to document their permission for you to use their image and likeness.

RIGHT OF PUBLICITY AND GETTING PERMISSION

Have a project that involves people? You might want to talk to an attorney if you think this will be either controversial (and the people would not be happy), will be shown in a gallery or museum (will be more public), or have a commercial component to it.

Using Reference Photographs

Artists and makers use reference photographs all of the time. A new U.S. Supreme Court case makes it clear that if you are using the reference photograph for the same purpose as the original (for example, making a colorized version of the photograph for a cover of a magazine), then you need to obtain a license.

If you are a student using a photograph as a reference, that's really not a problem. But if you are using that same photograph for commercial products, you may need to *clear the work*, meaning get permission to use the copyrighted works (See Studying Commercial Versus Non-commercial Uses via Fanworks, page 101). For example, an artist used an Associated Press (AP) photograph of Barack Obama without permission to make campaign posters; AP sued. For more on this topic, flip ahead to Fair Use Basics (page 77).

Using Stock Images

If you are using stock images (photographs or other kinds of images) from a stock library such as Getty Images, make sure to read the license. Each image can be different and can carry restrictions. For example, a lot of times the license doesn't allow alteration or derivative works, and you can get into trouble if you do so. Make sure you can do what you want with the photograph.

Getting the Right License to Create Derivative Works

Most times, the license from a stock image library is only for reproducing the image, not creating a derivative work. If you want to make a derivative work, make sure to get a license. You could find your work held up in trying to register it or even found to be infringing, even if you have legally purchased a license, but not the *right* license.

Unsplash

Unsplash is a site for free downloadable images that you can use or contribute to. It is a stock photography company. You can use the images, even without giving credit.

Here is the license: "Unsplash grants you an irrevocable, nonexclusive, worldwide copyright license to download, copy, modify, distribute, perform, and use photos from Unsplash for free, including for commercial purposes, without permission from or attributing the photographer or Unsplash. This license does not include the right to compile photos from Unsplash to replicate a similar or competing service."

We like Unsplash because of their broad grant of rights. In their own FAQ, they even note that their images can be used as references for illustrations and paintings which can be sold as long as they were not created by automated means.

To review the Unsplash terms of service for yourself, go to unsplash.com/terms.

Photographs on Covers or for Commercial Use

If you are using a photo on the cover of something, like a book, an album, or similar, or are using it commercially, there is more scrutiny. Get the right licenses. Get permission. Fair use will likely not help. Selling something using someone else's work is usually not good.

If you place an image in a book where there is comment and criticism about the image, that is likely fine, but if you put it on the cover to sell the book, that is likely not fine.

Photographs and Videos of Events

We live in a social media world where events want you to broadcast your images and even short videos. The venue that grants access to the event can set the terms. Venues can put whatever restrictions they want because people are on *their property*. These are *access controls*, rather than copyright. For example, a museum may state that "You can come into our museum, but you cannot take photographs of the exhibits."

We also see a lot of bootleg videos of concerts and other shows. What is interesting about this is that you do not get a copyright on the unauthorized video. And if the performer wanted, they could sue you for unauthorized recording, even if they are not recording it themselves. It's called the anti-bootlegging statute, and it is part of the Copyright Act of 1976. There's a pretty significant divide on this between the law and what people actually do every day.

Dallon Weekes of the band I Don't Know How But They Found Me performing at Bottom Lounge in Chicago.
Photo © Sidne K. Gard

Registering Photographs at the U.S. Copyright Office

You can register a single image up to a group of 750 images at the U.S. Copyright Office under one registration! You also can take photographs of works that you are registering (for example, a sculpture), which would register the sculpture, rather than the photograph (see Registering Your Creative Work, page 121).

STILL LOOKING FOR MORE ON PHOTOGRAPHS?

Here is the U.S. Copyright Office's information about photographs and copyright. copyright.gov/engage > types of work > copyright for photographers.

BAD PARABLE

PART II
Borrowing

You're in a museum in front of a Van Gogh. It's beautiful, it's moving to look at. While others are coming up to take selfies or admire the art, you have found somewhere to sit with a canvas and whatever art supplies the museum has allowed you to bring in. You work tirelessly to replicate the Van Gogh in front of you, trying to learn from old masters by retracing the steps they once went through.

Or maybe, you're sitting on your couch with skeins of yarn all around you and knitting needles in your hand as you watch a TikToker explain how they made a beautiful sweater. You follow along each step, each stitch, to learn the techniques.

We learn by borrowing and often we create by building off ideas and works that came before us and inspired us. Creating and borrowing go hand in hand. Someday the work you create might inspire someone else. Someday you might want to sell your work or show it in a gallery. And the law helps us understand where the boundaries are and how we form relationships between our work and others' works.

In this part, you will learn about:

- **Permissible and impermissible use.** We give you a quick overview before going into borrowing others' works.

- **Public domain works.** You don't have to ask permission to borrow them. They are free and available for everyone to use. The question is when does something come into the public domain?

- **Asking permission.** The work is under copyright and you want to ask permission to use it. How do you do that?

- **Fair use.** This is an important legal concept. You can use someone else's work under certain conditions. We will take you through the test to determine if your use of someone else's work likely falls under fair use. We will also give you some examples to help you sort it out.

- **Using trademarks.** Makers use others' trademarks in their work. How do you understand when it is legal? We'll be teaching you the *Rogers* test to help you sort it all out.

- **The myth of the 10% work.** Have you heard people talk about only needing to change something by 10%? That's not how the law works at all, but let's talk about it.

- **How fanworks come into play.** Fanworks necessarily borrow from existing copyrighted and public domain works. How do you understand what fans do, and how it fits into the legal landscape?

An *Introduction* to Permissible and Impermissible Uses

From the beginning of this book, we've noted that copyright is not an absolute property right, meaning that others can use a copyrighted work **while it is under copyright**. These are sometimes called *permissible uses*: if a third party engages in these uses, it is not considered infringement. The most famous is fair use, but there are others too. And then there are uses that some refer to as *tolerated uses*: the copyright holder doesn't like them and they are probably not legal, but at this moment in our world, business choices are made and the copyright holder lets them go. Sometimes these are also called *fans celebrating* (see How Far Can You Go? A Different Perspective on Enforcement, page 166).

Finally, there are impermissible uses. Those are just not cool, but people do them anyway. That's *infringement* (see Copyright Infringement, page 145). Your actions can be so bad, you can actually go to jail for criminal copyright infringement (see Criminal Liability, page 159). Plagiarism is another form of infringement (see What About Plagiarism?, page 160).

Permissible Uses

Permissible uses come in a number of varieties. Let's take a look.

You Own the Work!

You take a photograph of an orange. Awesome! That's your photograph. You took pictures of animals at the zoo? Awesome, too! You may have to get permission from the zoo for commercial use of the images, because you are on their premises.

Permission

You can ask the copyright holder for permission to use the work. This includes a *license*, either exclusive or non-exclusive to engage in one of the exclusive rights (copy, distribute, make derivatives, public display, and/or public performance). You can also obtain an assignment, where ownership is transferred to you. This must be in writing, and can include specific rights or all of them, (see Licensing, page 136).

It isn't hard to ask permission. Just ask! For this book, we have asked permission to use a number of photographs. As part of that permission, we have asked if the author wants to be attributed or not. You can email and ask. You can ask in person. Just memorialize it. You can create a simple contract for permissions, but do get permission in writing.

Here is an example:

> I, [Your Name], as the copyright holder of the photograph(s) mentioned below, hereby grant permission for their use with a non-exclusive, perpetual, worldwide license for the use [explain use]. I retain full copyright and ownership rights and request appropriate attribution as specified. No license fee is associated with this non-exclusive, perpetual worldwide license.

When you ask someone for permission to use their copyrighted work, or alternatively, their right of publicity, you can keep the agreement simple. But get everything in writing.

For copyrighted works be sure to include:

1. Person's name

2. The Work

3. Whether the use will be commercial or noncommercial

4. Whether there is payment

5. Whether you will be making a derivative work from the person's original work

6. Whether the permission is for an exclusive or non-exclusive right to use

7. That the person has the right to give permission

8. Whether attribution is required

For permission to use someone's image be sure to include:

1. Person's name

2. Right to use the image and likeness of the person

3. Whether the use will be commercial or noncommercial

4. Whether there is payment

5. Whether you will be making a derivative work from the person's original work

6. Whether the permission is for an exclusive or non-exclusive right to use

7. That the person has the right to give permission

8. Whether attribution is required

9. Whether 18 and older, legal age (and if not, consent of parent or guardian)

First Sale Doctrine

You purchase a copy of a pattern and fabric.

You can do many things with the pattern. You can make it, write on it, lend it to a friend, donate the pattern after you use it, and even throw it away. The copyright holder does not control the physical copy once you purchase it. This is called the *first sale doctrine*, and is sometimes referred to as *exhaustion*.

But the First Sale Doctrine does not allow you to make copies of the book or pattern (except under Fair Use Basics, page 77) You can't copy the pattern and then give copies out to your friends. This violates the exclusive right to copyright and distribute under the Copyright Act of 1976. If your friend likes the pattern, show them where they can legally purchase it, too.

And another even bigger issue. **First sale doctrine does not apply to digital copies.** First sale doctrine does not apply to digital copies. First sale doctrine does not apply to digital copies. It bears saying many times. You can't legally email or make a copy of a PDF for a friend. There's no first sale doctrine. Instead your purchase of that digital copy is seen as a license, a non-exclusive license, usually with restrictions like using it only for personal use and no making copies. Sometimes a license, like on software, will allow you to place that software on two computers. This was true of our automated software for the Grace longarm system. We could place the software on two different tablets. That was the license limit. Read the license for digital works. It will tell you what you can and can't do.

A physical copy gives you more freedom to share. A digital copy does not. For example, as part of our project, we bought a couple of copies of the *Splendid Sampler* book and ripped the pages up, sent the patterns to different people, and they sent the versions they made back to us. First sale all the way.

Take away: no sharing of digital copies, unless the copyright holder allows that. (See What is a Creative Commons License?, page 119.)

First sale is a super important concept for copyright. We couldn't have used books stores or you couldn't resell your car without it (because the car contains copyrighted software). You couldn't bring magazines to a guild meeting for recycling, and you couldn't rip a book to pieces, make it into fabric, and do other crazy art things to it. (Yep, you guessed it, Sid did that.)

Back of *Bodies of Water* quilt © Sidne K. Gard made of paper from novels, batting, fabric, paint, and thread.

Upcycling and First Sale

Generally, clothing is not protectable by copyright. Fabric might be, but first sale takes care of that. Want to repurpose clothing by cutting it up? Or a quilt into a skirt? First sale allows for this! It's important to note that there may be trademark issues. There was a case where rapper Lil Nas X used Nike shoes to create his own "Satan" shoes and "Jesus" shoes that were artistic expression. They sold for $1,018 a pair. The Satan shoes sold out in less than a minute. Nike sued over the Satan shoes, but not the Jesus shoes. The case was settled.

Derivative Work and First Sale

So, you make something with a found object or a copyrighted thing. You paste it into something or decoupage it onto a table. Can you? There are two competing cases (with the exact same company) that give us no clear answer.

Licensed Fabric and First Sale

Fabric featuring licensed images, such as Mickey Mouse or Star Wars, is sometimes labeled on the selvage as for personal use only. You've purchased it, so, the question is can you use for-personal-use labeled fabric to create finished items to sell, for example, on Etsy? Is it possible to restrict the first sale doctrine? It is not clear.

Classroom Uses

Section 110 of the Copyright Act of 1976 provides exceptions to exclusive rights in certain situations. One of these is face-to-face teaching in a non-profit educational institution. Section 110(1) allows students to perform a play in a classroom or show an entire film in that same classroom. This does not hold true if that same school puts on a play or shows a film and charges admission. This also doesn't apply to handouts or other reproductions, **only to certain exemptions of performances and displays.** It is important to reiterate that this only applies to non-profit educational institutions, not for profit, this doesn't work everywhere. And, this only covers the right to perform or display, not to copy.

Library Uses

Section 108 of the Copyright Act of 1976 concerns special allowances for libraries and archives. Some of these are for preservation purposes. Interlibrary loans and patron copies are also part of this, as are photocopy machines in a library. The library does not have liability when you make a copy of something at the library. They have a special exemption.

Fair Use

Fair use is a term that many people know. We're going to go through what it is and how to apply fair use in the next chapter, Fair Use Basics (page 77). Fair use allows for uses by third parties without permission while the work is still under copyright for specific purposes. Typical uses are criticism, comment, news reporting, scholarship, research, parody, and teaching.

- Fair use has also been used in technological instances like indexing (think Internet searches) and time-shifting (think home video recorders).

- Fair use is the mechanism that allows us to comment and criticize works, such as writing book reviews and biographies.

- Fair use also allows us to make physical and digital copies for research, scholarship, personal use, and in some cases, classroom use.

- Fair use allows you to make parodies.

We will be discussing fair use in more detail (see Fair Use Basics, page 77 and Art and Fair Use, page 86).

Not Cool: Infringement

It may seem like people can do whatever they want with your work, but that is not true. Determining whether copyright infringement has occurred is a complicated test, which we'll explain in Copyright Infringement (page 145). In short, a copyright holder can bring a lawsuit or file a small claim against unauthorized uses of their work. Copyright infringement usually takes the form of either literal copying or being substantially similar. Let's look quickly at both.

Literal Copying

You make a copy of a compact disc. This is literal copying. Literal copying of copyrighted work without permission is copyright infringement.

Substantial Similarity

You see a quilt of a ladybug. You think, "I want to make one that is like that but a little different." Though the quilts are not exactly the same, the question is, is the amount you took from the original quilt okay? The question will be: was there infringement, and if so, are there any permissible defenses. We will go into this in great detail shortly in Copyright Infringement (page 145).

Identifying
the Public Domain

When you are creating, you may want to include or build upon older works. Those may be in the public domain! When a work is in the public domain, it is free for all to use in any way (barring certain trademark uses that still carry protection). So, when is a work in the public domain? In the United States, the copyright term depends on several factors.

> *When a work is in the public domain, it is free for all to use in any way (barring certain trademark uses that still carry protection).*

Very Old Published Things? In the Public Domain!

Every year you see the list of new works entering the public domain as of January 1st, which is Public Domain Day.

In the United States, the maximum term of works published anywhere in the world before 1978 is 95 years from first publication. Here's the formula:

publication date + 95 years = term of the copyright

So, the 96th year is the first year the work is in the public domain.

This applies to all published work, regardless of where they are published. This pertains exclusively to United States territory.

However, this calculation does not apply for other countries. Remember the concept of Territoriality? See U.S. Copyright Sits in a Global World (page 18).

Date of First Publication Anywhere	Enters the Public Domain
1928	2024
1929	2025
1930	2026
1931	2027
1932	2028
1933	2029
1934	2030
1935	2031
1935	2032

Publication is Key

One key element is that the work **has to be published**—which means anything that has been circulated out in the world without restriction. Anything that was sold, offered for sale, gifted, or given away without restrictions is considered to have been published.

Before 1923

You will sometimes see "before 1923" as the date for public domain content. This is because for a long time, the public domain was frozen and no new works were added to the public domain. The term of copyright had been lengthened, and for twenty years nothing was added. The Copyright Term Extension Act, sometimes called the Sonny Bono Copyright Term Extension Act, was passed in 1998, and it added twenty years to the current terms. So, from 1998 to 2018, no published works came into the public domain in the United States. In 2019, we started to see works again come into the public domain. And so each year, many groups announce the new works that are coming into the public domain, which for some is a huge celebration. For a long time the answer to when something was in the public domain was "before 1923" but no longer. Works before 1923 had a maximum term of 75 years. Works published between 1923–1977 have a maximum term of 95 years.

The Term Could Be 95, 28, or Zero Years

Copyright terms are messy. The maximum term for works published before 1978 is now 95 years. But there were requirements for these works along the way that may have caused them to lose their copyright before the 95 years is up. We will discuss this in It Depends, January 1928-March 1989 (page 68).

Many works did not gain copyright protection at all, because they did not include © on the publication. (See Copyright Notice, page 114.) Other works, if published during a certain time period, had only 28 years. Whatever happened, the maximum possible term for any published work between 1923–1977 is 95 years.

Mickey Mouse and Winnie-the-Pooh Come into the Public Domain

In 2022, Winnie-the-Pooh entered the public domain in the United States The first book, *Winnie-the- Pooh* was published in 1926. We had to wait two more years, until 2024 for Tigger to join the gang, as he was first published in *The House at Pooh Corner* (1928).

The Disney version of Pooh is still protected, but the original drawings and the characters themselves are now in the public domain. Pooh's red shirt came later, and so it was still protected for a while. So if you're gonna use Pooh, put him in a different outfit or let him be naked.

Also in 2024, *Steamboat Willie*, *The Gallopin' Gaucho*, and *Plane Crazy*, three early Walt Disney animated shorts, entered into the public domain. Really? Yes! But again, like Pooh, there are a few things to note.

First, the trademarks are still protected both for the Mickey crowd and Pooh's world. You can't use them to identify a good or service. And second, only those are in the public domain. Any further character development is still under copyright.

There are many more works that are in the public domain, and each year more join Mickey and Tigger!

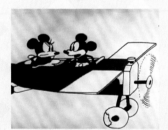

Still from *Plane Crazy* (1928)

Still from *Steamboat Willie* (1928)

Minnie in a still from *The Gallopin' Gaucho* (1928)

Ernest H. Shepard illustration from original *Winnie-the-Pooh* book (1926)

Ernest H. Shepard illustration from *The House At Pooh Corner* (1928)

Off Limits: Always Under Copyright

In contrast to old works, **new works (those published since 1989) are always protected by copyright**. So, if a work meets the copyrightable requirements, it is protected for a long time! Why is this so? Works before 1978 are measured under the Copyright Act of 1909. Then, in 1978, the Copyright Act of 1976 took over. So, as you have probably realized, copyright is a bit complicated. We're going to look at different clumps of dates to understand what happens under the new 1976 Copyright Act.

Published Works March 1, 1989 to Present

There are a bunch of works that are not in the public domain no matter what, as long as they meet the copyright subject matter and originality standards. Everything that was published on or after March 1, 1989 is still protected by copyright. For more on current terms, go to How Long Does Your Copyright Last?, page 111.

Now, you could use these works under an exception or get permission, but they are not in the public domain.

Unpublished Works, 1978-Present

All unpublished works from 1978 to the present are protected. There is no need to do anything, not even add a copyright notice (see Copyright Notice, page 114). None of these are in the public domain.

It Depends: January 1928-March 1989

Sometimes these works are protected by copyright, and sometimes they are not! There are a lot of works between 1928 and March 1989, which is where we're going to dive in more deeply. There are a few tricks that are fun and cool, but for the most part it is detailed work.

Domestic versus foreign works. There are different rules for domestic and foreign works. We're going to look at works from the United States first, then from other countries.

Published versus unpublished. We're going to look at published first, then unpublished.

Dates. We're going to pay close attention to the dates.

Copyright notice. Copyright notice doesn't impact whether you have copyright now, but it did until Feb 28, 1989. Yep, that's late. So, let's start with that!

Let's learn some key concepts before diving in.

Copyright Notice Was Required Before March 1, 1989

If you find a work **first published in the United States** before March 1, 1989, and it does not have a proper © or copyright notice, that work is in the public domain. Wild, right?

Copyright notice is the © symbol or the word copyright. Until March 1, 1989, a published work had to have a © notice in order to have copyright protection. If it did not, then it was in the public domain. Then, as of March 1, 1989, it became optional, meaning that works with or without copyright notice are protected by United States copyright law. There are still benefits to including copyright notice (see Copyright Notice, page 114).

Renewal Was Required Before January 1, 1964

If you find a work from the United States that was published before 1964 and it has a copyright notice on it, the next step in the investigation is to see if the work has a renewal record. You can do this by checking one of a few available databases.

Books Published Before 1964

For books, you can search Stanford's Copyright Renewal Database. Enter the book title or author name. See what turns up. If you find a renewal record, the copyright term is 95 years from publication. If you don't, the term was 28 years at most, and so it is in the public domain. (The work could have been in the public domain upon publication, if there was no copyright notice). If you don't find any records and the work was first published in the United States, that work is likely in the public domain. Likely, but not definitely because the records and searches are not perfect.

**STANFORD
RENEWAL RECORDS**

Want to search for book renewal records? It's easy! Just head over to exhibits.stanford.edu/copyrightrenewals

Everything Else Published Before 1964

For works published before 1950 that are not books, turn to records published by the U.S. Copyright Office called the Catalog of Copyright Entries (CCE). The CCEs are most easily accessed at the Internet Archive, archive.org/details/copyrightrecords. There are numerous volumes and they can be painstaking and complicated to search. There are different volumes for different media types and years. If you find a renewal record, the work is still under copyright. The record should have and "R" and then a string of numbers. If you don't find a record that begins with the letter "R" with a string of number, then it is in the public domain.

If the work was published on or after January 1, 1950, you should search the records at the U.S. Copyright Office website at copyright.gov/public-records. Researching the copyright status of older works would be a book topic of its own, but the U.S. Copyright Office offers a number of options and online guides to aid you in your search. You are again looking for a record with "r" for renewal.

Table for U.S. Works Published Before 1978

	Rule	Information You Need
Works published anywhere 95 years ago or more	In the public domain in the United States	Publication date
Works published first in the United States between 1929 and 1963	Depends Step 1: Do you see a © notice? No. It is in the public domain. Yes. Go to step 2. Step 2: Did you find a renewal record? No. In the public domain. Yes. Copyright will expire 95 years after publication.	Copy of the work to see if there is copyright notice Renewal Record information
Works published first in the United States between 1964 and February, 1989	Is there a copyright notice? No. In the Public domain. Yes. Copyright will expire 95 years after publication.	Copy of the work to see if there is copyright notice

Unpublished Works Before 1978

An unpublished work does not fall under the categories in the Table for U.S. Works Published Before 1978 (page 69). Unpublished works are measured using a different part of the Copyright Law, referred to as Section 303(a). Before 1978, unpublished works were protected by state law, and then in 1978 they were brought into the federal system. To do that, the law needed a transition period, and that's what Section 303(a) is all about. Let's take the example of a diary written in 1910.

As long as the diary was still unpublished as of January 1, 1978, the term is now the longer of the life of the author plus 70 years or December 31, 2002. So, let's say that the diary was written by Pauline Stig, who died in 1920. The term would be the longer of 1920 + 70 years, or 1990, or December 31, 2002. The longer in this case is the fixed date. But there is more.

Section 303(a) was made to give all unpublished works an opportunity for the next step: publish the work and get more time. If that unpublished work was first published between 1978 and 2002, the term is the longer of life of the author plus 70 or December 31, 2047. Exciting! If Pauline Stig's heirs (authorized copyright holders) published her diary for the first time between 1978 and 2002, then the work gets protection through December 31, 2047. This provides incentive to publish unpublished works.

Note: for anonymous works and work for hire, the term is measured on 120 years from creation, not life plus 70 years.

Foreign Works

Foreign works follow all of the rules of domestic works, but foreign works get a second chance if the owner messes up, particularly on copyright notice and renewal. But the rules are complicated. That means that you have to be careful in using foreign works because they likely had their copyright *restored*. Many foreign works came into the public domain in the United States either because they did not include the needed copyright notice, or if they did have notice, they did not renew the work within the 28-year window. So, if you don't see a copyright notice or find a renewal record, that is not the end of the conversation for foreign works. You should assume that the law allows that work to be protected for the full term—95 years from publication for works published before 1978. If you are interested in using foreign works, you can find more information in Durationator Copyright Files by Elizabeth Townsend Gard (Just Wanna Publications), available at Amazon.

Pre-1972 Sound Recordings

Before 1972, sound recordings were not protected by federal law. Now they are. That means that we have special rules for when sound recordings come into the public domain. This is different from the musical compositions or text that is incorporated in the sound recording.

Date	Sound Recording	Text/Musical Compositions	Notes
Recordings first published before 1923	December 31, 2021 All of these works are now in the public domain.	Public domain	
Recordings first published between 1923 and 1946	100 years from publication	Max term: 95 years from publication Check for © notice (if not there, PD) Check renewal: If no renewal, PD	Underlying work could be public domain earlier if domestic and no copyright notice, or if notice but no renewal
Recordings first published between 1947 and 1956	110 years from publication	95 years from publication Check for © notice (if not there, PD) Check renewal: If no renewal, PD	Underlying work could be public domain earlier if domestic and no copyright notice, or if notice but no renewal
Recordings first published between 1957 and Feb 1, 1972	February 15, 2067	95 years from publication Check for © notice (if not there, PD) For works 1957–1963, check renewal: If no renewal, PD	Through 1964, underlying work could be public domain earlier if domestic and no copyright notice, or if notice but no renewal. Domestic works between 1964–1972 require copyright notice.
Unpublished works	February 15, 2067	Life + 70 or December 31, 2001, whichever is longer Or if first published between 1978 and 2002, then longer of life + 70 and December 31, 2047	Since 2018, this option for longer publication had passed when the pre-1972 addition was added to the Copyright Act of 1976.

60,000 Pre-1972 Sound Recordings in the Public Domain

There are many sound recordings that are now in the public domain—the sound recordings and the text/music it is recording. All recordings published before 1923 are in the public domain. And all recordings that are 100 years from publication. So, that moves each year! Because the sound recording term is longer by five years than the text/music, you don't have to do the text/music math.

Want to listen to some public domain sound recordings? There are many sites that now have some of these recordings. See, for example, the National Jukebox at the Library of Congress, loc.gov/collections/national-jukebox

The Strange Case of Artwork

There's one more area you should be aware of relating to the public domain: artwork. Artwork can be defined in many ways.

Most people believe that the date associated with the painting is the public domain date. However, estates and owners often don't always agree that to be the case. That date we see referenced for paintings is usually the date of creation and not publication date. For example, you may find that someone is claiming that a 1909 painting is still under copyright. That's because they are claiming a later date for publication.

Here are a few things to know:

- When copies of the artwork were distributed to the general public, that constituted publication, and to be under copyright, you have to follow the rules for its time period (For example, copyright notice, renewal, and so on.) to determine the date it comes into the public domain. So, that's something to investigate. When the work was displayed at a museum, did they also sell or distribute copies? Merely displaying the work in a museum is not enough. That does not and never did constitute publication.

- Outside murals without visible copyright notice before 1978 are in the public domain; so too are government-funded art, for example were created as part of the Works Progress Administration or 1930s federal government funded arts programs.

- Unrestricted art sales or offer for sale (sold, lent, gifted, or distributed) counts as publication. No copyright notice before 1989? In the public domain.

- Copies made of the artwork for the general public also constitute publication, and if there was no copyright notice before 1989, then they are in the public domain.

Note: Once again, the rules for foreign works are different. And all of these rules are only for determining the copyright status in the United States.

Museums and Open Access

In recent years, many museums have started to provide copies of their collection online, and with that, they are including downloadable copies of works they feel are in the public domain and/or they own and are willing to allow people to use. Here are a few of the institutions that are doing this:

- The Metropolitan Museum of Artmetmuseum.org/about-the-met/policies-and-documents/open-access

- Smithsoniansi.edu/openaccess

- Art Institute of Chicago artic.edu/open-access/open-access-images

- The Cleveland Museum of Art clevelandart.org/open-access

- Pratt Museum library.pratt.edu > images > online image resources > open access image resources

- Whitney Museum of American Art whitney.org/open-access

- National Gallery of Art nga.gov/open-access-images.html

Each museum includes information of what you can do with the images, and if/when you need to ask permission. These images generally are designated as public domain with the label "Creative Commons Zero" (CC0) (see What is a Creative Commons License?, page 119).

The museums also sometimes mark them as "OA Public Domain," meaning Open Access Public domain, and they also often indicate in a tag "Public Domain."

The Realist View on Copyright

If a work is in the public domain, you can use it any way you want. But sometimes getting to that answer is hard. So, you weigh your options and make decisions on how to determine if you can use the work, and what you need to do to be able to use the work.

When does it matter that you get the copyright term right? That's part of the question you should be asking yourself. If Elizabeth posts a photograph of her 1972 kindergarten class, does it matter that she didn't get permission from the copyright holder? (And who is the copyright holder? The photographer? The school? So many questions follow). However, no one really cares, and we do it all of the time.

There are a few key questions you should ask yourself: attribution, control, and money. Are you Netflix making a series based on a short story? That has higher stakes than posting a school photograph from the 1970s. Part of what we must do in the real world is sort through these variables and make a decision.

WHEN IT MATTERS, CONSULT AN ATTORNEY

If you are using public domain work for a commercial project, or something where using the image without permission might hold up the whole project, you might want to consult a lawyer. We see that major movie studios have been known to pay licensing fees on public domain content just to make sure there aren't problems. Lawyers help us weigh the risks involved in our actions.

Orphan Works

Orphan works are works still under copyright, but no one can find the copyright holder. The Copyright Act of 1976 doesn't really have a way to fix this problem, but here are a few thoughts.

1. Check to see if there is a registration record at the U.S. Copyright Office. That may tell you who the copyright holder is or give you further clues on how to contact the copyright holder (see Everything Else Published Before 1964, page 69).

2. Run a risk assessment. Who is going to potentially sue you? Consult an attorney if you are really worried. For the most part, if you have searched for the parents, the copyright holders, and can't find them, that lessens the likelihood of suing but is not a guarantee. But also note: you may find the copyright holder, and they just don't respond. This is not an orphan, just an annoying copyright holder.

3. With common, non-protectable objects, if you are using something like a common quilt that has no identification of the owner, there is low risk. The copyright holder would have to prove that they hold the copyright, and then register the work (if it is a domestic work). It's just a lot of steps.

But if you are doing anything significantly commercial, beware of the orphans.

Layers of Copyright, or the MUD System

When we look at a copyrighted work, we may actually be looking at layers of copyrighted and even public domain works. So how do you know when the different parts are in the public domain? We call this the *MUD system*: main, underlying, and derivative works.

- Main work: In the MUD system, we label that first work, "Main." We now create relationships between the main work and the rest of the works that we are reviewing.

- Underlying work: This could be a short story, or something that the main work is based upon.

- Derivative works: Works that have the main work included may have enough creativity to secure an additional copyright. The main work's term remains the same. The derivative work has a term on the new material. In the example below, the radio play may be considered a derivative work of the original in that any new components made for the radio would be added to the original work. The performance is a derivative of the derivative radio play, with the main work's copyright still in play.

The Philadelphia Story **play by Philip Barry**

Expression	MUDS Analysis
Original Play	Main
Performance of the Play	Derivative 1 of Main
Radio adaptation of the play	Derivative 2 of Main
Performance of Radio Version of the Play	Derivative 1 of Derivative 2
French Translation of Script	Derivative 3 of Main

You have to analyze each individual work to determine its copyright status, and the relationship of that work to know whether it is in copyright or in the public domain. Let's take Winnie-the-Pooh as an example.

Winnie-the-Pooh

Expression	Status	MUDS Analysis
Winnie-the-Pooh character, published in *Winnie-the- Pooh* book (1926)	Public domain (longer than 95 years from publication)	Main work
***Winnie the Pooh* movie (2011)**	Copyright	Derivative 1 of main work
***Winnie-the-Pooh: Blood and Honey* movie (2023)**	Copyright	Derivative 2 of main work

The movie *Winnie the Pooh* (2011) was an authorized licensed version of the original characters to Disney, and this version is not in the public domain though the underlying versions of the character and story are. Once the main work, the original, was in the public domain, a horror film was created in 2023. That is also protected, even though the underlying characters from the main work are not.

What Can You Do With Public Domain Works?

Anything!!!! Here are some rules to remember:

- We know that anything published over 95 years ago is in the public domain.

- We know that anything first published in the United States before 1989 that does not have © notice is in the public domain.

- We know that everything (published and unpublished) after Feb 1989 is still under copyright.

The middle time: 1920–1980s are more complicated.

Unpublished works before 1978 are measured differently.

Aggressively claim the public domain. Enjoy, share, and love, but do not freak out if someone else also makes their own art with the same underlying public domain work. The whole point of the system is that we all play and enjoy.

Explore! There are so many resources out there with public domain images that you can include on your quilts, make fabric with, and so much more.

One great example of using public domain is that elements of Fritz Lang's film, *Metropolis* (1927), which as of January 1, 2023 is now in the public domain, appeared in *GHOST Agents*, a flip book.

◆

Use Public Domain Works

Don't be shy. Don't be scared. Maybe, start with something really old, like from the 1800s. An advertisement from an old magazine. There are so many possibilities.

We also love ephemera from before 1989. These are things such as tickets, menus, and posters that people made but didn't put a © notice on. ***This applies only to works from the United States being used in the United States.***

And take a look at the novels, movies, and sound recordings that have entered the public domain in the last few years. You will find so many including Sherlock Holmes, Minnie Mouse, *The Great Gatsby*, and so many more. And each year, there are new ones entering the public domain!

Play, make your own versions, copy public domain texts onto a quilt. Imagine using them anyway you want. Just don't pretend you were the original author.

If you are using a public domain image that might also be used as a brand or logo, make sure to read Using Trademarks (page 90) for more information.

Fair Use *Basics*

What is Fair Use?

Fair use is one way you can use a copyrighted work while it is still under copyright. When you quote from a book in a book review, that's fair use. When you take a bunch of images and do collage art, that could be fair use. Fair uses come in many shapes and sizes.

Fair use has become a very important force in our copyrighted world. Google searches are possible because of fair use. Scholars, artists, news reporters, librarians, teachers, and so many others rely on fair use for their daily work. Fair use allows us to comment, criticize, and make fun of works still under copyright.

We have had the concept of fair use around for almost 200 years in case law, but it wasn't until the Copyright Act of 1976 that it was added to the copyright statute. Fair use is found in Section 107 of the Copyright Act of 1976 (17 U.S.C. § 107). Fair use applies only to works potentially infringed in the United States. Traditionally, fair use is usually analyzed after we have evaluated whether infringement occurred, but that is not always so on a practical level. For our purposes, we are presuming that a copyrighted work has been used without permission. The question is will fair use apply?

Fair use has two parts: the preamble and the four factors. The preamble includes examples of when it is okay to use a copyrighted work without permission including for "criticism, comment, news reporting, teaching (including multiple copies for classroom use), scholarship, or research." The courts have added a few other uses to the list including parody (which falls under criticism and comment) and some technical uses of works, including Internet searches.

But that's just the first step. You have to evaluate your use by doing a four-factor test. There has to be a reason that you are using someone else's work, and we have to figure out if that use is fair. We look to the four-factor test that comes after the preamble. You ask four questions, about the original work and the potentially infringing work, which we are calling the unauthorized work. Let's look at each factor. This is something you should get familiar with if you want to use fair use as part of your practice.

Four-Factor Test

Fair use balances the copyright holder's rights with the unauthorized user's needs (some even say rights).

The four-factor test looks at, well, four factors:

- The first factor looks at how the unauthorized user is using the copyrighted work.

- The second factor turns to the nature of the copyrighted work—basically, is it fact or fiction.

- The third factor asks how much the unauthorized user took from the copyrighted work, both quantity and quality.

- The fourth factor asks if the taking by the unauthorized user harmed the economic market for the copyright holder, in other words, does it compete with or take away the financial opportunities of the original work.

Note: the four-factor test is a little bit different if you are commenting, criticizing, or parodying an original work. We'll get to that in more detail. In short, we don't want copyright holders to keep people from criticizing or making fun of a work—that's part of the democratic bargain. And so, fair use adjusts to take that into consideration.

First Factor: The Purpose and Character of the Use

Section 107(1) states "The purpose and character of the use, including whether such use is of a commercial nature or is for non-profit educational purposes;". You first look at unauthorized work. There are a number of parts to this first factor.

NON-PROFIT OR COMMERCIAL USE

- **Is this a non-profit educational use?** If so, this often weighs in favor of unauthorized use. Courts are more likely to find in favor of the use when it is for non-profit or educational purposes, but not always. Examples of uses under this category are scholarship and research. It it is about the *use*, and not just whether the user is at a non-profit educational institution. So, if you are copying a ton of workbook pages instead of have students purchase it, this will not be good, even if you are a non-profit.

- **Is it a commercial use?** This often weighs against unauthorized use. Things that are considered commercial include selling the potentially infringing product but also includes images used in an advertisement for the potentially infringing project; a copyrighted image on a product that someone is selling; or on the cover of a book, where the use is again without permission (to sell that book). And, of course, in commercials.

TRANSFORMATIVE

Taking a copyrighted work and doing something different from its original purpose *transforms* the authorized use. There are a number of kinds of transformative uses, but in the last twenty years, transformation has really become key.

The concept of "transformative" has had a long history. But a new case helps us understand transformative. In the U.S. Supreme Court case *Andy Warhol Foundation for the Visual Arts, Inc. v. Goldsmith* (2023), a reference photograph was used without permission to create a series of Prince silkscreen prints by Andy Warhol. The original photographer sued. The court found that the purpose of the original (to sell to magazines, including for cover images) was the same as the Andy Warhol versions (also sold to a magazine for a cover), and therefore it was not transformative.

Original Goldsmith photograph of Prince

One of the Andy Warhol silkscreen prints based on the Goldsmith photograph and used as a cover by Conde Nast.

The U.S. Supreme Court did something cool. It addressed how Warhol's use of Campbell soup labels in his work contrasts with the cover art. Referring to the *Campbell's Soup Cans* series, here the Court saw the use as transformative, as Warhol was commenting and criticizing on commercialism. The Court wrote, "an artistic painting might, for example, fall within the scope of fair use even though it precisely replicales a copyrighted advertising logo to make a comment about consumerism. The purpose of Campbell's logo is to advertise soup," explains the Court. "Warhol's canvases do not share that purpose. Rather, the Soup Cans series uses Campbell's copyrighted work for an artistic commentary on consumerism, a purpose that is orthogonal to advertising soup. The use therefore does not supersede the objects of the advertising logo."

This is really important. Do you see the distinction? The fair use must not replace the original use, it must be different in *purpose*. **That's the first factor.** The Supreme Court even includes an image of print of Warhol's Soup Can art. Warhol uses the copyrighted soup can label for artistic commentary on consumerism. And it conjures up the original to shed light on the original work itself. That's fair use in action. Note: the court does not get to the other factors, because those were not challenged from the Second Circuit Court decision, which had all favored Goldsmith. It was only the first factor that was on appeal.

The unauthorized use has to be different from the original use. Otherwise, if any interesting addition or adaptation of the original work qualified, it would gut the derivative rights of the original copyright holder under Section 106, see Making Derivative Works (page 32). To qualify as fair use, the unauthorized use has to be something different.

In short, to be transformative, the use of a copyright work must have a different purpose than the original. But that is just the first factor in looking at fair use. We have three to go. Now, being transformative is not always required. It is just part of the analysis of the first factor.

One of Warhol's *Campbell's Soup Cans*, which the *Andy Warhol* case referenced as art.

Second Factor: The Nature of the Copyrighted Work

Is the original work fact or fiction? Fictional works get more protection. Artwork gets more. Factual works get less. History, directions, and other non-fictional copyrighted works do not get as much protection under the fair use analysis.

The court believes that fictional, artistic, expressive works deserve greater protection, as opposed to facts that are available to everyone. A phone book gets less protection than a sculpture. Photography is sometimes seen as fact, sometimes as moving more toward fiction and art. It's a tricky one.

Third Factor: The Amount and Substantiality of the Portion Used in Relation to the Copyrighted Work as a Whole

How much did the unauthorized user take? The amount is analyzed both for its **qualitative and quantitative quantities**.

In terms of quantity, there is no set amount that constitutes the right "amount" that is "fair", but to be on the safe side, the less borrowed, the better.

We also see the concept of the *heart of the work*, meaning that if you take the key essense of the work then there's no reason to buy the original. That's not fair to the copyright holder. Think of it this way, if what you are doing is a market replacement that is not a fair use.

Fourth Factor: The Effects of the Use Upon the Potential Market for, or Value of, the Copyrighted Work.

This is often seen as one of the most important factors. Is the unauthorized user using the original work in a way that makes the unauthorized work a market replacement or taking away licensing opportunities? If that is the case, the court is less likely to find fair use.

Unpublished or Published

There's one more element to Section 107: "The fact that a work is unpublished shall not itself bar a finding of fair use if such finding is made upon consideration of all the [above] factors." That's the last bit of the statute. This means that fair use can be applied to any work, not just ones out in the public, although courts often do sometimes differentiate between whether the work had been circulated by the content owner (for example posted online) or kept unpublished (such as grandmother's diary in the attic). Somehow, keeping it out of the public's view remains important.

Fair Use and Comment, Criticism, and Parody

Commenting, criticism, and creating parodies are evaluated a little bit differently under Section 107, and they have become an important part of how we think about fair use. We do not see the term "parody" in the Preamble. This falls under "comment" and "criticism." The concept of commenting, criticism, and creating parodies has become a very important area of fair use. We see the analysis of comment, criticism and parody falling primarily under the First Factor and the Third Factor.

The key case is a case that concerns a parody of the Roy Orbison and William Dees song "Oh, Pretty Woman", and to explain the four-factor test when it comes to parody, we'll use this case. In 1989, the members of 2 Live Crew, a popular rap group, collectively wrote a song, "Pretty Woman," a comical take on the original song, a parody. They wanted to share writing credit with the original authors, and they contacted Acuff-Rose, the copyright holder, to obtain a license. They enclosed a copy of the song. Acuff-Rose, in their response, denied the use (and and refused payment of a fee): "I must inform you that we cannot permit the use of a parody of "Oh, Pretty Woman"." Did that stop 2 Live Crew? No, it did not. The song appeared on their album *As Clean as They Wanna Be*, with the title "Pretty Woman". Within a year it had sold 250,000 copies. Justice Souter, writing for the U.S. Supreme Court, does a four-factor fair use analysis.

Checking the First Factor: Purpose and Character of the (Unauthorized) Use

Transformativeness

The question is whether 2 Live Crew's use merely "supersedes the objects" of other original creation, supplanting the original, or instead adds something new, with a further purpose or different character, altering the first with **new expression, meaning, or message**. In other words, **whether and to what extent the new work is transformative**." And with this case, the era of transformativeness begins. Souter writes, "the more transformative the new work, the less will be the significance of other factors, like commercialism, that may weigh against a finding of fair use."

What is a Parody?

Souter turns to the question of what makes something a parody. "For the purposes of copyright law, the nub of the definitions, and the heart of any parodist's claim to quote from existing material, is the use of some elements of a prior author's composition to create a new one that, **at least in part, comments on that author's works**." The parody must have critical bearing on the original work.

If it uses the original work, merely to "get attention or to avoid the drudgery in working up something fresh," the borrowing is not a fair use. **Satire** does not get protection under fair use. Here is the difference. Parody mocks the original, while satire uses the original to mock something else.

The court found that 2 Live Crew's version "reasonably could be perceived as commenting on

the original or criticizing it, to some degree." The rap song "juxtaposes the romantic musings of a man whose fantasy comes true, with degrading taunts, a bawdy demand for sex, and a sign of relief from paternal responsibility. The later words can be taken as a comment on the naivete of the original of an earlier day, as a rejection of its sentiment that ignores the ugliness of street life and the debasement that it signifies."

Commercial Nature

What about the commercial nature? It is, after all, a commercial rap song that people purchase on an album. Commercialism is only one element in the four-factor test. But the court still takes time to address it. An advertisement will likely fail the fair use test, but commercial use of a work does not, in itself, mean a failure of the test. This is particularly true with parody, commenting, and criticism.

For the first factor, the court sides with 2 Live Crew. It's a parody, that's the nature of unauthorized use, and the fact that it is on an album doesn't defeat the first factor.

Checking the Second Factor: Nature of the (Original) Copyrighted Work

Based on this factor, the Roy Orbison version is a creative, expressive work, which holds a higher "value of materials used" than a work of non-fiction or facts. This is found in favor of Acuff-Rose (the copyright holder of "Pretty Woman".)

Checking the Third Factor: Amount and Substantiality of the (Unauthorized) Portion Use

There is a difference in the third factor with regard to parodies. While you can't take the heart of the work generally, using the heart of the work is okay in parodies. If you are creating a parody, commenting on a thing in a way that conjures up the thing (think Saturday Night Live), you can take the heart of the work because you need to do so in order to conjure up the original.

The commentary must comment on the original. That's key. It can't be used for convenience of form. As an example, as part of the *Campbell v. Accuff-Rose* case, the court addresses a book that used Dr. Seuss's *The Cat in the Hat* to tell the O.J. Simpson story. There was nothing about *The Cat in the Hat* that was being parodied. Instead, the book was being used to tell a different story, and the court labeled that satire. In terms of fair use, satire is bad. It doesn't constitute fair use. "Parody needs to mimic the original to make its point, and so has some claim to use the creation of its victim's … imagination, whereas satire can stand on its own two feet and so requires justification for the very act of borrowing."

"Pretty Woman" and the Fourth Factor: The Impact on the Market

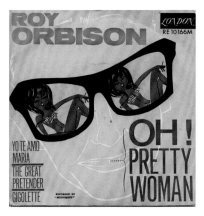

Did the use cause harm to the market, and would that kind of use cause problems for other copyright holders? The court did not find this to be a rap derivative (requiring permission) but a parody (requiring no permission).

A parody may harm the market, just like a bad review may shut down a play, but in this case, whether there is harm to the market of the original should not be taken into consideration. "This distinction between potentially remediable displacement and irremediable disparagement is reflected in the rule that there is no protectible derivative market for criticism." Souter explains, "The market for potential derivative uses includes only those that creators of original works would in general develop or license others to develop. Yet the unlikelihood that creators of imaginative works will license critical reviews or lampoons of their own productions removes such uses from the very notion of a potential licensing market."

There is no derivative market harm for critical works, including parody. We have now introduced you to fair use. Let's take a look at some examples of when the court found fair use, and when they did not. Then, the next chapter, Art and Fair Use, will dive deeper into the ways artists and makers can apply fair use.

Examples of Fair Use

Scholarship

You can quote and comment on others' works in your work. For example, you write a biography and use quotes from a number of letters and novels of your subject. You use only what you need of the letters for the commentary. You can't just wholesale print large chunks because they are interesting. The use of the art to illustrate an artist's work in a biography also constituted fair use. For more, see *Warren Publ'g Co. v. Spurlock*, 645 F. Supage 2d 402 (E.D. Pa. 2009).

Quotes as Part of Artwork

You take a quote from a poem and create a quilt using the quote and your interpretation of that poem. This constitutes fair use, comment/criticism, and transformative use.

Museum Exhibits

You can use photographs and other copyrighted works as part of an exhibit and even online catalogs as long as you are commenting on or criticizing the work. In the *Marano v. Metro. Museum of Art* 472 F. Supp. 3d 76 (2021) case, the court found that the use of a photograph of Eddie Van Halen playing his famous "Frankenstein" guitar at a concert was a different, transformative use when the Met put the photograph in its exhibit to discuss the instrument itself. This was not seen as commercial, even though the museum charges an entry fee.

Making Copies

Fair use also allows you to make copies for personal use. Two out-of-print fashion books were used for another book. As part of the research, the defendant author made copies of at least one of the out-of-print books. The copies were made for research purposes, and because they were out of print, there was no loss of commercial benefits. So, as a researcher, you can copy large swathes of out-of-print works. This doesn't speak to republishing those parts. *Duffy v. Penguin Books USA, Inc.,* 4 F. Supp. 2d 268 (S.D.N.Y. 1998)

Here's another example. We make a copy from five different books of how each approached the technique of creating perfect Flying Geese, a type of quilt block. We bring them to class to teach different strategies. Because it is a small amount, and the lesson is about comparing techniques that qualifies as fair use. However, if we copy a whole book or a good part of it, that is violating factor four and is unfair to the copyright holder because it becomes a market replacement for students.

Taking Bits of a Work

Collage artists take bits from a variety of sources and carefully craft a message that reflects on the sources. That is fair use.

A documentary film used clips from other films, and the court found it transformative because the clips added to the scholarly commentary that amounted to "more than mere narration." They had used snippets of *shtetl* scenery in a montage. "This documentary aims to teach and enlighten its audience about Aleichem's work and Jewish history." The works might have also been in the public domain, which would then not require fair use. This is an important theory, but the court does not do a public domain analysis. Also, each clip was less than 1.5% of the film and qualitatively minimal, and did not include the heart of the work. *Nat'l Ctr. for Jewish Film v. Riverside Films, L.L.C.,* No. 5:12-cv-00044-ODW (DTB) (C.D. Cal. Sept. 14, 2012).

In another documentary film, *Burlesque: Heart of the Glitter Tribe* (2017), used eight seconds of the chorus of a song "Fish Sticks n' Tater Tots". The use was found "incidental" to the film's purpose of providing "commentary on the burlesque art form" and it was used "as it happened" in the performance.

But see *Elvis Presley Enters., Inc. v. Passport Video*, 349 F.3d 622 (9th Cir. 2003), where the use of clips of Elvis in a sixteen-hour long video documentary was ruled as not constituting fair use. The documentary was commercial, and not a scholarly critique of historical analysis. The clips were also not transformative and were an excessive amount.

Many clips were used repeatedly, and market harm for licensing could be presumed. What we see is that transformative, scholarly (noncommercial), short uses are key in surviving a fair use analysis.

And another. A case about a 1974 boxing match between Muhammad Ali and George Foreman, where clips were used in a documentary film, between 41 seconds and 2 minutes. While the documentary was commercial in nature, it was a combination of commentary, criticism, scholarship, and research. The footage was not the focus of the documentary, and so little was used. The court also noted that the historical nature of the clips weighed in favor of using them under fair use. *Monster Commc'ns, Inc. v. Turner Broad. Sys., Inc.*, 935 F. Supp. 490 (S.D.N.Y. 1996).

Artists' Reel

An actor used film excerpts in her performance acting reel to help her obtain future casting. The films had been shown at festivals, but the actor's use was before commercial release. The Court found the use was transformative because it was to further her career by showcasing her acting for casting purposes. *Bain v. Film Indep., Inc.*, No. CV 18–4126 PA (JEMx), 2020 U.S. Dist. LEXIS 141859 (C.D. Cal. Aug. 6, 2020)

Not Fair Use

Here are things that courts have found not to be considered fair use.

Sanitizing and Condensing a Novel Without Permission

You can't condense a novel and sanitize it for children. You have to get permission. That's the copyright holder's decision. (Unless the books are in the public domain, and then go ahead!) For a deeper dive into this topic see *Penguin Random House LLC, et al. v. Frederik Colting and Melissa Medina, d/b/a Moppet Books*, No. 17-cv-386 (S.D.N.Y. Sept. 8, 2017)

Karaoke

Distributing lyrics with a karaoke system without obtaining a license is not considered fair use. This is not considered a teaching tool, it is not transformative, and is clearly commercial. To see an example of this exact situation see *Leadsinger, Inc. v. BMG Music Publ'g*, 512 F.3d 522 (9th Cir. 2008).

Commercial Copies

You can't make photocopies of copyrighted works that do not pass the four-factor test in a commercial photocopy shop for students to use as "course packages." Photoshops can't do that and still won't. You can see this in action in *Princeton Univ. Press v. Mich. Document Servs., Inc.*, 99 F.3d 1381 (6th Cir. 1996) The same is true for copies within a work environment. Employees copied journal articles and circulated them rather than getting more copies of the journal. This was not considered fair use. See *Am. Geophysical Union v. Texaco, Inc.*, 60 F.3d 913 (2d Cir. 1995) for a more in-depth look at this situation.

Teachers Ripping off Teachers

One teacher steals another teacher's work, and uses it without asking permission. That's not a fair use. In this case, it was about teaching cake decorations. The defendant copied fifty percent of the plaintiff's work. The court did not find that the use was fair. Don't be a teacher who steals from another teacher. See *Marcus v. Rowley*, 695 F.2d 1171 (9th Cir. 1983).

Celebrities Using Photos of Themselves from Social Media Posts

A paparazzi photographer took a photo of defendant model Emily Ratajkowski leaving a flower shop, and then Ratajkowski reposted the photograph to her Instagram Stories, which was deleted within 24 hours. The photographer filed a copyright infringement suit. The court found that the model's use was not transformative, that it had an impact on the potential market, and so fair use did not apply. Emily could not post the photo of herself on her Instagram. The photographer held the copyright. To take a closer look at the case, see *O'Neil v. Ratajkowski*, 563 F.Supp.3d 112 (S.D.N.Y. 2021). We should keep a watch on this one to see if it is reversed.

In another social media case, *Newsweek* used a photograph without getting a license, the court found for the photographer. No fair use. See *McGucken v. Newsweek LLC*, 19 Civ. 9617 (KPF), 2022 U.S. Dist. LEXIS 50231 (S.D.N.Y. Mar. 21, 2022)

Using the Emmy Statuette for Your Own Awards

You can't use the Emmy Statuette on your YouTube channel for the "Crony Awards" where you replace the atom with a COVID-19 virus because they both are awards shows, the use was commercial. The Crony Awards used the Emmy as satire, and not parody. See *Nat'l Acad. of TV Arts & Scis., Inc. v. Multimedia Sys. Design, Inc.*, No. 20-CV-7269 (VEC), 2021 U.S. Dist. LEXIS 142733 (S.D.N.Y. July 30, 2021)

Random Use of Some Else's Work

The play *Hand in God* used one minute and seven seconds of the comedy routine, *Who's On First?* as part of a way to impress a girl, using sock puppet characters. The play did not get a license to use the skit. The Second Circuit Court found that the use was commercial and that it was not transformative because the work was performed as the original was, and if this was transformative then any character in any play could sing a song or perform a comedy routine without obtaining a license.

Looking at the second factor, the work was fictional and creative. Reviewing the third factor, there was substantial copying of the routine without permission. And for the fourth factor, they could have gotten a license. Their use also didn't have any bearing on the plot. The use of *Who's On First* was to show the character's ability to memorize and could have been anything. See *TCA Television Corp. v. McCollum*, No. 1:16-cv-0134 (2d Cir. Oct. 11, 2016).

Copyrighted Eyewear Used in Advertisement

Using someone else's copyrighted work in an advertisement, even nonfunctional decorative eyewear, without obtaining permission is not good, and is rarely ever considered a fair use. It's crossing a line. You are using someone else's work to advertise your own. To see how this played out in the real world check out *Davis v. Gap, Inc.*, 246 F.3d 152 (2d Cir. 2001).

FAIR USE IN A COMMERCIAL CONTEXT

If you are planning to use fair use with a commercial product, we encourage you to consult with an attorney. Many publishers will not allow fair use, and you also may have to warranty any liability if there is a lawsuit or fair use is not applicable. Fair use is great for book reviews and student projects, but if you are doing anything more substantial, hire an attorney.

Art and Fair Use

You now know the basic concept of fair use, and some examples of what has been considered fair and not fair. This chapter looks at specific examples within art.

Don't Be a Market Replacement

As we've talked about already, in 2023 the U.S. Supreme Court handed down the *Andy Warhol* decision. If you are using the work for the same purpose, you need to get a license. Fair use doesn't work. The court also addressed this in earlier cases, namely a series of cases with the artist Jeff Koons.

Jeff Koons was sued multiple times for his work in his *Banality* series. The most famous lawsuit involves a photograph of puppies by a professional photographer, that Jeff Koons had remade and colorized into a 3-D sculpture without getting permission for the underlying image. *Rogers v. Koons*, 960 F.2d 301 (2d Cir. 1992). The court found that Koons's work didn't fall under fair use. Sounds like Andy Warhol, just 30 years earlier, right?

Postcard by Art Rogers entitled *Puppies* (left) next to the sculpture by Jeff Koons called *String of Puppies* (right). Koons did not get permission to use Roger's work. The court did not find fair use.

Collage Art is Better

Fourteen years later, both Koons and fair use had become more savvy. Here Koons had taken a commission to create a series of collage paintings, titled *Easyfun-Ethereal*, and as part of that had included images from advertisements and his own photographs, which were scanned into a computer and then the resulting image was printed as a template for his assistants to paint billboard-sized 10' × 14' canvasses. He made seven of these, and one, *Niagara* is the subject of the lawsuit.

Original photograph by Andrea Blanch *Silk Sandals* as published in the August 2000 issue of Allure Magazine (left) next to Koons's collage and colorized version entitled *Niagara* (right)

Koons had taken the legs from an advertisement, and as he did with *Puppies*, altered the image, this time including colorization and changing the orientation. The legs were taken from a photograph, entitled "Silk Sandals by Gucci" and owned by Andrea Blanch, from the August 2000 issue of *Allure* magazine. Koons positioned these legs with other images of legs taken from other sources, and not all of the original picture had been taken, just the legs and feet had been lifted off the background and used out of context. Koons explained that he juxtaposed women's legs against a background of food and landscape and stated that he intended to "comment on the ways in which some of our most basic appetites—for food, play, and sex—are mediated by popular images." He further explained, "By re-contextualizing these fragments as I do, I try to compel the viewer to break out of the conventional way of experiencing a particular appetite as mediated by mass media." How would the court view this use of someone else's professional photograph? The court found that Koons's use of the *Silk Sandals* legs was "transformative." The court explains, "Koons asserts—and Blanch does not deny—that his purposes in using Blanch's image are sharply different from Blanch's goals in creating it."

The court articulates a test:

> The test for whether *Niagara's* use of *Silk Sandals* is transformative, then, is whether it "merely supersedes the objects of the original creation, or instead adds something new, with a further purpose or different character, altering the first with **new expression, meaning, or message**."

Koons had learned how to make his work transformative. Compared to his earlier art where he was sued and lost, now he started to think about transformative fair use as an artist—if he was going to use others' work without permission, he had to start thinking about *why* he was using them as part of the process. And that prhase "new expression, meaning or message" also became key as well.

Using Others' Art in a Commercial Setting

Fair use will likely not apply if your use is a market substitute for the original. That's the *Andy Warhol* case. If you are using an image that is still protected by copyright, you likely need permission to use that work.

First Sale Doctrine and Art

Artist Tom Forsythe made art out of Barbie dolls, creating a series of photos called *Food Chain Barbie*, where Barbie was posed in different kitchen appliances, and even as part of enchiladas. The court found the use to be transformative with a parody quality. *Mattel Inc. v. Walking Mountain Prods.*, 353 F.3d 792 (9th Cir. 2003). This spawned many others to create art with Barbie. (There's Barbie-in-a-Blender Day each year now).

Using Images Online for Your Website

If you are using someone else's photograph on your website, the best advice is to get permission. It's just not wise to take a random photo from an Internet search and put it on your website. There are bots searching for unauthorized use of photos, and doing so will get you into hot water, even if a court later decides it is fair use. The era of using photos without consequences seems to be over. And now we have the Copyright Claims Board, a place to bring your complaint of someone using your photograph without permission. (See Copyright Claims Board, page 162).

Another Angle: Code of Best Practices for Visual Arts

Best Practices in Fair Use for the Visual Arts by the College Art Association addresses ways to think about fair use. This is one of many projects coming out of the Center for Media and Social Impact at American University. They have created best practices for fair use for documentary filmmakers, poets (Elizabeth was a legal reviewer on this one), and also artists, which you can find at cmsimpact.org/report-list/codes.

The *Code of Best Practices for Visual Arts* was co-sponsored by College Art Association and funded by the Andrew W. Mellon Foundation with additional support provided by the Samuel H. Kress Foundation. To produce the guides, they have conversations with the art community (or whichever group they are working with) to understand the norms and customs of the community and how they interact with fair use. These have been significantly impactful. These guides reveal that it is not just artists who need fair use protection, but also those who teach art, display art (museums), and those who comment on and criticize art. You can read the full Code for yourself at collegeart.org > Standards & Guidelines > Intellectual Property > CAA's Code of Best Practices in Fair Use for the Visual Arts. Let's take a look.

For each of their basic principles, they describe a situation, a principle, and limitations. We're going to look at the principles.

Analytic Writing

They begin with those who are commenting on and criticizing art: "In their analytic writing about art, scholars and other writers (and, by extension, their publishers) may invoke fair use to *quote, excerpt, or reproduce* copyrighted works, subject to certain limitations…" The limitations include the amount needed to analyze the work at issue. This is a traditional fair use space. We all need to be able to look at a painting, and then be able to write or comment about that painting, and even have a photograph of that painting so that the reader can follow along.

Teaching About Art

They then turn to the classroom. "Teachers in the visual arts may invoke fair use in using copyrighted works of various kinds to support formal instruction in a range of settings, as well as for uses that extend such teaching and for reference collections that support it, subject to certain limitations …" You can make copies, for example in a slide show, to discuss different forms of contemporary art, or to provide instructions on the same technique through the ages. Those are both examples of using visual arts in a formal instructional setting. And we have other parts of the Copyright Act of 1976 that supports this as well.

Making Art

For our makers, this third point is the heart of the question. What can artists do with others' work that fall under fair use? Here is what the guidelines suggest. "Artists may invoke fair use to incorporate copyrighted material into new artworks in any medium, subject to certain limitations..." The limitations include that the artist should include materials creating "new artistic meaning," and should be justified by the artistic objective, with

Artists may invoke fair use to incorporate copyrighted material into new artworks in any medium, subject to certain limitations...

artists able to explain the rationale for the use and why they are integral to the meaning of the new work. And when using the work of someone else, make sure to cite the source when possible. We also know that this is more limited after the *Andy Warhol* case; it can't be a market substitute for the original. "New artist meaning" was a key element in many fair use cases. It seems that at the moment, it is really whether the original and potentially infringing use serves the same purpose, and if the infringing use is a market substitute for the original. If so, then there is no fair use. Get a license.

But it seems like their "making art" analysis doesn't go far enough. What about reference photographs? What about public domain works? What about non-protectable elements? We know this is a more nuanced conversation.

Museum Uses

They turn to institutional uses of others' works. "Museums and their staff may invoke fair use in using copyrighted works, including images and text as well as time-based and born-digital material, in furtherance of their core missions, subject to certain limitations..." Here we see that the guidelines recognize that museums and other spaces that house cultural objects need spaces within fair use. They want to be able to preserve and display the works that they have. And we see that courts have agreed, allowing museums to use copyrighted images in exhibits (as long as they meet the fair use requirements, including not a market replacement. You can have an exhibit about book covers over the years, without getting permission to display them. That serves a different purpose than selling the individual books. You can even put that display online.

The guidelines turn to online access of materials, making sure these are included. It is interesting that they have expanded the definition to not just traditional museums, but also memory institutions.

Using *Trademarks*

This is not a book about trademarks! (That's *Just Wanna Trademark for Makers,* [by C&T Publishing] the other book we wrote!). But trademarks get used creatively in copyrighted works, so it is important to understand why and how this is possible. Usually, this falls under the First Amendment, which is another way of thinking about fair use. Trademark law borrows legal concepts from copyright law to allow uses such as fair use.

What is a Trademark?

A trademark can be any word, name, symbol, or image that conveys the source of a product. A logo, a brand name—we see them all of the time.

They help us distinguish between potato chips, glue, and hotels. The function is to identify the source of the goods or services. "Trademarks can of course do other things: catch a consumer's eye, appeal to his fancies, and convey every manner of message. But whatever else [a trademark] may do, a trade-mark is not a trademark unless it identifies a product's source (this is a Nike) and distinguishes that source from others (not any other sneaker brand)." *Jack Daniel's Properties, Inc. v. VIP Products LLC,* 599 U.S. 140 (2023).

Key Trademark Terms

Source Identifiers

Trademark law focuses on source identifiers: names, logos, and other elements that identify a good or service.

A trademark must be a source identifier for a product or service. Trademarks are most effective when consumers see your mark and choose your goods or services because they identify it as the one they want. They help customers/consumers find products faster (reducing the search cost) and remember what they like and don't like.

Goodwill

Goodwill is what you think about a particular version of a good or service because you identify the trademark and have feelings about it. Goodwill connects to the source identifiers. The goodwill you have toward certain source identifiers is why you buy one product over another or why you know to recommend Service A over its competitor, Service B.

Companies build up goodwill surrounding their trademark through advertising, marketing, and word of mouth. As the trademark becomes known, the goodwill attached to it can become worth a great deal of money and an intellectual property asset of the company.

Goodwill Isn't Always Good

Goodwill doesn't mean that consumers must think good things about your products—goodwill is whatever they think of when they see your product. For example, maybe consumers know to avoid buying a certain type of rotary cutter when they see a particular logo.

Expressive Use of a Trademark

You can use someone else's trademark as expressive, either in language or in art. Think, "the Rolls Royce of thread." It conveys that the thread is expensive and precious. There are a number of instances where trademarked goods and services themselves can be used within permissible uses.

Likelihood of Confusion

Likelihood of confusion] is the key concept in trademark: does your mark likely confuse customers as to the source of that good? We do a multi-part test to determine that. We will discuss this more fully shortly, see The *Rogers* Test: Determining Source Identifier or Expressive Content (page 92).

Dilution

If you have a famous mark, then you may also have protection from *dilution*. This is when someone uses a famous brand to increase the recognizability of their brand. This comes in two forms: **blurring** and **tarnishment**. *Blurring* is when you trade on someone else's fame, like Federal Expresso. That blurs Federal Express with your coffee shop. *Tarnishment* is when you take a famous brand and do naughty things. The famous example is an adult film called *Debbie Does Dallas*, where girls wore Dallas Cowboy cheerleading uniforms, and well ... the Dallas Cowboys organization wasn't pleased.

The *Rogers* Test: Determining Source Identifier or Expressive Content

If you use someone else's trademark as a source identifier, even as a parody, that is not permitted. It's a commercial use of someone else's property. See the recent U.S. Supreme Court case *Jack Daniels v. VIP*, 599 U.S. 140 (2023).

But you can use it as expressive content. So, how do you know if you are using something as a source identifier versus expressive content? We have a case, *Rogers v. Grimaldi*, 695 F. Supp. 112 (S.D.N.Y. 1988) which established a test.

In 1986, Federico Fellini's film *Ginger and Fred* told the fictional story of two Italian cabaret performers who made a living by imitating Ginger Rogers and Fred Astaire. Ginger Rogers was not happy. She sued over the use of her name in the title and believed the film gave a false impression that she had endorsed the film and therefore, violated her right of publicity, and defamed her by presenting her in a negative light.

The *Rogers* court found that "literary titles do not violate the [Trademark Act] 'unless the title had no artistic relevance to the underlying work whatsoever, or if it has some artistic relevance unless the title explicitly misleads as to the source or the content of the work" as cited in Mattel, Inc. v. MCA Records, 296 F.3d 894 (9th Cir. 2002).

Trademark law adopted the test. This was seen a test to see if there would be confusion as to the source of the work, that is being endorsed by Ginger Rogers. The filter was determining whether a likelihood of confusion test could be applied. If there was some artistic relevance and it was not explicitly misleading, then the likelihood of confusion claim under trademark law *could not go forward*. The test was applied to many things beyond titles, as we will see shortly.

In short: Is the trademark being used as a trademark, or is it being used as something expressive and/or an artistic non-trademark use?

The *Rogers* case was quickly adopted and expanded. But just because something has expressive elements does not mean it falls under *Rogers*. A trademark or trade dress can be expressive, if the use is also used as a source identifier, then it fails the *Rogers* test.

The test is as follows:

1. Does the use of the trademark have some artistic relevance to the underlying work? In other words, is the use something artistic or expressive? If YES, then go on to question 2.

2. Is the use not explicitly misleading as to the source of that work? The next step is to make sure that your artistic or expressive use is not going to mislead customers of the original company's products and/or services.

Expressive Use: The "Barbie Girl" Case

The case, *Mattel, Inc. v. MCA Records*, 296 F.3d 894 (9th Cir. 2002), written by Judge Kozinski, starts out with this sentence: "If this were a sci-fi melodrama, it might be called Speech-Zilla meets Trademark Kong." Konzinski is known for his creative writing in opinions.

Judge Kozinski begins with Barbie, the doll, describing her origins in the 1950s as an adult collector's item, and then turning into the mega toy that she is. "Barbie has been labeled both the ideal American woman and a bimbo … She remains a symbol of American girlhood, a public figure who graces the aisles of toy stores throughout the country and beyond. With Barbie, Mattel created not just a toy, but a cultural icon." and (high-pitched singing) "Barbie. The song made it to the Top 40 list (and anyone who was a teenager at that time can probably still sing the lyrics!) Mattel sued in 2002.

Aqua is a Danish band that created a song called "Barbie Girl" on their album *Aquarium*. The song is about Barbie's life, with the band members acting out the parts of Ken. When they released "Barbie Girl" "as yet, only dreamed of attaining Barbie-like status." (And who says court cases are dry and boring!)

Kosinski gets down to analyzing the case. "A trademark is a word, phrase, or symbol that is used to identify a manufacturer or sponsor of a good or the provider of a service," explains the Judge.

The question is how the First Amendment interacts with the property right awarded by the United States Patent and Trademark Office (USPTO) to the trademark holder. Judge Kozinski suggests that some marks become part of our language, like "the Rolls Royce of its class," or "What else is a quick fix, but a Band Aid?" We use the mark to express concepts; they have become part of our vocabulary. They are not, in this case, being used as a source identifier, but we recognize the qualities of the mark to describe something else. "Simply put, the trademark owner does not have the right to control public discourse whenever the public imbues his mark with meaning beyond its source-identifying function." Kozinski then turns back to the Mattel case.

Here, Aqua used Mattel's mark, both as the title of the song and as the subject of the song. "The song pokes fun at Barbie and the values that Aqua contends she represents … The song does not rely on the Barbie mark to poke fun at another subject but targets Barbie herself." This sounds a lot like the copyright case, *Campbell v. Acuff-Rose*, right? He cites this and other cases.

Kozinski applied the *Rogers* case. The use of the word "Barbie" in the title was relevant to the underlying work and was artistic/expressive, and the song does not explicitly mislead as to the source of the work. Aqua's use of the title "Barbie" was not trademark infringement.

So, that's the test. Using a trademark in an artistic way: is the use relevant to the underlying artistic work being created, and does the use explicitly mislead as to the source of the work?

Failing the *Rogers* Test: The Jack Daniel's Case

VIP is a dog toy company that parodies popular beverage brands with funny names: "Dos Perros" for Dos Equis and "Doggie Walker" for Johnny Walker. VIP registered trademarks for many of their joke names, along with their line of toys "Silly Squeakers." Each funny name was registered with the USPTO as a source identifier for that particular toy.

Then, VIP thought up "Bad Spaniels" for a toy based on Jack Daniels. The joke was it was "No. 2" rather than No. 7, and the toy was full of potty and pee humor. The toy was the same shape, size, and color as a bottle of Jack Daniels. And "Bad Spaniels" was used on the tag as a source identifier.

The tag included a disclaimer that the product was not associated with Jack Daniel Distillery, but disclaimers are just not enough. Jack Daniels sent a cease and desist letter to VIP to stop selling the toy. VIP responded by bringing a *lawsuit* that they were neither infringing or diluting the Jack Daniel brand because it was a parody, that it was an expressive artistic work. The case went through the district and appeals court, and ended up at the U.S. Supreme Court.

This recent case helps us understand the source identifier versus expressive content divide further. The company used their jokey version of Jack Daniels to not only make fun of the product, but also to identify the source of their version. You can

make fun of a product, and even sell that product, but you can't use it as a source identifier. Ever.

Elena Kagan, Associate Justice of the Supreme Court of the United States, delivered the opinion for the court. She begins, "This case is about dog toys and whiskey, two items seldom appearing in the same sentence." Jack Daniel's has numerous trademarks on its bottle and label for whiskey, named "Old No. 7." It is a well-protected and well-known mark.

The court believed the *Rogers* test did not apply.

University of Alabama v. Moore

Another case of using the *Rogers* test is in the case of *Univ. of Alabama Bd. of Trustees v. New Life Art, Inc.*, 683 F.3d 1266, 1279 (11th Cir. 2012)

Daniel Moore is a painter who, since 1979, has focused his work on famous University of Alabama football scenes. For the first eleven years, Moore had no relationship with the university. Then, in 1991, he signed a dozen licensing agreements with the university for market-specific items. His work appears on calendars, mugs, and other items.

He also continued to create and sell paintings and prints that were not subject to the licensing agreement, and some that he had created before the agreement. In 2002, the University of Alabama told Moore he needed to get permission to depict their uniforms because the uniforms were trademarks in the unlicensed paintings and prints. Moore disagreed because he said he was using them to depict historical events—the football games. The University of Alabama sued Moore in 2005. The Eleventh Circuit Court divided the discussion between the paintings, prints, and calendars, and mugs and other mundane products. What did they mean by mundane products? Coffee cups and other mass produced items usually found in gift shops.

The court concluded that the First Amendment interests in artistic expression outweighed any consumer confusion, and so no trademark infringement occurred. The court turned to the *Rogers* test. They noted that other Circuits had applied the *Rogers* test, including to a parody of *Cliff Notes* called *Spy Notes* (*Cliff Notes, Inc. v. Bantam Doubleday Dell Publishing Group*, 718 F. Supp. 1159 [S.D.N.Y. 1989]); and an artist who had painted a collage of Tiger Woods images (*ETW Corp. v. Jireh Publ'g, Inc.*, 332 F.3d 915, 918–19 [6th Cir., 2003]). All found that the uses had artistic relevance to the underlying work, and did not mislead as to the source of the work. All of the examples were found to be protected by the First Amendment against a claim of false endorsement and/or trademark infringement. Then they turned to Moore.

The court explained, "Selling the copyrighted drawing itself may not amount to a trademark infringement, but its placement on certain products very well might." Creating an artwork under *Rogers* is one thing; commercializing it on mugs and other gift shop items is quite another.

Copyright Versus Trademark

In earlier chapters we noted that certain early versions of Mickey and Winnie-the-Pooh came into other public domain, see Identifying the Public Domain (page 65). However, just because they are in the public domain doesn't mean that they aren't still source identifiers under trademark. Don't use them as your source identifier. The same is true with many other popular public domain but trademarked characters. Research needs to be done before considering any use of a public domain item as a trademark.

Sometimes you may want to use a property that is in the public domain, but you also want to create trademarked products. You may then obtain a license from the content holder, as they may hold the trademarks. Think Mickey. Think Sherlock.

Other Permissible Uses of a Trademark

Nominative Use

You ask someone "What is your favorite batting?" They can answer that question, "The Warm Company," even though the name is trademarked. If we can't name the things in our life, we will be paralyzed.

Elizabeth has to be able to say "I'm a law professor at Tulane University." She's using Tulane's trademark in that instance, but it is to identify her place of work. Sid has to be able to say they're a student at the School of the Art Institute of Chicago. It's identifying their place of study. You can do that. Comparative advertising uses that. "Wonderfil is so much better than Angelfil." (We made up that last company).

However, claims must be truthful and verifiable if numbers are used. "Four out of five dentists … " (But now we're getting into advertising law).

The concept of nominative use comes from two cases: one about New Kids On The Block, and another about Terri Welles, a former Playboy Playmate of the Year. In both cases, the courts agreed that you had to be able to name the thing you are discussing.

The New Kids On The Block case concerned a quiz offered by two media outlets asking readers to pay fifty cents to vote on which New Kid they preferred. The media outlets had to name the New Kids to offer the quiz. The courts did not agree with the New Kids attempt to block use of their trademarked name, "[w]hile the New Kids have a limited property right in their name, that right does not entitle them to control their fans' use of their own money. Where, as here, the use does not imply sponsorship or endorsement, the fact that it is carried on for profit and in competition with the trademark holder's business is beside the point." (*New Kids On The Block v. News Am. Pub.*, Inc., 971 F.2d 302 [9th Cir. 1992])

In the second case, Terri Welles had created an early website naming herself as 1981 Playmate of the Year. She used PMOY, Playboy, and Playmate in metatags, but she also used the phrase "Playmate of the Year" as wallpaper on her site. You could name someone like PMOY, but you can't decorate your website with it. That's nominative use. *Playboy Enterprises, Inc. v. Welles* (279 F. 3d 796 [9th Cir. 2002])

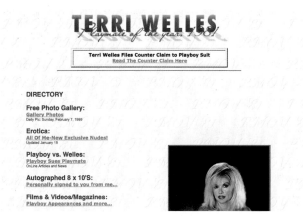

See the faint PMOY in the white background over and over? You can't do that.

Incidental Use of Trademarks

You are in an interview that is being recorded. You happen to be drinking LaCroix Sparkling Water. You are not endorsing the product, you just happen to be drinking it. This is called an incidental use. You are not using it as an ad, you are just depicting your life.

Descriptive (or Classic) Fair Use

In trademark, descriptive fair use is a little more complicated. Sometimes companies choose trademarks that describe their product, but over time, people identify the product with that company. Fish Fri for Louisiana, and allowed FISH FRI as a trademark, as a source identifier. But others could use "fish fri" as descriptive of a batter to fry fish. You can use that descriptive word, even if it is someone else's trademark, but you can't use it as a trademark.

For example, a cosmetic company, Chesebrough-Pond's USA Co., ran a campaign for Cutex lipstick using "Seal it with a Kiss!!," that asked customers to kiss a postcard and send it to someone they love. The owner of the registered mark SEALED WITH A KISS, Cosmetically Sealed Industries, Inc., a competing line of cosmetics, sued.

The court said that "sealed with a kiss" was common and being used in a descriptive sense, not as a source identifier of a product, and so qualified as descriptive fair use. "So long as the defendants [Chesebrough] in good faith are using the phrase in its descriptive sense and prominently identifying the product with the defendants' marks, the defendants incur no liability simply because the materials containing the descriptive phrase are so widely disseminated as to form some degree of association in the public's mind between the phrase and the product. That too is a risk the plaintiff [CBI] took in selecting as its mark a phrase that was not only descriptive but readily recognized by consumers." See *Cosmetically Sealed Industries, Inc. v. Chesebrough-Pond's USA Co.*, 125 F.3d 28 (2d Cir. 1997).

USING A FAMOUS TRADEMARK?

If you are using a famous mark in your work, consult with an attorney to run a dilution analysis. It may save you heartache and money in the end.

No 10% Change Rule ... But Maybe *90%*?

> You may have heard that if you just change ten percent of a copyrighted work, you are good to go. Or that you can copy ten percent of a copyrighted work. This is false.

How Did This Myth Get Started?

With the enactment of the Copyright Act of 1976 and the inclusion of fair use, two groups were created to study and come up with guidelines on the new relationship between fair use and copy machines, a new thing at the time, in connection to making copies for teaching.

The Classroom guidelines, the full name being *Agreement on Guidelines for Classroom Copying In Not-For-Profit Educational Institutions With Respect to Books and Periodicals*, was an agreement between authors, educators, and publishers in 1976, the same year as the enactment of the Copyright Act of 1976. This is **not** part of the law, and many saw it as too restrictive.

Here is what the guidelines say about how much a teacher can copy for classroom use in non-profit education settings with regard to books and periodicals. These are not designed for use by copy shops or for-profit shops.

Single copy. Teachers may, for scholarly research, copy a chapter from a book, an article from a periodical, a short story, essay, poem, chart, cartoon, or drawing.

Multiple copies. For classroom discussion: a poem less than 250 words, or not more than two pages; a complete article, story, or essay of less than 2,500 words; or an excerpt of no more than **1,000 words or 10%, whichever is less**; or one chart, graph, diagram, drawing, cartoon, or picture per book or per periodical. The copying must be at "the instance and inspiration of the individual teacher" and "the inspiration and decision to use the work and the moment of its use for maximum teaching effectiveness are so close in time that it would be unreasonable to expect a timely reply to a request for permission. Cumulative effect: it can only be for one course, and not more than one poem, article, story, essay or two excerpts may be copied from the same author, or three from the same collection in one class term; and not more than nine instances of copying for one course in one term. Copying can not be a substitute for an anthology or textbook. And no copying from consumables including workbooks and testing materials. Additional, the teacher can't charge students for the copies."

If you notice the part we bolded, you see where the 10% myth got its origins.

These are considered the *minimum* standards for educational fair use under Section 107. This was supposed to help teachers understand permissible copying. But they are not controlling in court. See *Marcus v. Rowley*, 695 F.2d 1171, (9th Cir. 1983). They are guidelines, not legally binding rules.

Moreover, these are fairly limiting guidelines, both in what they apply to and how much can be used. Other parts of the Copyright Act of 1976, including Section 108, are more expansive.

Cambridge University Press Versus Mark P. Becker

Since then, a bunch of the issues that arose have been litigated, including creating course packets (copies of portions of books, articles, and other copywritten materials that were bound for college students). This issue was litigated in *Cambridge University Press v. Mark P. Becker*, No. 1:08-cv-1425-ODE, 2020 U.S. Dist. LEXIS 35134 (N.D. Ga. Mar. 2, 2020). Cambridge University Press, SAGE Publications Inc, and Oxford University Press sued Georgia State for infringing their copyright in 6,700 works that appeared in their e-reserve system because Georgia State has "invited students to download, review, and print such materials without permission of the copyright holder."

Georgia State University (GSU) had a policy that allowed GSU professors to make digital copies of excerpts from books for students without paying publishers by using an e-reserve system. The books involved were research-based scholarly books and edited collections of articles by professors. Professors often put these books on reserve, where students could go to read assignments, or alternatively, they created course packets that students are required to purchase. The creation of course packets usually requires permission from publishers through the Copyright Clearance Center (CCC) (which helped fund the publisher's case at issue). But, instead of sending all students to use one or a few physical copies on reserve, at Georgia State, professors could now have librarians scan the excerpt from the published book, and then give access to GSU students on course-specific websites. This was the e-reserve.

The question that the Eleventh Circuit Court took up was whether e-reserves counted under fair use, or if licensing fees were required. The Eleventh Circuit Court turned to the four-factor fair use test.

Course Packets—First Factor

Was GSU's use transformative? The court found that the use was verbatim (digital) copies of the original and that the use, reading, was the same. GSU's use supersedes the original. The Eleventh Circuit Court also considered that GSU was a non-profit educational institution, part of the first factor. In previous course packet cases, the copying was done by a commercial entity; here it is done by GSU staff. The court found the use is the kind considered under fair use's first factor, even though it was not a transformative use. Educational uses are important. "Congress devoted considerable attention to working out the proper scope of the fair use defense as applied to copying for educational and classroom purposes, going so far as to include in a final report the Classroom Guidelines developed by representatives of educator, author, and publisher groups at the urging of Congress." Congress went to great lengths to include educational copying under fair use. So, the Eleventh Circuit Court agreed with the District Court that the first factor favors a finding of fair use.

Course Packets—Second Factor

The Eleventh Circuit Court found that the works were not merely factual, but contained "evaluative, analytical, or subjectively descriptive material," and so the Eleventh Circuit Courtfound the second factor to either be neutral, or even weighing against fair use. But they also said that the second factor did not have much importance in this case because the works are neither fictional nor unpublished.

Course Packets—Third Factor

Here the District Court had found the defendant had not used more than 10% of a work, or one chapter of a book with ten or more chapters.

The Eleventh Circuit Court responded: "The District Court's blanket 10 percent-or-one-chapter benchmark was improper." **No bright-line rules exist.** The Eleventh Circuit Court also said that previously commercial copying cases were not binding; instead, the court had to look to the defendant's pedagogical purpose, measured against the works.

The Eleventh Circuit Court explained that the District Court was right **not to use the Classroom Guidelines or the course packet cases**. But the District Court erred in using the 10%-or-one-chapter safe harbor. "The District Court should have analyzed each instance of alleged copying individually, considering the quantity and quality of the material taken—including whether the material taken constitutes the heart of the work—and whether the taking was excessive in light of the educational purpose of the use and the threat of market substitution."

Course Packets—Fourth Factor

The Eleventh Circuit Court agreed with the District Court that "the small excerpts the Defendants used do not substitute for the full books from which they are drawn," and no lost book sales were presented. Then they turned to CCC's licensing program for academic permissions, which the plaintiffs (and their litigation funder, CCC) felt was substantially harmed. The Court wrote, "the fact that Plaintiffs have made paying easier does not automatically dictate a right of payment ... The goal of copyright is to stimulate the creation of new works, not to furnish copyright holders with control over all markets. Accordingly, the ability to license does not demand a finding against fair use."

So, why do we need to know this? The Eleventh Circuit Court of appeals court did a fair use analysis and **rejected the 10% concept**. It's more complicated than 10 percent. And 10 percent was about copying for classroom use, and nothing more. Help stop the spread of the 10 percent myth.

What If Something is Changed by 90%?

Super Mario and Sanders Sides help us to understand when something is so dramatically changed from the original that it becomes something new entirely—and that is totally okay!

From Popeye Comes Super Mario

Super Mario: How Nintendo Conquered America by Jeff Ryan tells the origin story of Mario and his gang. In the days of arcade games Nintendo needed something new. The game designer started with the idea of making a game based on the cartoon *Popeye,* but a new live-action film just released. When they looked into it, Nintendo found that while they could eventually get the rights to Popeye, it would take years. So no Popeye.

But they had their core story: defeat the villain to save the girl.

They used archetype characters. Bluto became a big, angry gorilla. What a perfect antagonist. "A big, dumb gorilla won't let Olive Oyl—er, some other lady—go free … " The gorilla came from *King Kong,* named after a stubborn animal, the donkey: Donkey Kong. And Popeye turned into Mario. So, when you look at these characters and stories, do you see the original? Maybe, barely. Popeye was the starting point, but Super Mario was the result.

The Many Sides of Sanders Sides

Here is a weirder example of a derivative work moving so far from its original source that it becomes something new.

In 2016, Vine-star turned YouTuber, Thomas Sanders began a scripted video series on YouTube known as Sanders Sides. Thomas personifyied and portrayed different sides of his personality: he created the characters Creativity, Anxiety, Morality, and Logic. As the series progressed and gained a cult following online, two more sides were added, Deceit and Intrusive Thoughts, and all six characters were eventually given names beyond their personality trait.

The fandom that grew up around this web series created art, writing, role plays, and fan podcasts using these six characters as a starting point. Characters would be given different names, they would exist in different settings, have different relationships, and even different appearances until eventually they really began to become different characters. For more on fandoms and fan culture, see Studying Commercial Versus Non-commercial Uses via Fanworks (page 101).

Sid participated in this too. In high school, they joined a tabletop role-playing group (think Dungeons and Dragons) where each player based the character they were playing off of a Sanders Sides character. Sid and their friends then proceeded to play with these characters for four years. By the end of the game, the character Sid played stopped feeling and looking like a fan character and became their original character. The same was true for each of the characters their friends were playing as well.

Thomas Sanders as Janus "Deceit" Sanders in an episode of the *Sanders Sides* spinoff YouTube series *Sanders Asides*

Dee Adder, Sid's character, may still be associated with snakes and the color yellow, but he's a separate entity from Thomas Sanders's character, Janus "Deceit" Sanders. That's the 90 percent idea in action.

Studying Commercial Versus Non-commercial Uses via *Fanworks*

Crafters and makers often make works that are based on popular (or not so popular) famous television, movie, comic, and YouTube properties. Fans make for themselves, but they also sell their work. This chapter helps us understand fanwork, and the legal implications. Let's take a look at the role of copyright.

What is a Fandom?

Fan culture is a huge part of our modern world. There's a reason that franchises like Marvel and *Doctor Who* and even *My Little Pony* are so ubiquitous—the fans that support them. Think Taylor Swift and her Swifties, who together have made her a powerhouse. Fandom is how a lot of us find ways to connect to people and make friends. People spend hundreds of hours making beautiful fan works, sharing them online, and even, yes, selling them. And brands need fans, not just to be passive viewers, but active participants.

> *People spend hundreds of hours making beautiful fan works, sharing them online, and even, yes, selling them. And brands need fans, not just to be passive viewers, but active participants.*

Fandom isn't a new thing. In fact, fan culture can be traced back to the late 1800s when fans of the original *Sherlock Holmes* stories held public demonstrations after Holmes was killed off. Fast forward to the 1970s, viewers (often women!) watching the original *Star Trek* and similar shows shaped the more modern idea of fandom as fans started to create their own versions of the shows through zines and other forms of writing and art. Fast forward again, and the Internet exploded fan culture, allowing fans to find each other, converse, obsess, debate, and share in a huge new way.

But fan culture doesn't fit neatly with copyright. At all. And that sometimes stresses out the copyright holders, the lawyers, and, yes, the fans. Copyright law was originally designed to regulate booksellers not to steal from each other, and later other major content players. It was only with the Internet that fans and pirates (think uploading and downloading digital copies of music, movies, and television shows) started to engage in mass distribution in ways not previously possible, and not merely watching or listening to them. We've been trying to understand this struggle for years, and a lot has changed, especially in the last five or so years.

Why Fans Create Things

Fans create things to connect with and celebrate the properties that they love. This connects back to personhood theory—the idea that your creations come from your identity and connection. And it is awesome. People connect and find friends and places to discuss all kinds of things. And they create artwork, costumes, and stories because they love the fandom. Finding common interests and loves is an amazing way to connect to other humans, and so too is making things that reflect that love.

There are also people that create works *for fan groups*. Those are people who sell online and at fan shows. Sometimes they are also fans of a particular fandom and sometimes they aren't necessarily fans of a fandom but see the opportunity to sell their art or writing.

Can you see the difference between the two activities? One is personal. One is commercial. And sometimes, the personal and the commercial mix together. We will be looking at all of this in this chapter.

Creating Things Versus Copying Things—*The Three Stooges* Case

We went to FanExpo in New Orleans, Louisiana, and we headed to Artist Alley. That's our favorite part. We see different interpretations of fan culture, and you find gems. A lot of the artwork is putting different fandoms into a particular style or adding jokes or perspective to a particular character.

But there are also a lot of portraits of characters and actors. We talk about the difference as we walk through the convention. And we find ourselves thinking about the *Three Stooges* case, and revisiting *Andy Warhol*.

Gary Saderup was a celebrity lithographer. For over 25 years, he would draw charcoal sketches of celebrities, and then use those drawings to create lithographic and silkscreen masters for prints and T-shirts, which he sold. Then, Comedy III Productions sued him over the Stooges' right of publicity.

What is the right of publicity? The economic right to control your image. And even though the actors who played the Stooges were dead, the right of publicity in California lasts 70 years after death.

The question was, was this art or misappropriation of a celebrity's image? If he had just made the artwork, he would have been okay, but he reproduced his drawings in prints and T-shirts. The courts found his work to be merchandise, not art, and so not protected from the right of publicity. We saw the same questions in regard to football art in the University of Alabama case, (see University of Alabama v. Moore, page 94). And the court's decision in the *Andy Warhol* case says that if the art serves the same purpose as the original, reference photograph, that is not fair use.

And yet … we see many portraits of characters and celebrities. One catches our eye. An artist has a whole booth set up with pencil drawings. They are so reminiscent of the *Three Stooges* case. And yet, when we ask him if he has had any problems with copyright or right of publicity, he says no. He goes around the country with many copies of his prints. No one cares. Is it violating the law? Likely. Does it matter? Likely not in the current climate, but there could be two issues: the photograph he is using to create his sketches, and also the right of publicity of the people being sketched.

Fan Writing Versus Fan Art When it Comes to Intellectual Property

There are different expectations for fan art and fan writing, usually called fanfiction. Sid has done a lot of both as many fans do. But it's interesting to look at how different the culture around each fan art form is. Fan art has become much more mainstream and acceptable than its writing counterpart. Creators, actors, and writers from original intellectual properties (IPs) often even share fan art on their social media, sign fan art at convention meet and greets, and sometimes even own copies of fan art for the media they're part of. Fan art is pretty celebrated.

There are several different websites that act as a place to post fanfiction—the most prominent of which is Archive of Our Own (also known as Ao3). Ao3 quite literally does act as an archive for pretty much any kind of fanfiction you can imagine. Ao3 was made in response to other fanfiction sites like fanfiction. net having much more restrictive terms of service for what was allowed on their site and because many fandom-specific fanfiction sites would be shut down and the fanfictions would cease to be accessible when they did.

If we were following the exact law of copyright infringement with no wriggle room, both fan art and fan fiction often don't qualify for fair use.

Fanfiction writing still has a stigma to it in a way that fan art does not. This is in large part due to vampire novelist Anne Rice's aggressive anti-fanfiction message in the early 2000s. Rice's novels had a huge fan base, and because of that, along with the homoerotic nature of *Interview with the Vampire,* many people were writing fanfictions about her work.

Rice's response? "I do not allow fanfiction. The characters are copyrighted. It upsets me terribly to even think about fanfiction with my characters. I advise my readers to write your own original stories with your own characters. It is absolutely essential that you respect my wishes." To this day, this response is famous. She saw fanfiction as a problem. Not a celebration. She sent cease and desist letters to fans writing stories using her characters. To this day, many fanfiction authors still add a line before or after their posts stating that they do not claim to own the original work they are writing about.

Overtime, Rice's view on this seemed to have lightened to some degree (even admitting in 2012 that fanfiction can be a transitional space for young writers to experiment with), but within fan communities there is still a great deal of tension surrounding the legality of fanfiction.

Nevertheless, fanfiction remains a huge part of fan communities, and most fanfiction writers aren't being sent cease and desist letters. At its core, fanfiction isn't all that different from all those new *Great Gatsby* derivatives and retellings being published once a work is in the public domain. We see dozens of new versions of Great Gatsby, in many forms. And now, we also have a Broadway musical. These works are basically fanfiction, but they're fanfiction for public domain works. The financial investment becomes less risky once a work is in the public domain, but the fan creativity seems to continue regardless of the copyright status of the work. (See How Far Can You Go? A Different Perspective on Enforcement, page 166.)

Interestingly, authors of the original IPs that fans are writing about often don't want to engage with fanfiction because they don't want to unconsciously copy the writing of fans into the next installment of the original work. But there are also instances where fans who used to be fanfiction writers or fan artists later get hired to work on the franchise they used to be obsessed over as a fan. The hashtag #fanartgotmepaid on X (formerly known as Twitter) became a place where artists talked about their experiences of how being fans and making fan works ended up being part of the path to getting them various kinds of employment.

When Fanfiction Becomes a Bestseller

Remember when *Fifty Shades of Grey* became a huge deal and people kept talking about how before being published as a novel it was posted online as *Twilight* fanfiction? Well, this is something that is becoming increasingly common. So much so that a *Fifty Shades* fanfiction also was published as an original novel called *365 Days*. Yes, a fanfiction of a fanfiction, both of which became proper novels with film adaptations.

The young adult genre and the romance genre seem to be where these fanfictions turned novels mostly exist, which makes sense given the demographics and the implicit romance angle. From *Harry Potter* to Taylor Swift, there's a shocking amount of these. In fact, there are over fifteen novels that were once Star Wars fanfiction romantically pairing the characters Kylo Ren and Rey!

And legally, it's mostly okay. In a lot of ways, this goes back to the idea of changing 90% of an original work. (See No 10% Change Rule ... But Maybe 90%?, page 97.) How far removed does something have to be before it becomes an original work instead of a derivative? There are certainly no vampires in *Fifty Shades of Grey*.

Fan Conventions aka the Rise of Cons

Every weekend, there are hundreds of *cons*, comic and pop culture conventions around the country and world. And with each of them, you see authorized merchandise, usually at the front of the show, signings with celebrities (actors, comics artists, and the like), and an artists' alley. In this last section, you will find artists of all kinds and backgrounds selling their own versions of characters from a variety of cultural content—comics, TV shows, films, and more. And for the most part, they are not authorized to do this.

Their work does not fall under fair use. Their work often isn't transformative. But nonetheless, they go from show to show, making their living selling fan art. In the same spaces as authorized merch *and the actors and creators themselves* are occupying. Could they be shut down? There have not been court cases about this. But the possibility still exists.

Beware of Section 103(a)

Section 103(a) Reads "The subject matter of copyright as specified by section 102 includes compilations and derivative works, **but protection for a work employing pre-existing material in which copyright subsists does not extend to any part of the work in which such material has been used unlawfully.**"

Every fan artist should know Section 103(a). It's brutal. The idea is that you don't gain copyright protection in something that is considered an unauthorized and/or infringing derivative work if exceptions (like fair use) don't apply. We have two key cases to help us understand Section 103(a): one about *Rocky* and the other about the artist formerly known as Prince.

In 1993, Prince decided to go by a symbol instead of his name. Then, someone, Ferdinand Pickett, made a guitar using that symbol. Prince loved it, even playing a similar guitar in public, but not Pickett's. Oh no! Yep. Pickett sued. Prince had registered the symbol with the U.S. Copyright Office and obtained a valid registered copyright from the U.S. Copyright Office. The court found that Pickett had made an unauthorized derivative work of Prince's copyrighted symbol.

In another case, Timothy Burton Anderson wrote an unauthorized treatment (a proposal for a script) for a sequel to *Rocky*, after seeing Rocky III. He met with some big-deal people in LA, even with Sylvester Stallone himself at his Paramount office. But later, they didn't hire Anderson when they made *Rocky IV* and Anderson sued. Anderson had made an unauthorized derivative work, which is an exclusive right of the copyright holder, Stallone. And because it was unauthorized, *no part of the treatment* is protectable, because it relied on the original. The non-infringing portions that relied on the original were not protected either.

Does this mean that any fan art or fiction is not protectable by copyright? Is it available for anyone to use? It's unclear.

The Grey Area of Borrowing

In many ways, fanworks bring us to this idea of a gray area. Sometimes what fans do is legal under fair use, permissions, or the work is in the public domain. Sometimes it is just not legal, but no one cares. And then sometimes they do. The law may not protect the works fans make, because of Section 103, as described above. But most of the time, the law doesn't really come into play. For more see How Far Can You Go? A Different Perspective on Enforcement, page 166.

The *Copyright* Life Cycle Worksheet

On the next two pages you will find the Copyright Life Cycle Worksheet to help you keep track of what you are doing when you are creating a work. It also serves as proof of the work you have been doing (should you need it in a copyright scuffle), especially if you are keeping notes and dating them.

The Life Cycle Lesson

We are all creators of new works, but we are also all borrowers of others' works. There is a wonder in using old works, yesterday's photos, books we grew up on, all kinds of works. We sometimes borrow legally by asking permission, or within a particular defense like fair use, library exceptions, or classroom uses. Sometimes we borrow without permission.

But whatever we do, we are all creators and consumers of culture. We must recognize that whatever we create goes out into the world. That's the metaphor of the butterfly. Use the Copyright Life Cycle Worksheet to document your creative process every step of the way. Download a fresh worksheet for each work you make.

Download the Form

You can download the Copyright Life Cycle Worksheet too! Scribble on it. Fill it in. If you find the need to start over or you decide to fill it. If you find you need to start over or decide to use it for many projects, you can print a fresh copy.

To access the form through the tiny url, type the web address provided into your browser window. To access the list through the QR code, open the camera app on your phone, and aim the camera at the QR code, and click the link that pops up on the screen.

tinyurl.com/11566-documents-download

The Five Stages of a Copyrighted Work

Do you remember being in elementary school and learning about the life cycle of a butterfly? From egg to caterpillar to chrysalis to butterfly, it goes through a lot of changes. Well, the creative works we as makers create also go through a lot of changes. In a way, our art and our crafts have their own butterfly-esque life cycle.

The life cycle of a work arguably has **five** stages.

Stage 1: The Idea

Brainstorm and write/sketch down your ideas. As an artist, you think of an idea for a painting, a short story, or maybe a drawing. The idea grows. Until the idea is fixed in a tangible medium of expression (the painting is painted, or the sketch is started, the story is put down on paper), the idea remains just that: an idea. Copyright law in the United States protects works fixed in any medium. No term has begun until the idea is fixed. (See What's Your Idea?, page 25) You may also want to keep track of where your ideas came from to better understand how your work sits within both an artistic and a legal context. The Life Cycle has a place for that too.

Stage 2: Making the Creation

Let's make it! You have identified the idea. You then build it—you take common elements like shapes (see Identifying Non-Protectable Elements, page 34), and/or things that are already in the public domain (see Identifying the Public Domain, page 65) like the original Winnie-the-Pooh, and you create something new. You might be using works that are under copyright, either through permissions (see Permission, page 61) or fair use (see Fair Use Basics, page 77) and you are obviously making your own things too. Let's list them. There are a number of buckets to identify what source materials you are using for your creation.

Stage 3: The Work I Made!

You select, arrange, and create new elements and in the process, like a butterfly, a copyrighted work emerges.

On the form we've included a check box to mark whether your work meets the originality standard (see Originality Standard, page 29). You don't have to meet the originality standard, you just won't have a copyrightable work if you do not. That's okay, you just can't exclude others from using your work. You can indicate the type of work (see Types of Works, page 123). If you decide to register your work, you will have to decide whether it fits into the U.S. Copyright Office categories: literary, visual, performing, audiovisual, photographs, and sound recording. (See Registering Your Creative Work, page 121.) We've included a short place to include a description of the work, too!

Stage 4: Protection

In this section of the form you can note how you may want to protect your work. We'll be diving into the various ways you can opt to protect your work in Part III: Protecting, page 110.

Stage 5: Out in the World

Once your work is out in the world, all kinds of things can happen to them—good, exciting, and sometimes bad or frustrating. Get ready! Your work is about to start its journey and fly to places you might never have imagined. And with it, new eggs/ideas are created. And the copyright life cycle begins again.

Eventually, your work will enter the public domain, but that is a long time from now, unless you opt to share it sooner, which we'll dive into in What is a Creative Commons License?, page 119.

Words of Advice

Think through how you are using others' works and understand your justification. And if you care about your own work, put a © notice on it, Creative Commons rights statements, and register your work with the U.S. Copyright Office. You have put a lot of time into your creations. Make proactive decisions on what you want them to do out in the world, and be ok with what happens once they are out in the world. But also recognize that once they are out in the world, others will build upon your work—using your ideas, elements from your work that may or may not be protectable, and sometimes outright copying or stealing. It is the joy and frustration of copyright. It is part of the life cycle.

The Copyright Life Cycle Worksheet © 2024 by Elizabeth Townsend Gard and Sidney K. Gard is licensed under CC BY-NC-SA 4.0. To view a copy of this license, visit creativecommons.org/licenses > 4.0 Licenses > by-nc-sa

Copyright is fun, weird, and wild. Try your best. Record what you do in case someone is upset later, or if *you* are upset and you can prove your process.

The *Copyright* Life Cycle

Working Title	Author	Type of Author

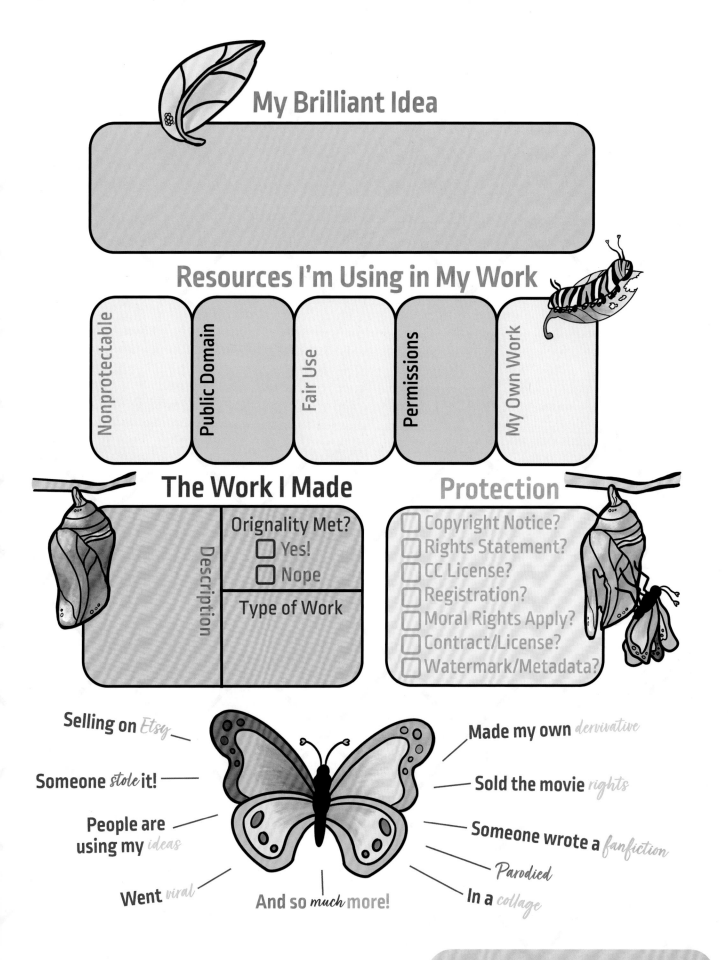

My Brilliant Idea

Resources I'm Using in My Work

- Nonprotectable
- Public Domain
- Fair Use
- Permissions
- My Own Work

The Work I Made

Description

Orignality Met?
- ☐ Yes!
- ☐ Nope

Type of Work

Protection

- ☐ Copyright Notice?
- ☐ Rights Statement?
- ☐ CC License?
- ☐ Registration?
- ☐ Moral Rights Apply?
- ☐ Contract/License?
- ☐ Watermark/Metadata?

Selling on *Etsy*

Someone *stole* it!

People are using my *ideas*

Went *viral*

And so *much* more!

Made my own *derivative*

Sold the movie *rights*

Someone wrote a *fanfiction*

Parodied

In a *collage*

PART III
Protecting

Okay, so, you've made the thing. It's beautiful. It's amazing. You want to show the entire world what you made. You might even want to make some money off the thing you made.

But something happens once the thing you made goes out into the world. Namely, other people happen. Other people might love your work so much that they want to make their own versions. Or they might want to make parodies of it, commenting and criticizing it. The question is what are they legally allowed to do with your work, and what can you do to either support or mitigate what they're doing?

In this part you will learn:

1 **Length of copyright for modern works.** You know about old works already, but how long does the copyright last on the work you just made?

2 **How to protect your copyrights.** You'll nail down the basics of protecting your copyrights, including U.S. Copyright Office registration, as well as when you might choose not to protect your works.

3 **Moral rights.** Learn about some special protecting rules that come along with the world of fine arts (which includes graffiti!), and learn why it's important to give credit where credit is due.

4 **Selling and transferring copyright.** How to give your copyright to someone else.

How *Long* Does Your Copyright Last?

You had an idea. You used non-protectable elements. You might have thrown in some borrowed elements—a public domain work, maybe you asked permission, or maybe you relied on fair use. And now, you've made something.

Let's go back to the Constitution! The U.S. Constitution requires that copyrights last for "limited times." U.S. Constitution, I.8.8. That means you gain protection and then at some point, the work you have created enters the public domain. We saw in the Public Domain chapter that when works come into the public domain can get messy, especially with works from the twentieth century. But good news for us! The copyright term for works created on or after March 1, 1989 are pretty easy to determine.

When you create a copyrightable work, a copyright begins.

The Term is Based on the Type of Author

Remember when we discussed the legal categories of authorship in Who is the Author?, (page 47)? We are revisiting this now in terms of how long the copyright term lasts. So, figure out what kind of author has created the work, then you can figure out how long the term lasts.

- **Single author:** Life of the author plus 70 years
- **Joint author:** Life of the last surviving author plus 70 years
- **Work for hire:** The shorter of 95 years from publication or 120 years from creation
- **Anonymous works:** the shorter of 95 years from publication or 120 years from creation

Other Factors

Now that you know the length of copyright, here are a few things to keep in mind.

1. This list applies to works created on or after January 1, 1978. For works before that, go back to Identifying the Public Domain, page 65.

2. For work for hire, you have to determine if it falls under employee or independent contractor. This is an important distinction! (See Work for Hire, page 50.)

3. This is the term for the United States. Each country is different. At this time, most countries are either life plus 70, like the United States, or life plus 50.

4. If you do not make your work commercially available in the last twenty years of the copyright, libraries are allowed to reproduce and distribute copies.

A Little Thing Called Termination Rights

You sign a contract for the movie rights to be made of your comic. It's your first big deal. It's not a great deal. The comic turns out to be a huge hit. You, the original creator, haven't made much from it. The Copyright Act of 1976 allows you to terminate that contract, that transfer of copyright, down the road.

Termination of transfer (also called "termination" or "reversion rights") is considered a "second bite of the apple." As long as it is not a work for hire, you can terminate the copyright rights as part of a contract and renegotiate the transfer or do something else with them. This is a complicated area of law. You have to wait at least 35 years from the date of the execution of the grant of copyright to trigger termination.

GET HELP FOR REVERSIONS

Think you might have a case for having rights revert to you? This would be a good time to find a lawyer. There is a small window, and a bunch of requirements.

TERMINATION OF TRANSFER CHECK TOOL

Want to check on the status of whether termination applies to a work? Go to the Termination of Transfer tool created by the Authors Alliance at rightsback.org.

What Happens to Your Copyrighted Works When You Die?

Copyright lasts for seventy years after your death. What is going to happen to all those lovely works once you die?

Well, there are two possibilities. You have made arrangements in your will for someone to take over as copyright holder, or you don't. If you don't, your intellectual property descends with your other property. But the problem becomes, people might not know that you have copyrights that are now theirs and then these lovely works become orphan works (see Orphan Works, page 74).

You can transfer copyright by will or by trust. You can also transfer your copyright during your lifetime. You must transfer it as a written assignment. Just saying you've transferred it is not enough. (See Licensing and Transferring Your Copyright, page 135.)

PLAN WITH YOUR LAWYER

Estate planning on copyright can get complicated, particularly if your copyrighted works have value. Consult an attorney.

What Happens If the Company that Owns a Work Goes Out of Business?

When a company that holds copyrighted works closes, it often creates a lot of orphans. Sometimes the company has sold their intellectual property assets, but oftentimes this has not happened (see Orphan Works, page 74). But it can get worse. Let's take a publishing company that goes out of business. The publishing company may have held the copyright on works, or they may not have—they only had a license to publish the work and the copyright remained with the author.

So, what are you to do? Do some detective work. You also can assess the risk of someone suing you for using the work.

Underlying Works

When you base your work on an earlier work, it is important to remember that the term of copyright of the underlying work may be different. Make sure to check the status of each work used (Layers of Copyright, or the MUD System, page 75).

Terms in Other Countries

The Berne Convention governs the minimum terms for copyright works. The United States joined this treaty late, and in part, was a holdout because of the way the Copyright Act of 1909 configured copyright terms. Since 1989 we have been in compliance.

So, if you are trying to determine the copyright status in other countries, they are likely a system where the minimum term is life plus 50, or the now standard term of life plus 70. There are a lot of differences when it comes to photographs and films, and usually, there is no category of work for hire. For example, in Europe, the term of a film is determined by the last surviving author of the following positions on the film: the principal director, screenplay author, the author of the dialogue, and the composer of music specifically created for use in the cinematographic or audiovisual work. Pretty complicated, right? Luckily we have the IMDB database to help us determine when a work is out of copyright! If you are curious, you can download the app or visit imdb.com

So, where do you begin? Look at the country's copyright laws and see the basic terms. It may get more complicated, and in that case, it is time to seek out a lawyer, or email Elizabeth! (Copyright terms are her speciality.)

Copyright Terms in Canada

As of 2022, Canada recently changed its terms of copyright from life plus 50 to life plus 70. Canada has done what the United States did in 1998, and extended the copyright term by twenty years. They did this as part of an agreement with the United States and Mexico. The term is not retroactive, which is good. So, works in 2021 had the term of life plus 50, and then in 2022, works now have the term of life plus 70.

So, in 2021, all works by individuals who had died in 1970 were out of copyright. In 2023, all works by individuals who had died 1971 and later will now be protected through 2042.

In Canada, the current terms are:

Individual: Life plus 70 years

Joint author: Life of the last surviving author plus 70 years

Author unknown: 75 years after publication, or 100 years after creation, whichever is shorter.

There are often additional terms for photographs, posthumous works, sound recordings, and Crown (government) copyright. The takeaway? The length of a copyright is different in Canada from the United States. Use resources to determine the status.

> **CANADIAN COPYRIGHT TERM AND PUBLIC DOMAIN FLOW CHART**
> Want to know more about Canadian copyright terms? Try this flowchart, created by the University of Alberta! Go to ualberta.ca/faculty-and-staff/copyright > licensed & royalty-free content > public domain > Canadian copyright term and public domain flowchart

Copyright *Notice*

Copyright arises automatically every time we create something, whether we are a two-year old creating art at preschool or a famous artist whose paintings are worth millions. No registration is needed.

But you can get more protection if you put a copyright notice on something and even more protection if you register the work with the U.S. Copyright Office. Let's talk about how that works. This chapter focuses on copyright notices. The next chapter discusses the related concept of rights statements. The last chapter in this trilogy is how to register your work at the U.S. Copyright Office.

In short, we think you should put a copyright notice on your works, but it is really up to you whether to register your work. You can decide what rights statement you want, which we will go over shortly. But by putting a copyright notice on your work, it is less likely your work will become an orphan. And we really don't want to create more orphan works.

There are three different terms to understand before diving in to giving notice.

Copyright notice. A copyright notice has three parts: the word, abbreviation, or symbol for copyright; the date; and the owner. For example the copyright notice on this book is © 2024 Elizabeth Townsend Gard and Sidney K. Gard. In this chapter we'll explore what it means, why to include it, and what should be included. A copyright notice is the first step to letting the world know you intend to enforce your property rights.

Rights statements. Rights statements are the portion usually near or after the copyright notice that tells the world what they can and can't do with the work. The most famous one is "All rights reserved." Copyright Rights Statements (page 118) explores what that means exactly and what the other options are, including "No rights reserved," "Some rights reserved," and Creative Commons rights statements.

Registration. Copyright arises automatically, but the way the system operates is that if you don't register your work, you have much less protection. In fact, without registering your work, you cannot go to court! So, while you do hold a copyright automatically, your protection is subpar. We'll talk more about strategies for registering your work, including costs and how to group your works to save money in Registering Your Creative Work (page 121).

Diving into Copyright Notice

Copyright notice tells the world who the copyright holder is and when the work was created. That is what we are covering in this chapter. Let's look at some key concepts related to copyright notice.

Publication

Notice is only required when a work is circulated in public without restrictions. An example of a restriction would be marking your work with "Draft. Do not distribute." A notice of a restriction should be placed on all copies that are going to be sold or distributed to the public.

The legal definition of publication has historically been complicated, but here is a basic guideline: If the work is being distributed to the public by sale, rental, lease, lending, or transfer of ownership, the work is published. A mere offer to sell (rather than actual sale) also triggers publication.

If a work is merely being displayed, this does not constitute publication, as long as there are no copies circulating to the public. For example, if you have a quilt hanging in a show, that is not considered published, but if you print postcards featuring that quilt to hand out, that would be considered published.

Basic Components of a Copyright Notice

There are three basic components; the word "Copyright" (or an abbreviation or the © copyright symbol), the date, and the copyright holder.

©, Copyright, or Copr.

Every copyright notice begins with ©, Copyright, or Copr. Any of these work, but © is considered the best, particularly if your work is going to be sold or distributed internationally.

The U.S. Copyright Office also accepts variants of the © notice. It must resemble the ©, and also alert readers that it stands for copyright.

Here are examples:

- The letter c with a parenthesis over the top.
- The letter c with a parenthesis under the bottom.
- (c
- c)
- (c)
- The letter c with an unenclosed circle around it.

But the U.S. Copyright Office does not allow:

- CO
- C
- C/O
- @ (for example, the letter a in a circle).
- The letter c with a circle attached to the bottom of the letter.
- The letter c in a square.
- [c]

You can also misspell copyright. These are the acceptable variants:

- Copyrighted
- Copywrite
- Copywritten
- Copyright Pending
- Copyright Applied For
- Copyright and Registered
- Registered U.S. Copyright Office
- Copy
- Copyr.

You don't have to get it exactly right to still gain protection.

Interestingly, just a rights statement alone, for example "All Rights Reserved" on its own does not work! It has to be accompanied by a variation of the word or symbol for copyright, the name of the copyright holder, and the date.

Name of the Copyright Holder

This is the name of the owner of the copyright. It, too, can be an abbreviation. It is usually the person/company that holds the rights to the copyright at the time of publication. For example, *Tender*, by Beth Hetland. © 2024 by Beth Hetland. Even though Fantagraphics published Beth's book, Beth holds the copyright.

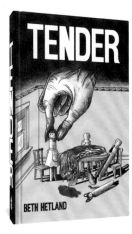

When looking at someone else's notice, the name on the notice tells us who the copyright holder is, at least at the time of publication. It's a place to start if you're researching the copyright ownership of a given artwork, book, or other work. The copyright might have been transferred to someone else, but it is a place to begin. The name, in combination with the date, also sometimes tells us how long the copyright lasts. For instance, Beth Hetland is likely the legal author and the copyright holder so the copyright term would be her life plus 70 years. If the copyright notice had said "Fantagraphics" instead, we would have to investigate if the book was a work-for-hire, instead of an individual author, and then the term would be 95 years from publication.

Deceased people cannot be named as the copyright holder, or register a copyright of a new work. It has to name the person who holds the rights. That's the point of copyright notice; to name and identify the person to contact, should one need permission.

Date

The notice usually includes the year of publication. For pictorial, graphic, or sculptural works, the year of publication is not required. Comic books and graphic novels usually include the year because they are literary as well as graphic art.

Location of Notice

Where copyright notice should be placed is an important topic in copyright law. It's a notice, people have to be able to find it. Different types of works have different placement requirements.

- **Literary works:** Ideally, notice would be on the title page, or the page following the title page, but it must be placed at the beginning. If there are no more than ten pages, the last page appears to also be acceptable. Note: Notice on a dust jacket is not acceptable.

- **Contributions to collective works.** Notice can be included on the title of the contribution page, or at the end of the contribution. You can also include the collective work copyright notice on the page with the book itself, as long as it is clear.

- **Artistic works:** The notice can be a label either on the front or back of the artwork, or on a mounting, matting, frame, or other materials where the work is durably attached.

- **Musical works:** The placement and requirements are same as literary works, but if embodied in a sound recording, notice is not necessary.

- **Sound recordings:** Notice can be on the label, the jacket that houses the disk, or other packaging, as long it is not something that is meant to be disposed of once the sound recording is open, for example, notice printed on the plastic seal around a compact disc wouldn't count because that is made to be disposed of.

- **Audiovisual works:** Be sure to place the notice near the title, with the end credits, at the beginning of the work, or at the end. If it is a boxed or physical set, it is likely also on the packaging. But it really needs to be on the audiovisual work itself.

- **Fabric:** For fabric and other reproductions that are sheet-like or strip material bearing multiple or continuous reproductions of the work, the U.S. Copyright Office has special rules. The notice can be on the fabric itself; the margin or selvage; the reverse side of the fabric; or on a tag or label attached to the spool or container holding the fabric. How far apart must the notice be? We have a number of cases that give variation on how far apart the notice must be, from once every time the pattern repeats, to nineteen inches to as much as 30 inches. Textile and fabrics also are not required to have the year included. For reversible works, the notice can go on any side, and it is okay if it is printed in reverse.

What If There is No Notice?

No notice *does not* necessarily mean the work is in the public domain. If the work was published after March 1, 1989, notice is not required. Assume that anything published after March 1, 1989 is under copyright.

The Advantages of Copyright Notice

Since March 1, 1989, copyright notice is not required in order to be protected by the Copyright Act of 1976. Why include copyright notice when it is no longer required?

Mine

By putting notice on your work, it alerts the world that copyright is being claimed. In the reverse, by not putting copyright notice on your work, you are signaling that you *are not likely* to claim copyright on the work, that you are more in a sharing mood. It also helps to prevent a work from becoming an orphan. Remember, orphans are works that are still under copyright but the copyright holder can't be identified or found.

Not Innocent

If you put a notice on a work and someone uses your work anyway, they are no longer an innocent infringer. They knew you claimed a property right. They used it anyway. In this case, the copyright notice has to be in proper form. Not innocent means that if there is a lawsuit, it could actually be willful infringement, in which case statutory damages could be significant. Innocence or

willfulness deeply impacts on the amount of money a court will award. Innocent infringers can have their statutory damages reduced to $200, while willful damages can be up to $150,000 per infringed work. Putting a proper copyright notice on your work makes a difference.

Identity

Because notice includes your name, it allows people to know who is claiming the property right and ideally can contact you (if necessary) for permission.

Time

The date of publication is required as part of copyright notice. This helps us understand when the clock started, and *when it ends*. The property right is not perpetual. We can do the math based on the date of publication, in some instances, of when copyright ends.

Copyright *Rights* Statements

The Rights Themselves

There are five basic exclusive rights the copyright holder gets *automatically upon creation without doing anything*. When we create a pattern, when we pick threads and make a cross-stitched wall hanging, when a kid draws a picture, when we typed this book ... anytime something is put into a tangible medium of expression, there's a copyright, and that copyright lasts for a long time. Let's take a look and understand each one of the rights. Section 106 of the Copyright Act of 1976.

Reproduction Rights

Copyright holders have the right to make copies of the original work. This is the basis of copyright: the right to copy. This includes both literal copying and creating substantially similar copies.

Distribution Rights

The copyright holder has the right to decide when and how a work is distributed to the public. Once the sale occurs, however, the copyright holder does not control subsequent sales, but not sales of copies made from the original object sold. This is called the First Sale Doctrine.

Public Display Rights

The copyright holder decides where and when the work is displayed publicly. This makes sense. For example, a painter can decide which galleries show their work.

Public Performance Rights

Except for artwork, the copyright holder controls when a work can be publicly performed during the term of the copyright. This means you can publicly perform artwork without getting permission to do so. Think of the recreation of great paintings as a staged show, for instance. That's a public performance of a painting.

Creating Derivative Works

The copyright holder has the exclusive right to create secondary works from the original work. These are called derivative works. As we've talked about, there are some exceptions (namely fair use) where others can use your work and make their own derivative works without permission. (See Permissible Uses, page 61.)

Rights Statements

Now that you know which rights you hold, you need to understand what choices you have when it comes to expressing your rights in relation to others' using your work, namely the general public. When you release a product, an artwork, or something else into the world, it is ideal to let the public know how you feel about the rights you hold and what they can or can't do with your work, and in what situations. In addition to making public rights statements, you could also create contracts and one-on-one relationships.

The rights statement, in conjunction with the copyright notice, alerts the world to the intentions of the copyright holder regarding what others can do. Sometimes there are additional words that communicate to the world permissible uses and restrictions on the use of the work.

There are three basic kinds:

- **All Rights Reserved.** The copyright holder wants to control as much as possible. This is the default, even if you don't include a rights statement.

- **No Rights Reserved.** The copyright holder sends their work out into the world. Anyone can do whatever they want with the work.

- **Some Rights Reserved.** The most common way to express "some rights reserved" has become using a Creative Commons license. This tells anyone who comes to the work what they can and can't do, without having to ask direct permission.

What is a Creative Commons License?

In the twenty-first century, with the rise of the Internet, people found that all rights reserved was a bit too restrictive. There are many times where the copyright holder is okay with people further distributing or sharing their work, using it to build new things (for example, making derivative works), and even using the work commercially.

The Creative Commons (CC) organization transformed how we think about rights statements. They created a system which allows a license from the copyright holder to be placed on the work so that anyone coming to the work would know the permissions and limitations in using that work. Using a Creative Commons license allows you to be more specific about what can and can't be done with your work.

Let's look at the key components you can choose:

- **Attribution.** You want your name/company included when someone else uses the work.

- **Share alike.** You allow people to use your work, but only if they also share what they make too.

- **No derivatives.** You allow people to use your work, but they can't make different versions. They can't change or add anything to your work.

- **Noncommercial.** You allow people to use your work, but they can't sell your work, or sell anything they make using your work, and they can't use it in a commercial context.

- **CC0 No Rights Reserved.** You disclaim all rights in the copyright and send it out into the world. There are no restrictions on how other people use the work, it becomes part of the public domain.

You can create a Creative Commons license at their website, creativecommons.org. A Creative Commons license tells the world what kind of license to the work you are giving them. You should still put the copyright notice in addition to these terms. Using Creative Commons works is an awesome way to add resources, and the rights statements are very helpful.

These aspects of the license get bundled into different standard licenses. There are six standard licenses available on the Creative Commons website.

Attribution (CC BY)

 This license allows you to distribute, remix, adapt, and build upon the original work but requires attribution to the original author. You can also use the work commercially and you can also make derivative works for the original work

Attribution Share Alike (CC BY-SA)

 This license allows you to distribute, remix, adapt, and build upon the original work but requires attribution to the original author. You can also use the work commercially. *But*, this license also requires you to share whatever you create in the same manner as you borrowed from the original work.

Attribution NonCommercial (CC BY-NC)

 This license allows you to distribute, remix, adapt, and build upon the original work. You must give attribution to the original author and you are restricted to using it only for noncommercial purposes.

Attribution NonCommercial Share Alike (CC BY-NC-SA)

 This license allows you to distribute, remix, adapt, and build upon the original work but requires attribution to the original author. You are restricted to using it for noncommercial purposes only, and this license requires you to share whatever you make in the same manner as the original work.

Attribution-No Derivatives (CC BY-ND)

 This license allows you to copy and distribute the work, as long as you attribute the original author, but you cannot make derivative work. This license allows commercial use.

Attribution-NonCommercial-No Derivatives (CC BY-NC-ND)

 This license allows you to copy and distribute the work, as long as you attribute the original author, but you cannot make derivative work. You are not allowed to use it for commercial purposes.

Public Domain Dedication (CC0)

 Often referred to as CC Zero, this license allows a creator to dedicate the work to the public domain, allowing you to distribute, remix, adapt, and create derivative works, without attribution or any restrictions. This is what a lot of the museums are using to let the public know which works are in the public domain. Some even offer high-resolution downloads and you don't have to ask permission from the museums to use it. (See Museums and Open Access, page 73.)

(See Museums and Open Access, page 73.)

MORE INFORMATION ON CREATIVE ...

More Information on Creative Commons Licenses

For more information on Creative Commons licenses, go to their website at creativecommons.org. They also offer a guide for creating: creativecommons.org > Licenses and Tools > Made with Creative Commons.

Choosing a Creative Commons License

Want help choosing the right license? Creative Commons has made a Chooser: creativecommons.org > Licenses and Tools > Choose a License > Our Chooser

Registering Your Creative Work

Copyright arises automatically upon fixation. When you make, write, or draw something, it has copyright. To have power behind that copyright, registration at the U.S. Copyright Office is necessary.

Why Register at the U.S. Copyright Office?

Many makers do not take advantage of registering their works with the U.S. Copyright Office. Unlike publishers, the movie industry and other industries, makers and artists have been slow to adopt registration. But we see that changing, as special categories like registering photographs and potentially 2D works, both designed with makers in mind.

So, why register your works?

- Registration allows you to sue in court, and if you win a lawsuit, you may elect to ask for damages up to $150,000 for willful infringement. Attorney's fees may even be rewarded in some cases.

- Registration also is helpful if you file a notice-and-takedown with a social media platform.

- Registration is required if you want to pursue an infringement in the Copyright Claims Board (small claims board at the U.S. Copyright Office), see Copyright Claims Board (page 162).

- Registration tells others in the world how to find you, in case they want to seek a license from you.

- Registration also allows U.S. Customs to seize illegal copies of your work for you!

Registration is important. It lets the world know that you care about your work and that you took the time to make a public record of its existence, and provide information about the work, including authorship.

A lot of artists and makers do not register their works. We get it. But in case you do want to register your work, we're going to go through the basics.

Register Now!

One important aspect is that registering when within three months of publication allows for a great deal of benefits. You are presumed to be the copyright holder, and statutory damages apply, if you choose that in court. If you wait until after the infringement occurs, you may not be in the best legal position, as actual damages are a lot harder to prove than statutory damages, which can range from $750 to $30,000 per work, and up to $150,000 for willful infringement. And it's worse for unpublished work. No statutory damages or attorney's fees apply unless the work was registered before the infringement occurred.

Some Basic Questions

Do I Need a Lawyer to Apply for Registration?

Nope! You can do it yourself!

How Do You Register a Work?

It's easy. You go to the U.S. Copyright Office's website copyright.gov You have to choose a category to register the works: literary, visual, performing arts, or sound recording.

Deposit Requirement

As part of the copyright registration process, you must deposit a copy of your work. This is either a digital or physical copy. The requirements depend on the type of registration you choose, but now copies are more often digital.

Application Overview

So you want to register your work with the U.S. Copyright Office? Let's look at the basic steps.

1. Get Your Account

The U.S. Copyright Office has a system called the Electronic Copyright Office (eCO). You need to make an account to apply for copyright registration.

2. Choose and Fill in the Online Application

There are a lot of different types of registration applications. It's a bit confusing and ridiculous. But you have to know your options and choose the right application.

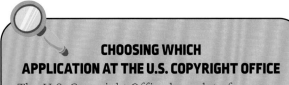

CHOOSING WHICH APPLICATION AT THE U.S. COPYRIGHT OFFICE

The U.S. Copyright Office has a lot of resources to help you fill in the forms, decide which application, and more. Visit copyright. gov/registration

3. Get the Specimens Ready

You will likely be filing your application digitally, and so you will need electronic materials related to the application: an image, a sound file, a spreadsheet, or other files. Each type of application has different requirements. You need to know those requirements and get them ready.

4. Pay the Application Fee

Each type of application has a different fee. You pay that when you file the application. If your application is denied, you do not get the money back. For example, the range is $45 for one work, to $55 for 750 photographs. For more information, look to the fees section of the U.S. Copyright website copyright.gov/about/fees.

5. Wait

You may have correspondence from the U.S. Copyright Office. But it is really the approval process and no additional hoops that you have to go through. (Unlike trademark, where the application is published for review by the public, and patents, where there is a long and difficult review process.)

Before You Start

Before you begin your application it is important for you to determine what you are and are not claiming. A copyright application will ask you to specify certain aspects of your copyrighted work: what you are claiming, and at the same time, what elements you are not claiming. In other words you are identifying and disclaiming pre-existing works. Let's look at an example.

For example, if you are creating a new version of a Jane Austen novel. You are going to disclaim the original novel, because it is in the public domain. You are claiming your new adaptation of the work. Make sense? You want to show the U.S. Copyright Office that you recognize that some aspects of your work are not being claimed, while others are. Here is an example from the U.S. Copyright Office:

> Theresa Tell creates a collage that combines her own artwork with logos from a number of famous companies.

Here Theresa could claim the "selection and arrangement of pre-existing logos with new two-dimensional artwork added." She would disclaim as pre-existing: "pre-existing logos incorporated."

Registering a Derivative Work

Only the copyright holder has the right to prepare derivative works, and therefore register them. You can receive permission to create a derivative work in the form of a license or assignment, of course. To register a derivative work you have to have information regarding previous registrations of pre-existing underlying works. Include information on what was previously published, who owns those previous publications, describe the new material added to make a derivative work, and describe any pre-existing work or works that the work is based on, as well as including the new material itself.

Registering a Compilation

Much like derivative works, you have to make clear what is pre-existing and what is new. You are only gaining a copyright on the new materials. You may also be gaining protection on the selection, arrangement, and coordination of the compilation.

Types of Works

Copyright law divides types of works into categories: literary, performing arts, artistic (including photographs and architecture), and audiovisual works. If you decide to register your work, you choose the category as part of the process.

Literary Works

This includes books, patterns, and other written materials. The list from the U.S. Copyright Office includes:

- Fiction
- Nonfiction
- Poetry
- Directories
- Catlaogs
- Textbooks
- Reference works
- Advertising copy
- Compilation of information
- Computer programs
- Databases

Letters, Diaries, and Private Correspondence

Letters, diaries, and private correspondence are protected as literary work. The author of the writings, rather than the recipient, generally holds the copyright. So, Elizabeth writes a letter to Sid and sends it to them. Elizabeth still holds the copyright in that letter (see The Copyright is Distinct from the Object, page 33).

Computer Programs, Including Apps

Computer programs are registered as literary works, and again, goes to the expression of the idea, rather than the idea itself. Source code (statements and instructions written by a human) and object code (the conversion of programming language to machine language) are registered as one work, and not separately.

Interviews

Interviews can be written or recorded. To claim copyright, the work must be fixed (put in writing or recorded). They can be registered as either a literary work (written) or performing arts (recorded). So, the form matters in choosing which category to register the work. Interviews are weird for another reason. The U.S. Copyright Office has divided the interviewer and interviewee into two separate copyrightable parts. They are separate. That is, unless they both agree and claim the work as a joint work, or that one party transfers ownership to the other.

COPYRIGHT AND INTERVIEWS

If you are doing an interview, make sure to have a form that transfers or states the copyright so that if you want to register it or claim copyright, that aspect is clear.

Performing Arts

This category includes musical compositions, dramatic works, sound recordings, and choreographic works. **The list from the U.S. Copyright office includes:**

- Musical works, including any accompanying words
- Sound recordings
- Dramatic works, including any accompanying music
- Choreographic works
- Pantomimes
- Audiovisual works
- Motion pictures

Musical works (the sound recording or audiovisual recording) may be distinct from the musical compositions. Choreographic works are also included in this category.

Artistic Works

The category is called pictorial, graphic, and sculptural works, which include two-dimensional and three-dimensional works like photographs, prints and art reproductions, maps, globes, charts, diagrams, models, and technical drawings, including architectural plans and after 1990, architectural buildings themselves! These include:

- Fine art (for example, painting and sculpture)
- Graphic art
- Photographs (although a separate category with registration)
- Prints
- Art reproductions
- Maps and globes
- Charts and diagrams
- Technical drawings, including architectural plans
- Models
- Applied art (the aesthetic elements separable from the useful article)

Cartoons, Comic Strips, and Comic Books

These are generally categorized as artist works, but they can also be registered as literary works. It will depend on what is most dominant: text or images.

Installation Art

When applying to register installation art, identify the copyrightable content, and use terms like sculpture, painting, and photographs. The U.S. Copyright Office suggests using the phrase "a series of sequentially and thematically related photographs interspersed with drawn and painting images to create a larger work of authorship." Compendium III, Section 918. You are describing the copyrighted works, where the parts add up to one creative work. Obviously you would change it to replicate what you are actually doing.

Maps

Maps are considered a part of visual arts and they have been a category since the first U.S. Copyright Act, the Copyright Act of 1790. You must meet the originality requirement, as always.

Photographs

Photographs have their own special category. In this category, you can register up to 750 photographs on one registration form.

Motion Pictures and Other Audiovisual Works

This category includes movies, television shows, video games, music videos, and animations.

◆ ◆ ◆

Many Types, Many Opportunities

When you think of arts, crafts, and other making forms, think of all of the categories the works may fall into.

Let's use quilting as an example. Where do quilts fall?

- The quilt itself is an artistic work.
- A book about quilting is a literary work.
- A pattern booklet is a literary work.
- The fabric in the quilt is an artistic work.
- YouTube videos about making the quilt are audiovisual works.
- Podcasts about quilting are performing arts.

◆ ◆ ◆

Which Application?

When you are registering a copyright, you are registering a particular type of work (for example, a visual artist) with a particular application (for example, a group of unpublished photographs). So, you have to know both the type of work and proper application, and there are different rules along the way for different types of applications.

To determine the type of application you need, first go to the U.S. Copyright Office's website. The different types of applications change all of the time, and will likely change more as the U.S. Copyright Office modernizes.

Individual work: this is a registration for one work

Group works: this allows you to register a bunch of works under one registration application, saving you money. Two that are particularly useful are **unpublished works** for up to ten works and **photographs** for up to 750 works.

Basic Information for the Registration Application

As you work your way through the registration process, here are a few things to consider:

Author. Unless you are filling an application out for someone else, or you have created the works in the course of your employment (and you are not for tax purposes an independent contractor), you are likely the author. (See Who is the Author?, page 47)

Claimant. Unless you have assigned, transferred, sold, or licensed your rights to someone else, you are likely the claimant. If you have done any of the above, then the person controlling the copyright is the claimant.

Limitation of claim. Here is where you disclaim anything that you are not claiming. So, if you recognize that some parts of what you are doing are in the public domain, for instance, or are based on another's work, you can enter that info when requested.

Rights and permissions. Who is allowed to give out rights and permissions? Usually, this would be the author, but you could put someone else down.

Correspondent. Who the U.S. Copyright Office contacts if they have questions.

Special handling. If you check this box, you are expediting your application (usually in expectation of litigation), and you will pay a hefty fee. You would do this if you believe there has been infringement of your non-registered work and you are planning to go to court. This would allow you to register the work quickly. It would not cover you for any infringement that occurs before the registration certificate is issued. But it will quickly allow you to be able to go to court and collect statutory damages if you win. Special handling usually takes around five working days and costs an extra $800.

You then pay the fees, and submit copies of the work. You can either upload or mail copies.

Do You Need to Register Everything? No. Not at All.

You should register works you feel are valuable—that if someone swiped them you would be very unhappy. The blog post you wrote this morning? Well, probably not. But maybe if that is really important to you maybe you will.

If you think you would pursue an infringement, then you should register. If you are a "let the chips fall where they may" kind of person, then you really don't need to register. But again, take note, the big companies—they register their works. They know that without registration, the copyright isn't very strong.

How Long Does the Process Take?

It's actually not that bad! Right now, the U.S.Copyright Office reports about 3 to 4 months.

WANT TO CHECK THE PROCESSING TIME?

The U.S. Copyright Office has a way of doing that! Visit, copyright.gov > Registration > Registration Processing Times and FAQs.

Moral Rights

Imagine you take pictures at a museum and post them online. You didn't include a photo of the information card listing the title, author, and date of the work. Suddenly people are screaming in the comments for the information. Why? The **right of attribution**, in other words the right to be named, is something people personally care about. And systems, laws, and norms have developed around that. We are going to look at this from a number of angles.

We hear this a lot when someone copies someone else's artwork "Couldn't they have at least attributed the work to me?" Those are moral rights. They are distinct from economic rights (the right to copy, distribute, and make derivative works.) They are about the identity and integrity of the artist that made the work.

The concept of moral rights comes from the French legal concept, *droit moral*, which is the idea that when an artist creates something that is so core to who they are, they get moral rights. This is a European, civil law concept that the United States has been very slow to adopt. The work you create is an expression of *you*, more than merely the economics of the work, and that should be protected as well.

The concept of moral rights is older than copyright. Wild, right? Copyright begins with the printing press in the 1400s. Moral rights, the right to be named and given integrity, goes back to Roman times.

Now, moral rights are seen around the world, in nearly every country. But in the United States, moral rights only attach to specific kinds of fine art and under certain conditions. There are different ways law and our larger society approach the idea of moral rights.

Moral rights under copyright law. The Visual Artist Rights Act (VARA) is found under Section 106A of the Copyright Act of 1976. A small, select group of works ("fine art") are given special additional legal protection.

Metadata, attribution, and the copyright act.: This falls under the Copyright Act as well, which legally limits the removal, alteration, or falsification of metadata related to a copyrighted work, and may impact potentially infringing activities like striping copyrighted works of their identifying information and creating deep fakes (a deep fake takes a video or photo with a person in it, and replaces it with someone else's likeness. This is often used with the help of AI, and makes it seem like someone did something that they had not actually done).

Creative Commons licenses. As part of the Creative Commons licensing system, you can require attribution as part of the permission to use the work.

State law. As theft, under state law, often called passing off, unfair competition and misappropriation.

Contracts. Contracts and private ordering systems an include specific terms that require the author/artist to be named.

Norms. As custom and courtesy in many fields of arts and crafts the artist/maker is included.

The U.S. Copyright Office actually described moral rights as a "patchwork" of state, federal, contract, and private ordering systems. Moral rights also have to be balanced with the First Amendment and fair use.

Best Practices: Give Credit Where Credit is Due

We will be reviewing a ton of laws. However, the shortest and easiest way to deal with moral rights is to, **give credit where credit is due**. That sounds simple. It is. There may be instances where you are creating a work from non-protectable elements, or you have contracted around not providing attribution (for example, graphic illustration). But giving credit is a simple way to avoid anyone's feelings getting hurt.

Art, Craft, and Quilt Exhibitions

The application forms for entering your work in a craft fair, quilt show, contents, and other spaces vary, of course. But some things should be standard, regardless of what the organizers ask you to fill out. And if you are an organizer, consider the elements below.

Never take credit for someone else's work. If you are using a pattern to make a quilt, include the designer's name of that pattern. Ideally you would include if someone else did the quilting, give them credit, and even a link of where they may purchase or find the pattern. The same is true for knitting, crocheting, cross-stitching, and other crafts.

Make sure the label clearly gives everyone involved the attribution they deserve. If you are not including someone who contributed to the work, make sure there is a contract that agrees they will not be included.

Respect your fellow artists. If your work was inspired by others, include that on your information tag.

Follow the customs and practices of your art and/or craft. We see different communities have different standards of sharing and territoriality.

◆ ◆ ◆

The Visual Artists Rights Act (VARA): Copyright Law and Moral Rights

Under VARA, there are two basic kinds of moral rights:

Right of attribution: the right to be named (or not named)

Right of integrity: the right to prevent prejudicial distortion of your work by distortion, mutilation, or modification

In 1990, the United States added VARA through the Copyright Act. Section 106A addresses the rights of attribution and integrity for certain authors under the Copyright Act. But your work must qualify under visual arts as defined by the Copyright Act of 1976, and most creative works are not covered.

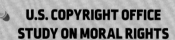

U.S. COPYRIGHT OFFICE STUDY ON MORAL RIGHTS

The U.S. Copyright Office conducted a comprehensive report on Moral Rights in 2019 called Authors, Attribution and Integrity, copyright.gov/policy/moralrights.

Works of Visual Art

Only certain work under the visual art category gets moral rights protection in the United States. That is *not true around the world*, where most countries have a vibrant and extensive moral rights system. The definition of a work of visual art becomes important. That is found in 17 U.S.C. Section 101. Under that section, a **work of visual art"** is—

(1) a painting, drawing, print, or sculpture, existing in a single copy, in a limited edition of 200 copies or fewer that are signed and consecutively numbered by the author, or, in the case of a sculpture, in multiple cast, carved, or fabricated sculptures of 200 or fewer that are consecutively numbered by the author and bear the signature or other identifying mark of the author; or

(2) a still photographic image produced for exhibition purposes only, existing in a single copy that is signed by the author, or in a limited edition of 200 copies or fewer that are signed and consecutively numbered by the author.

A work of visual art is something unique, or with 200 copies or less. The focus seems to be on fine art and gallery art, but in recent years, graffiti cases have successfully used VARA in court.

Not Everything Qualifies for Moral Rights

The list of what does not qualify for moral rights protection in the United Statesis long. Let's take a look.

- **Anything that is not a work of visual arts.** Remember, it's the Copyright Law's definition and not your idea of what counts as a work of visual arts.

- **Works for Hire.** If a work is categorized as a work made for hire, VARA does not apply. If you forgot the definition of work for hire, see Work for Hire, page 50). This includes specially ordered commissioned works and works made within the employment context (remember independent contractors do not fall into this last one).

- **Any commercial art, merchandising item, or packaging.** This usually includes graphic design, illustration, and photography aimed at a commercial purpose.

- **Any applied art (where the art serves as part of utilitarian objects).** Applied art is not defined in VARA, leaving courts scrambling. Applied art is usually defined as art created with a specific, practical purpose including industrial designs.

- **Non-copyrightable art.** If a work does not qualify for copyright, it also does not gain moral rights protection. There's a case about a wildflower display in Chicago, where the court found the garden not protectable by copyright, and therefore cannot be protected by moral rights. That seems obvious, but you have to have a copyright to have moral rights.

- **Preparatory works including models.**

- **Site-specific works.** While not listed in VARA, some courts believe they are not included.

The Rights

So what moral rights do the authors of visual arts actually have?

Right of Attribution

The right to claim authorship of the work. The author also has the right to prevent the use of his or her name as the author of any work of visual art which he or she did not create.

Right of Integrity

This is the right to prevent the use of the author's name as the author of the work of visual art in the event of a distortion, mutilation, or other modification of the work, which would be prejudicial to his or her honor or reputation. One common example is putting a religious piece of art next to excrement art.

Right Against Destruction of Works by Authors of Recognized Stature

There is a right to prevent any intentional or grossly negligent destruction of a work of recognized stature. The term "recognized stature" is not defined by the statute. The court in *5Pointz II* looked to the appropriate community and context for the particular medium, in this case graffiti.

There are exceptions to these protections under VARA.

Specifically, these rights are limited by three exceptions:

- A modification that is the result of the passage of time or inherent nature of the materials does not violate VARA.

- Modifications resulting from conservation or public presentation (including lighting and placement) are not considered destruction, distortion, mutilation, or other modification (unless modifications are caused by gross negligence) also does not violate VARA

- VARA applies to original works only, and not copies or reproductions of the original

Exercise of the Rights

Ownership of the copyright, the work itself, and the VARA rights are each distinctly separate. Only the author, whether or not the author is the copyright holder, has VARA rights. The rights may not be transferred, but the rights may be waived by express agreement in writing by the author. The writing must identify the work, and the uses of that work to which the waiver applies.

Duration

How long do moral rights last?

In the United States

- **Works created after June 1, 1991:** (VARA's effective date): life of the author (they expire at the death of the author)

- **Works created before June 1, 1991 and the artist no longer holds the copyright title:** no rights under VARA.

- **Works created before June 1, 1991 but the artist has not transferred the copyright:** the term is the same as the copyright term (usually life plus 70 years). See How Long Does Your Copyright Last?, page 111.

Many have commented on the weirdness of the duration of VARA, and that works where the title was transferred before June 1, 1991 do not gain VARA protection. See Section 17 U.S.C. Section 106A(d).

Remedies

You can get the same remedies as under the economic rights portion of the Copyright Act: injunctions, impounding, actual damages, statutory damages, costs, and attorney's fees. (See In the End, What Do You Get?, page 143.)

Statutory damages for moral rights begin at $500 and go up to $20,000, and if willful, $100,000. If the violation was deemed an innocent infringement, the damages can be reduced to $200.

No Registration Required

Moral rights happen automatically for works of visual art. VARA does not require that a work be registered with the U.S. Copyright Office to be protected. But there are also no criminal penalties related to moral rights.

Waivers

Moral rights are a personal right to the author of the work. You cannot assign your moral rights to someone else. However, you can waive them, meaning you agree not to enforce moral rights. That means there are fewer encumbrances on a copyright that you may be licensing or assigning to someone else. The waiver can be a standalone document or incorporated into a contract. Only the author/creator of the work can waive moral rights, and not the copyright holder, should it be someone different.

Writing a Waiver

Sometimes contracts will require you to waive your moral rights, and that is allowable by the law.

Elements to include in a waiver:

- The name of the author

- That the waiver can be conditional or unconditional, and can be revokable or irrevocable.

- The name of the works the waiver applies to

- That you are waiving your moral rights

- The jurisdiction the waiver applies to

- Who the waiver is made in favor of [the company asking for it]

- Whether the waiver extends to sub-licenses, assignees, or successors

If one joint author waives their rights, it waives the rights of all joint authors, even if they are not privy to the contract, 17 U.S.C. Section 106A(e)(1).

Also, the transfer of the copyright *does not* automatically create a waiver of moral rights. These are separate, and the waiver of moral rights, like an assignment of copyright, must be in writing and signed by the author(s), 17 U.S.C. Section 106A(e)(2).

Graffiti Artists Win $6.75 Million for Moral Rights

The first photo shows the graffiti as it was. The second photograph shows the unauthorized whitewashing before the court made a decision on the status.

Gerald Wolkoff had given graffiti artists permission to cover his warehouse located in Long Island, Queens, New York, with art. The graffiti had been going on for years, and the warehouse artwork was curated and supervised by Jonathan Cohen. It included over 21 artists. It was spectacular and became known around the world. It was famous.

Then, in 2013, Wolkoff decided to tear down the 200,000-square-foot building to put up luxury apartments. Under VARA, Cohen and sixteen other artists filed for a temporary injunction order to keep that from happening. Here's where the case gets complicated. The court denied the request on November 12, 2013, and stated that a written opinion was soon to follow. The case was not done, as there were more issues to work out. But before that could happen, and before the written opinion was issued, on November 19, 2013, in the middle of the night, the evening before the judge issued his opinion on the preliminary injunction, Wolkoff painted over all the graffiti with white paint. Then on November 20, the next day, the court had decided that the artists were not entitled to protection under VARA to prevent the destruction of the building. The question remained whether the artwork had achieved the recognized stature needed to keep the work from being destroyed, but that a court would have to decide whether the artist's work had achieved the required recognized stature. Now the artwork was destroyed. This was a game changer. The question, in this first case, was whether the graffiti artist had achieved the recognized stature required by VARA for right of integrity. The judge denied the preliminary injunction because it was not clear that the artists met the stature requirement. But before the decision came down, Wolkoff whitewashed over all of the graffiti, including putting smiley faces in white paint on some of the art.

When the decision came out, the decision included the sentence: "the defendants are exposed to potentially significant monetary damages if it is ultimately determined after trial that the plaintiffs' works were of 'recognized stature.'"

Cohen II is the amended complaint after the destruction. *Cohen II* went to trial, and the same judge found all but four of the pieces met the recognized stature requirement under VARA. The judge awarded the maximum amount of statutory damages for willfulness under the Copyright Act; $150,000 per piece, and with 45 pieces, the total came to $6.75 million. The judge included that it didn't matter if a work was temporary or permanent. The decision was applied by Wolkoff.

The Second Circuit Court sorts out the test for recognized stature. "A work is of recognized stature when it is one of high quality, status, or caliber that has been acknowledged as such by a relevant community." In other words, you use expert testimony to help understand, rather than leaving it up to a judge, reminding us all that courts have an aesthetic non-discrimination policy. The court reiterated that a work can be temporary or permanent under VARA (as long as it lasts more than a few seconds). The court also found Wolkoff's actions to be willful destruction, allowing for the maximum in damages. *Castillo v. G&M Realty, L.P.*, 950 F.3d 155, 163 (2d Cir. 2020), cert. denied, 2020 U.S. LEXIS 4495 (2020);

The Relationship Between Copyright and Moral Rights: Paula Nadelstern

Moral rights might just save you, or at the very least, beef up your claim. Paula Nadelstern, an award-winning quilter, found out that a major hotel chain had used her quilts as models for their lobby rugs. Paula Nadelstern sued for copyright infringement. For examples of her work, visit paulanadelstern.com.

The quilts copied by the hotel chain copied quilts that had been published in one of her books. Her publisher, C&T Publishing, had registered the copyright with the U.S. Copyright Office. Paula's legal team also included a VARA claim on the quilts themselves.

From the original complaint: "Defendants Couristan, Hotel Corporation, and Hilton have willfully violated plaintiff's rights under Visual Artists Rights Act, 17 U.S.C. Section 106A by manufacturing, casting to be manufactured, importing, vending, distributing, selling, displaying and/or promoting carpets which are direct copies of plaintiff's unique works of visual art (kaleidoscopic quilts) … " More specifically, the complaint asserted that the defendants violated Paula's 106A(a)(1)(A) right to claim authorship (attribution right) and 106A(a)(3)(A) right to prevent intentional distortion, mutilation, or other modification which is prejudicial to her reputation (right of integrity). The parties settled.

Part of the settlement was that she got her name on a plaque near the carpets and also her name (attribution) on the website. The settlement also required the hotel to replace the rugs when they are worn, and in doing so, pay an additional royalty fee, likely part of the right of integrity portion of the settlement.

What is most interesting, and something to think about, is that VARA did not require Paula to register the quilts, and she *had not* registered the quilts, only the book about the quilts. However, she was still able to succeed because of the way the statute is structured to sue on VARA claims. The book copyright covered copyright infringement; VARA covered moral rights regardless of registration.

Integrity of Copyright Management Information

One other tool artists now have is Section 1202 of the U.S. Copyright Act of 1976, which was added in 1998. This part of the Copyright Act prohibits people from removing key metadata from a copyrighted work.

This includes:

- The title

- Copyright owner

- Terms and conditions of use

- Performers in non-audiovisual works

- Writers, performers, and directors credited in an audiovisual work

Is Section 1202 limited to the digital realm? The U.S. Copyright Act doesn't say, but courts have recently interpreted it more broadly.

Stripping or altering metadata from an image comes with a potential penalty of $2,500 to $25,000 plus attorney's fees.

Section 1202 also prohibits the act to induce, enable, facilitate or conceal infringement by providing copyright management information that is false, or distributing or importing for distribution, copyright management information that is false. An example of Section 1202 is when someone tries to take off the copyright notice from copyrights, or strips those photographs of all the metadata.

Licensing and *Transferring* Your Copyright

> As the copyright holder, you have the exclusive right to decide who uses your work, and that is usually done through licensing and/or transferring your copyright. You can also exploit your copyright yourself, do nothing at all with it, give it away, or share it. It's yours. You get to decide.

Selling Works: Things to Think About

Usually, when you sell works, the copyright remains with the author, unless explicitly included as an assignment in writing.

Often, you are selling copies of the work, like prints, or the work itself, like an original quilt, or even patterns. In each of these, the copyright remains with the copyright holder. You can use a Creative Commons license to indicate what the buyer can do with the work, see What is a Creative Commons License? (page 119)

Copyright Agreements

Someone else wants to use your work, and is asking for permission. Awesome! Let's understand your basic options.

Assignment

An **assignment** assigns the copyright to someone else. You can assign some of the rights (for example, right to copy or right to make derivative works), or all of the rights. Once you assign a right, you no longer have the legal right to that right. You could include something in the contract that still allows you a license to that right. But generally, you give up the right to that right in that work. This is a transfer of your copyright.

You can only transfer copyright by a written agreement, which **must be signed**.

You have to decide what you want to transfer: all of the Section 106 rights, or something specific. The specific rights you can assign are reproduction, distribution, derivative, public display, and public performance. Additionally, you can assign the movie rights to your story, but keep the derivative work sequel rights.

Here are some things you need to include in a copyright transfer agreement:

- The name of the copyright holder and the name of the new owner.

- The name of the copyrighted work

- What rights are being transferred? Remember, you don't have to transfer all of the rights.

- Confirmation that the Copyright holder has the right to transfer ownership.

- If any attribution of moral rights remains with the copyright holder.

And then, you and the other party sign the agreement. You should also let the U.S. Copyright Office know that you have assigned the copyright to someone else. You can do this through the website copyright.gov.

There is no specific form to create an assignment. And you can even assign future copyrighted works that have not yet been created. Think of an artist commissioned to create a mural. The contract includes an assignment of copyright. The mural does not yet exist, but the contract assigns the copyright in the work.

TRANSFERRING A COPYRIGHTED WORK

You may want to consult a lawyer when transferring a copyright in a work, particularly if it is of significant value. You want to make sure not only that you are the legal copyright holder, but that you are transferring the rights you wish to transfer, and if you have residual uses allowed with those rights.

Licensing

Licensing comes in two flavors: exclusive and non-exclusive.

Exclusive Licenses

Exclusive licenses look a lot like assignments. You are allowing only one party, person, or company to use the work, and/or control specific rights attached to the work. You guessed it, exclusive licenses have to be in writing with a signature. The license can be for a particular time or territory, and it can revert back to the copyright holder.

Non-Exclusive Licenses

You allow someone to use the work, but others can too. Non-exclusive licenses do not need to be in writing or have a signed agreement, and they can be implied. Elizabeth invited and paid for Amy to come on trips to take photographs of quilts. No specific written agreement was put in place, but because Elizabeth paid for the trip, supplied some of the equipment, and directed what Amy took pictures of, there is an implied non-exclusive license. Now, if Elizabeth wanted an assignment or an exclusive license to use the photographs, she needed to put a contract, in writing, in place. Make sense?

Creative Commons licenses are non-exclusive licenses. (See What is a Creative Commons License? page 119.)

Copyright Transfer for Other Reasons

Copyrights can be transferred due to bankruptcies, mergers, and divorce. They can also be transferred by a will or through law if there is no will.

BAD PARABLE

WOW! NO WONDER THIS VIEW INSPIRED BOTH YOUR BLANKET AND KAT'S STORY.

YES! I'M GLAD WE CAME BACK HERE.

AND I'M GLAD I READ UP ABOUT COPYRIGHT.

OH, YEAH. WHAT DID WE ALL LEARN?

MY STORY WAS COPYRIGHTED THE MOMENT I PUT PEN TO PAPER. BUT I WENT THE EXTRA STEP OF INCLUDING A COPYRIGHT NOTICE ON THE ZINE I MADE. THIS WILL HELP PROTECT MY WORK!

KAT AND I WERE BOTH INSPIRED BY THE OCEAN BUT MY CROCHET BLANKET DOESN'T INFRINGE ON THEIR STORY BASED ON OUR SHARED INSPIRATION.

SIMILARLY, I USED GRANNY SQUARES, WHICH ARE COMMON BUILDING BLOCKS, FOR MY BLANKET. I CAN'T COPYRIGHT THOSE BUT MY OCEAN THEMED PATCHWORK BLANKET MIGHT BE WORTH FILING COPYRIGHT FOR.

I MADE SCARVES WITH A BASIC KNITTING STICH! I CAN'T COPYRIGHT THIS BUT THAT'S OKAY. I MADE THIS SCARVES TO DONATING, NOT TO PROFIT.

BEACH BOY

I'M A CREATIVE PERSON WHO WORKS WITH DIFFERENT MEDIUMS AND CREATES ART THAT IS BOTH DERIVATIVE AND NON-DERIVATIVE.

UNDERSTANDING COPYRIGHT HELPS ME KNOW WHAT I DO AND DON'T HAVE CLAIMS TO LEGALLY, NO MATTER THE ENDEAVOR!

I LOVE YOU, COPYRIGHT!!

PART IV
Enforcing

You've had an idea, used resources to make it, and created something. You decided on the protection level you wanted for your work. And now, something happened, or you are worried that something may happen. Or, you are thinking of making something that might be just a little risky. This is the chapter for you. You will learn:

- **Copyright infringement.** You'll find out what it is and how courts analyze whether there is copyright infringement.

- **Plagiarism.** Get the scoop on what this is and how it is different from copyright infringement.

- **Copyright Claims Board.** If you have a potential copyright infringement claim under $15,000, this may be the venue for you. Learn how it works.

- **The real world.** We look at real world situations to help you understand how frequently copyrights are being enforced, and how much give and take there actually is.

When Things Go *Wrong*

Imagine that you get an email from a friend. Someone has swiped your original design.

That depends on:

- Whether the work you created is copyrightable in the first place (See Part I: Creating, page 12)

- Whether you have included copyright notice (see Copyright Notice, page 114)

- Whether you have registered the work (see Registering Your Creative Work, page 121)

- Where the alleged infringement occurred

- What is alleged

- And most importantly, whether you care

Assuming the work is protected by copyright, and that there is infringement, there are a number of things you can do when you believe someone has infringed your work. But it can go both ways. What if someone thinks *you* have infringed their work? We'll discuss that, too.

Just remember to breathe. Maybe get some ice cream (or a glass of wine), and take a moment. It can be upsetting when someone has allegedly infringed on your work or when someone gets mad at you for something you might be infringing on. But this is part of the ecosystem of creating, and there are ways to make things better.

Mechanisms for Addressing Infringement

Currently, we have a number of options.

- **Be an enforcer.** If you want to be an enforcer, register your work. Send a cease-and-desist letter. You can use the social media platforms with a takedown submission. And, in some cases, you can sue for infringement, but only if you have a registration certificate from the U.S. Copyright Office. You can also now file a claim with the Copyright Claims Board. (See Copyright Claims Board, page 162.)

- **Win over your infringer.** You could contact the person who is infringing. Explain things to them, and see if they want a license to use your work. You could, of course, combine this with enforcer mode.

- **Other options.** Ignore it. Appreciate that you created something worth stealing! Make more things. Keep them to yourself next time so people don't steal. Use it as a social media opportunity.

Remember that fame comes with piracy. Hollywood studios have whole teams that work on piracy, and they still have problems. It's part of the world that we live in, especially in a digital environment. Craft and quilt patterns, for example, are a lot easier to replicate and steal than fabric or a complicated tool. Someone might try to make their own version of a PFAFF sewing machine, but it will take a lot more to make a knockoff machine than copying a crochet pattern of a penguin.

Going Down the Enforcer Path

So, you've decided. You have registered your work. You have hired a lawyer. You are taking the infringer to federal court. Or maybe you just want to send a cease-and-desist letter. Perhaps you are going to try the new small claims system at the U.S. Copyright Office. Or maybe you will file a notice and takedown with a social media platform. Whatever way you decide to enforce your copyright, you should make sure you *have* a copyright, that there was unlawful copying, and that no exceptions apply to the behavior.

We will be looking at copyright infringement in detail, but for now, let's look at the steps you should be taking in any situation where you are suddenly really mad and ready to enforce.

Step One: Was There Copying?

Look at what was taken from the original and used in the allegedly infringing copy.

Look to see if the elements copied are:

- In the public domain (and therefore anyone can use them)

- Independently created (made without access to the original work)

If there was copying of copyrightable elements, the courts then move on to the next step.

The copying doesn't have to be exact; it can be substantially similar. And if the original had been distributed widely to the public that often goes towards proving access and even subconscious copying.

Step Two: Was There Inappropriate Copying?

Next you have to see if the original and the allegedly infringing work is inappropriate copying. Jump ahead to Copyright Infringement (page 145) to determine whether the copying was inappropriate.

Step Three: Are There Potential Reasons That the Use is Lawful?

There are many permissible uses and reasons for someone using another's work.

You should check to see if any of these apply.

- **Fair use.** If fair use applies, you probably shouldn't try to enforce the copyright. This is true especially with social media takedown notices. For example, if you file a takedown notice with a social medial platform, you swear upon penalty of perjury that you have done a fair use analysis as the copyright holder. So, check to make sure there may not be a reason. (See Fair Use Basics, page 77.)

- **First sale doctrine.** They are not copying, but using something they purchased lawfully.

- **Authorized uses.** They have a license or assignment to use the work.

This is just a sampling of the kinds of reasons that someone could use a work and that the law sees it as okay, even if you don't. Let's turn to some of the situations we see for enforcement, starting with social media platforms' use of notice and takedown as a means of combating copyright infringement.

Notice and Takedown

The notice and takedown system was enacted as the Online Copyright Infringement Liability Limitation Act, a part of the Digital Millennium Copyright Act of 1998. It protects platform hosts from liability as long as they have a system in place to address alleged infringement, among other things.

If your work has been infringed and the infringement is occurring on an online platform, you can notify the platform to take the infringing content down. Each social media platform has a way to address potential infringement. You can find each platform's notice and takedown process through a quick Internet search for [platform name] notice and takedown.

Each social media platform has their own system, but they all ask for the same basic information.

They will want:

- Your confirmation that you are, or represent the copyright owner

- Your full contact information

- Descriptions of your copyrighted work and the allegedly infringing work

- Instruction on how to locate the infringing content on the platform's site, some platforms specifically request URLs

- Your declaration that you, in good faith, believe that the content is, in fact, infringing and that there are no permissions in place to allow the use the content

- Your affirmation that the information in your claim is accurate

- An electronic signature

Before filling out that form it is very important that you do your own fair use analysis (see Four-Factor Test, page 77) to make sure that what the alleged infringer is doing is actually illegal, even if you don't like it. Following a court case that involved a mom, a dancing baby in a walker running around a kitchen joyfully bouncing to a Prince song playing in the background, the court determined that copyright holders must do a fair use analysis before they complete a notice and takedown form.

This is known as Section 512(f) under the Copyright Act of 1976. This is a claim for misrepresentation. This is someone filing a notice-and-takedown and "knowingly materially misrepresents … that the material or activity is infringing … " Not doing a fair use analysis can potentially be a misrepresentation of the situation.

Again, what this means is that if you are filing a notice, you have to consider whether there are fair uses that might apply. And if you don't, and you lose in court (if it gets there), you could be responsible for damages. Hmmm … This could be a little clearer, don't you think?

This includes analyzing for the following:

- **De minimis use** (See Just a Little Bit: De Minimis Copying, page 146.)

- **Independent creation** (See Independent Creation, page 147.)

- **Source material is in the public domain** (See Identifying the Public Domain, page 65.)

- **License to use** (See Copyright Rights Statements, page 118, What is a Creative Commons License?, page 119, and Licensing and Transferring Your Copyright, page 135.)

- **Rogers test applies** (for trademark and right of publicity) (See The *Rogers* Test: Determining Source Identifier or Expressive Content, page 92.)

- **Commenting or criticizing original work** (See Fair Use Basics, page 77.)

- **News reporting** (See Fair Use Basics, page 77.)

- **Parody** (See Fair Use Basics, page 77.)

Some systems ask you to confirm specific lists like the one above; others just ask you to confirm that you have met the Section 512(f) requirements (without any understanding of what that is or where it comes from.

Once you file a notice and takedown with a platform, the alleged infringer is notified. They are given the opportunity for counter-notification, to explain why they used the materials. That is then forwarded to you, the person making the complaint. You then have fourteen days to file a complaint in federal court to keep the work from being posted again. If that does not occur, the platform notifies the counter-notifier that they can repost the content. That's their whole system.

If you receive a notice and takedown. First, don't panic. Evaluate your use. Why do you think they are upset? Is it legitimate? Were you both relying on something in the public domain? Independent creation? Fair Use? If you feel like the work shouldn't have been taken down, file a counter-notice. If the original complainer doesn't file a legal action against you in court within fourteen days, you can put it back up if you want. Alternatively, you can keep it down, even if you are in the right. It's okay. And how likely is someone to file a complaint and take you to court? Not very, but it is still a risk. You might want to talk to an attorney.

IT'S GETTING LEGAL

So, if either you are ready to fight or someone else is, hire an attorney. Sending an angry letter—and it doesn't have to be angry, is an art. It's worth the money to hire someone with the expertise. Also, threatening someone with legal action has potential consequences in so many ways. Don't do this on your own.

We also see that sometimes copyright holders reach out to the alleged infringers to work it out. You might try that as well. Sometimes the copyright holder even withdraws the notice!

Cease and Desist Letters

Someone is allegedly infringing on your work, and you want to tell them to stop doing something, or pay a license fee, or destroy their copies. A cease and desist letter is one tool to achieve that goal. A cease and desist letter is sent when you think someone has infringed your copyright, trademark, patent, or trade dress, there has been a contract problem or harassment. In order to be infringing, there are different criteria for each. Note: We are only covering copyright infringement in this book, and so other related issues are beyond the scope of the materials.

What is a Cease and Desist Letter?

This is a letter you send directly to the alleged infringer to tell them you are not happy. Cease and desist letters should be crafted to attempt to attain the outcome that you want. Think about what you really want out of it. Do you want the infringer to stop using your work? Do you want them to destroy the infringing work? Do you want them to pay a licensing fee? Do you want them to credit you?

There is something important to realize. If you threaten the infringer with a lawsuit, you may actually have to do that, and they could file suit against **you** first.

Before you send a letter or have a lawyer send a letter, there are a few things to do, including some homework, as described previously. You know you have a valid copyright, you are aware that there are no exceptions, and that the alleged infringer had

access and they substantially copied your work. Also, you should think about the tone of the letter and who will be reading it. The record industry famously sent threatening letters to 8-year-olds and grandmothers for illegally downloading music. It did not go over well. They are still seen as villains.

Something to consider when setting the tone is who are you sending it to, what kind of relationship you want with them, are you going to be friendly or threatening, and what is the goal.

Here is what the letter needs to contain:

- Information

- The name and address of both parties.

- Description of the activities. Describe the activities so that the receiver is put on notice and knows that you are aware of the behavior.

- (Optional) You could include a full legal *complaint*, the document you file in federal court, meaning that if they don't agree, you will start a copyright lawsuit. This is very aggressive, and pretty expensive. You should likely hire an attorney and also be ready to engage in litigation. This could be insanely costly as well. Once you start a fight, it can get really complicated and expensive fast. So, this is not for the faint of heart.

WHAT IF YOU RECEIVE A CEASE AND DESIST?

If you receive a cease and desist letter, evaluate, and investigate the claim. Stop your activity if you are in the wrong. Negotiate a license, if that is something you want to do. Can you ignore it? Maybe. In any case, talk to a lawyer.

Social Pressure

Over the last two years, we've seen another approach. When someone is infringing, or the community thinks they are infringing, social pressure in the form of social networks is powerful. It's something to think about. We've seen this quite a bit on social media platforms, in YouTube videos, and in person. The copyright owner demonstrates the theft and tells people about it. They often ask people to boycott the alleged infringer. We've also seen it backfire in pretty spectacular ways.

In the End, What Do You Get?

So, you decide to take someone to court. You spend a lot of time and money. If you sue someone, what is the end game? There are three possibilities: injunction, damages, and/or destruction.

Injunction

Stop doing that! This can either be temporary or permanent. Injunctions are granted to prevent future infringements, either temporarily while the court case develops or permanently, as a result of the outcome of the case.

Damages

This can include actual damages by the infringement and profits gained by the infringer, or statutory damages (if the work is registered with the U.S. Copyright Office). With statutory damages, you do not have to show your actual damages and profits, which can be a hard thing to do with copyright cases. The award of statutory damages is between $750 and $30,000 per infringed work. If willful damages are found, the damages can rise to up to $150,000 per infringed work. If it is found that the infringer was not aware of infringing, for example, an innocent infringer, the damages can be reduced to $200.

Destruction

Destruction of the inappropriately copied items can be mandated after the copyright case concludes as part of the remedy.

Seizure or Impoundment

The seizure or impounding of inappropriately copied items can happen when the copyright case is ending.

Costs and Attorney's Fees

The American system assumes that each side will pay their own costs and attorney's fees. It's only in rare situations that costs and attorney's fees are awarded. These are not automatically awarded to the winning party, it is up to the court to decide. The determination on whether attorneys' fees will be awarded is based on the conduct of the non-prevailing party, whether the lawsuit was frivolous, the non-prevailing party's motivation, whether settlement attempts were in good faith, whether the losing party was objectively unreasonable, and whether deterrence and compensation for the behavior is necessary. The idea is that if someone is being uncool there should be consequences. But if there is a real issue to litigate, no one should be punished for showing up to court. So, you can win, but you can still have a lot of debt coming out of the lawsuit. That's part of the price of going to court.

Copyright Claims Board: A New Alternative

Starting in June 2022, the U.S. Copyright Office created a small-claims online space to resolve differences. It is called the Copyright Claims Board, and it allows for disputes under $15,000. We will be discussing the details more in Copyright Claims Board (page 162). But in short, it allows people to voluntarily resolve differences with the input and structural guidance of the U.S. Copyright Office. We are still learning how this will impact on resolving copyright disputes.

A Note on Innocent Infringers

If a work has a copyright notice attached, there is no defense of innocent infringement. It is also not a defense that you just didn't know it was under copyright. Copyright applies a strict liability approach; copyright doesn't care about whether you knew or not. The court can reduce damages to $200 if someone claims to be an innocent infringer and there was no copyright notice. 17 U.S.C. Section 504(c)(2); Section 401(d); Section 402(d).

If a work has a copyright notice attached, there is no defense of innocent infringement.

Copyright *Infringement*

Copyright infringement is the unauthorized use of the rights of the copyright holder. We have already explored elements of infringement when we talked about fair use, a defense of copyright infringement (see Fair Use Basics, page 77). This chapter dives into how courts look at infringement suits, which helps us understand how we should also view it. We will spend a great amount of time on the right of reproduction, the key right, and also touch on the right of distribution and the right to make derivative works.

Right of Reproduction

The right of reproduction is the key to copyright: you decide who, when, and in which manner people can make copies of your work. You can license the right to copy or you can sell that right. The right to copy is fundamental to copyright. This is Section 106(1) of the Copyright Act of 1976. We will look at two ways that the right of reproduction is infringed: exact copies, sometimes called literal copying, and substantial similarity.

Literal, Exact Copies

Cheryl makes a pattern. Jaki takes that pattern, scans it, and posts it online in a Facebook group. Jaki has made an exact copy.

We talk about this being piracy. Pirates steal exact copies and then either try to sell the unauthorized copies, or sometimes, just post it on the Internet. This is **literal copying**. If there is literal copying, you are done with the analysis. There is copyright infringement. The more complicated questions come with substantial similarity.

Substantial Similarity

While not an exact copy, there are enough similarities that the actions may be infringing. Next, you have to figure out how to determine if the similarities are with the plaintiff's original work (rather than independent creation or a public domain work), and also if the copying is inappropriate and infringing. We will be looking more at how substantial similarity analysis is done in Substantial Similarity Test (page 149). The tests and the words to describe the process may vary by jurisdiction, but the basic ideas are the same.

Once you determine there has been copying and that copying is inappropriate copying, the next question is whether there are defenses that explain the use, for example fair use. You can also have a situation where the common work between the two works is in the public domain (see Identifying the Public Domain, page 65). And of course, the problem may turn out to either be that the original work is not actually under copyright (see Originality Standard, page 29) or that the infringement is really about non-protectable elements (see Identifying Non-Protectable Elements, page 34) rather than the selection, arrangement, and coordination of those elements.

Additional Defenses to Copying

We have already looked at fair use in quite a lot of detail (See Fair Use Basics, page 77.) And you know about the First Sale Doctrine, as well as the joy of public domain works. However, before we learn about the various copyright infringement tests that courts have developed, let's look at some of the defenses to infringement.

Just a Little Bit: De Minimis Copying

When is copying just little bits of something *not* enough to infringe on the Section 106(1) reproduction right? We talk in copyright about *de minimis copying*—so small that it doesn't really impact on the economics of the original work. The full Latin phrase is *"de minimis non curat lex,"* meaning "the law does not concern itself with trifles."

The law also doesn't concern itself with the dessert, trifle • *Photo © Timothy Krause*

De minimis copying became particularly prickly when things were filmed in the background in movies or documentaries and then the copyright holders claimed copyright infringement. A pinball machine in the film *What Women Want*, a baseball game playing in the distance while an interview was taking place, and a baby dancing to a faintly heard Prince song in the background are all real-world examples. The focus of each of these uses was not the copyrightable work, but somehow parts of them were now part of a new work.

In *What Women Want* the pinball machine was not the focus of the scene, and it was only on screen for a very short period of time. None of the characters talk about the pinball machine, and the pinball machine is not even fully shown. The court ruled it *de minimis*—no copyright infringement.

A still from the film *What Women Want*, showing the pinball machine in the background.

A more recent case in 2018 involved graffiti. In *Gayle v. Home Box Office, Inc.*, 17-CV-5867 (JMF) (S.D.N.Y. May. 1, 2018), HBO won a case involving a scene from the TV series, *Vinyl*, where a woman walks by a dumpster tagged with graffiti that says "art we all." Here the graffiti was barely visible for less than three seconds, was not the focus of the scene, and one would barely have noticed it at all. Fleeting uses, the court explains, are *de minimis*.

Compare *Gayle* to a decision by the Second Circuit Court two decades earlier involving a poster of Faith Ringgold's *Church Picnic Story Quilt*, which had been a key case in the *de minimis* conversation. *Faith Ringgold v. Black Entertainment Television*, 126 F.3d 70, (2d Cir. 1997). Faith Ringgold is a famous artist that is best known for her narrative quilts. She began as a painter, but switched to painting on fabric, adding quilting elements and writing stories into her quilts, the first of which was *Who's Afraid of Aunt Jemima?* (1983). Ringgold also writes children's books, including *Tar Beach* (1991), which is based on her quilt of the same name, and has become very very famous.

In the television series *Roc*, a poster of Ringgold's quilt was used on nine different occasions for a total of 26.75 seconds **without permission**. HBO and BET raised the *de minimis* defense. The court rejected it. The High Museum had a license to sell poster reproductions of the quilt. The poster was used as set decoration in *Roc*. To determine whether *de minimis* applied in this case, the court turned to the Library of Congress's royalty rates to be paid by public broadcasting entities for the use of published pictorial and visual works, which distinguishes between a featured and background display, setting a higher royalty rate for featured.

Images used in public broadcasting require a fee, the court explains. A featured image is defined as "a full-screen or substantially full-screen display for more than three seconds." The court cites 37 C.F.R. Section 253.8(b)92). Background images are defined as less than full-screen display, or full-screen for less than three seconds. The court applied this to the case, finding that the poster was visible for a total of 26–27 seconds. Moreover, the poster was chosen because of its significance as recognizable, and well suited for set decoration for an African-American church scene within the television show. "The *de minimis* threshold for actionable copying of protected expression has been crossed."

One commentator, Mitchell Zimmermann, suggested that to be *de minimis* a work must not be observable—that the time you see the work is short (under three seconds) or that it is blurred and unidentifiable. The pinball case would suggest inconsequential as well. Here again, the pinball machine was not in focus, and not very visible. *De minimis* requires the use to be incidental and brief, preferably out of focus, in the background, not significant to the plot, and not readily discernible.

De minimis has been a significant topic of conversation with music sampling—how much can you take, and does *de minimis* apply? That is beyond the scope of this book, but it is an important issue.

Independent Creation

Copyright allows for different creators to create the same work independently of each other. For example, two people can each create a rainbow quilt. Neither knew about each other. Neither will be infringing on the other.

Subconscious Copying

Imagine that in 2004 you saw a very cool quilt at the International Quilt Festival, but you have since forgotten about it. You didn't take a picture of it, because your phone didn't have a camera at that time. In 2018, you make a quilt that turns out to be nearly identical to the 2004 quilt. You didn't remember the Festival quilt. You post your quilt, and it becomes the cover of your new book, which sells millions of copies. The original copyright holder of the quilt sees it and gets very angry. If the original quilt qualifies for copyright protection, the court will likely see this as subconscious copying. You had access to it. You copied it, even though you didn't remember seeing it.

There are cases regarding subconscious copying in music all the time. The court often looks at the availability of the work in general, as well as your own experience with the work. So, when an artist told us that he never looks at things on the Internet, that's not necessarily the test—personal awareness of the image. If the original work is popular and widely available, an individual's personal experience will not matter. If a work is well-known enough, the court will assume access, and then look to see how similar the two works are.

If the original work is popular and widely available, an individual's personal experience will not matter.

Public Domain and Other Non-Protectable Elements

Public domain and non-protectable elements have to be taken into consideration because they are also defenses. If you need a refresher, see Identifying the Public Domain, page 65, and Identifying Non-Protectable Elements, page 34. Non-protectable elements and works in the public domain can be used by everyone, it's just a matter of determining how similar the use is, and whether that use is protectable. If you make the same changes to a public domain image as someone else, that could be seen as infringement.

Using Someone Else's Version of a Public Domain Work

You find a work in the public domain and you make something. Awesome. You find someone's interpretation of the public domain work and you copy that. Not so awesome. Here is an example. *Tufenkian Import/Export Ventures, Inc. v. Einstein Moomjy*, 339 F.3d 127, (2d Cir. 2003) concerned two carpets, both using the same public domain source. James Tufenkian took two public domain images and put them together, modifying them on his computer. He used different components from the public domain images, and added some bits of his own creation, including stick-figure animals and castle-like figures. Two years after Tukenkian's work had been marketed, a competitor, Bashian, hired one of Tufenkian's former employees to help him design a rug. Bashian's design team was familiar with Tukenkian's rug, and Bashian admits some copying occurred. There were new elements, but they were using the same public domain elements. So, you have the original, the simplified version, and the copy of the simplified version. The court found the copy of the simplified version infringing. You can't do that. You can't take someone else's choices using a public domain work and copy them.

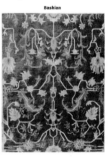

When you take images from the public domain, edit and add additional creativity, you gain copyright in that version of the public domain work. It doesn't mean that others can't use that same public domain image, but they cannot mimic what you did with that same image.

Beanie Babies Look Nothing like Actual Cows and Pigs

Nature, including cows and pigs, is not protected by copyright (see Identifying Non-Protectable Elements, page 34.) We have another example in a famous case about Beanie Babies. Ty, the manufacturer of Beanie Babies sued another toy company for copying their pig named Squealer, and their cow named Daisy. The defendant said that cows and pigs were in the public domain. The court

Squealer is on the right, and the infringing "pig" is on the left.

said, not *these cows and pigs* ... because the Beanie Babies hardly looked like public domain cows and pigs! *Ty, Inc. v. GMA Accessories, Inc.*, 132 F.3 11967 (7th Cir. 1997).

Substantial Similarity Test

Now that you have a good understanding of acceptable defenses to copying, let's loop back to how to determine if there are enough similarities to constitute inappropriate copying. Remember that the first step is to determine if the original work has a valid copyright. Once you have established that the next step is to see if there was substantial copying.

The courts have developed a number of tests to determine if things that seem substantially similar are infringing. The questions are generally the same from court to court, but may differ depending on the jurisdiction. The court will first determine if there was *copying in fact*. This is the first step. When there is no direct evidence of literal copying (for example, burning a compact disc), courts look at circumstantial evidence: whether the defendant had access to the plaintiff's work, and the degree of similarity between the two works. They are trying to determine there was copying in fact.

Access. The courts look at how popular the work was and where the work was available. The court also looks to direct points of access to the work by the defendant (for example the plaintiff emailed a copy of their work to the defendant in preparation for a podcast interview.) The court also looks at general, public access. Other considerations could be: whether permission been granted to use the copyrighted work through a license, a Creative Commons license, or one-on-one.

Degree of similarity. This one is more complicated, which is why we'll be taking a deep dive into this topic. The courts will seek to determine how and why they are they similar and if it subconscious copying, direct copying, or a case of using common public domain reference materials.

Substantial similarity is a two part test. The access plus degree of similarity is part one. If there has indeed been copying in fact, then the courts move to determine part two, **inappropriate copying**, which can be a long, drawn out comparison between the plaintiff's and the defendant's works.

Interestingly, one of the key cases used to teach law students is *Boisson v. Banian, Ltd.*, 273 F.3d 262 (2d Cir. 2001), a quilting case! But first, we begin with the classic case of *Nichols v. Universal Picture Corp.*, 45 F.2d 119 (2d Cir. 1930), cert. denied, 282 U.S. 902 (1931). In this case from 1931, Judge Hand set out what we now refer to as the levels of abstractions test. *Nichols v. Universal Picture Corp.*

Judge Hand suggested that when looking at whether there was copyright infringement, there were **levels of abstraction** "Upon any work ... a great number of patterns of increasing generality will fit equally well, as more and more of the incident is left out. The last may perhaps be no more than the most general statement of what the [work] is about, at times might consist only of its title; but there is a point in this series of abstractions where they are no longer protected, since otherwise, the [author] could prevent his "ideas" to which, apart from their expression, his property is never extended. Nobody has ever been able to fix that boundary, and nobody ever can…"

So, we all still do this abstraction test—and it is painstaking. What are the big concepts? What are the details? What was taken? Let's see it in action with *Boisson v. Banian, Ltd.*

In 1991, Judi Boisson of American Country Quilts and Linens, a twenty-year quilt industry veteran, designed two Alphabet Quilts, which she named *School Days*. Both quilts were designed on a five-by-six blockgrid and featured hand-drawn alphabet letters. Boisson selected and arranged the various colors and placement of the letters. Boisson included a copyright notice on the quilts, and she registered the quilts with the U.S. Copyright Office. Judi regularly registered her works. She has over

90 copyright registrations at the U.S. Copyright Office.

Vijay Rao (doing business as Banian) decided to start selling quilts by importing them from India and selling them through boutique stores and catalog companies. In 1991, he ordered pre-made quilts, shown to him by a third party, and then after requesting modifications, reordered the quilt in 1994 and 1995. In 1998 Boisson initiated a lawsuit claiming copyright infringement and Banian voluntarily withdrew the quilts at issue from the market. Boisson sued Banian.

The case started in district court, where the quilts were not found to be infringing. Boisson appealed to the Second Circuit Court. The Second Circuit Court found that while the alphabet and the use of colors was not protectable, Boisson's **selection, arrangement, and coordination of non-copyrightable elements was protectable.**

Substantial Similarity Test in Boisson v. Banian

Copyright Registration

Because Boisson registered both *School Days* quilts the same year she designed them, and within five years of first publication, the Copyright Act of 1976 provides the **presumption** that she holds valid copyrights. 17 U.S.C. Section 410(c). The registration of the works is the first step in being able to file a copyright claim. And there are also potential statutory damages available, should they be awarded (which is rare).

Substantial Similarity

Since Boisson had a valid copyright, now the court had to determine if it was literal copying or circumstantial copying. The quilts were not identical. So, on to circumstantial copying. Was there opportunity/access and are the comparative quilts similar?

The court first looked at whether there had been **actual copying of plaintiff's work**. Banian did not dispute that there was actual copying.

Next the court had to dig into the degree of **originality/substantial similarity**. The court looked at individual elements of the quilt to see how original each element was.

First, the alphabet. The alphabet is in the public domain, and Boisson did not dispute this.

Next, the court looked at the layout of the alphabet. The district court found that to be in the public domain, but the appeals court did not find "the alphabetical arrangement of the letters in the five-by-six block format required some minimum degree of creativity, which is all that is required for copyrightability." These factors create a presumption that the layout is original and therefore a protectable element. Therefore, if defendants want to contest this presumption, they bear the burden of proving that this particular layout is not original. The defendant did not provide enough proof to show that the layout was in the public domain. If Banian had done a better job indicating that the layout of the alphabet was in the public domain, the case might have turned out differently. Lesson: If a work is registered, and you (the potential infringer) believe it is a public domain pattern, you have to put together a good case as to why it is, otherwise the court will presume that it meets the originality standard, and if registered with the U.S. Copyright Office, that the registration is valid.

Then, the court looked at the color. Color, by itself, is not protectable, but as part of the selection, arrangement, and coordination, it might be.

So, the court found access plus substantial similarity, which meant that the court went on to see if there was inappropriate coping.

Improper (or Inappropriate) Copying

Once the court found substantial similarity, they then turned to evaluating whether there was improper copying.

The general test for improper copying is the *ordinary observer test* but the court felt that would do the analysis injustice. The ordinary observer test asks whether an average lay observer would be predisposed to overlook the differences between the works and consider the overall aesthetics of the works the same.

With works taken from the public domain (in this case non-protectable elements), the court suggested that the more discerning *total concept and feel* test be applied. With this text, you look at the total concept and feel of the two works, but at the same time recognizing the public domain elements. "In the present case, while use of the alphabet may not provide a basis for infringement, we must compare defendants' quilts and plaintiffs' quilts on the basis of the arrangement and shapes of the letters, the colors chosen to represent the letters and other parts of the quilts, the quilting patterns, the particular icons chosen and their placement."

Boisson's School Days 1 Quilt

Banian's ABC Green Quilt

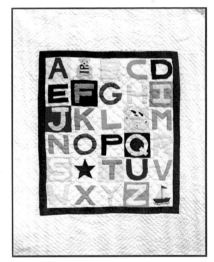
Banian's ABC Navy Quilt

Copyright infringement cases often do a detailed analysis of the differences and similarities between two works. This case is a good example of what you see in numerous cases, and helps you understand when something you make might infringe on something someone else has made. You can do this analysis yourself. Remember the 10 percent myth? This would be its legal mate—how much do you need to change a work to not be infringing? That's really what Boisson and the other infringement cases teach us.

The court turned to comparing the quilts. In their first comparison, the court found "an enormous amount of sameness" with Boissen's *School Days 1* versus Banian's *ABC Green Version(s)*. Both have the same formation of the alphabet, with different icons filling in the last row. Boisson's *School Days 1* has a cat, house, single-stared American flag, and a basket. Banian's *ABC Green Version 1* has a cow jumping over the moon, a sailboat, a bear, and a star.

The court then did a comparison letter by letter. Here are some of the analyses they did. (We are not making you review the entire alphabet).

A: Both quilts: dark blue on light blue background

B: Both quilts: red on white background

D: Both quilts: polka-dots on light blue background

F: Boisson's: white on pink; Banian's: pink on white background

G: Both quilts: green background

H and L: Both quilts: blue on white background

M: Both quilts: yellow on white background

N: Both quilts: green on white background

O: Both quilts: blue on polka-dot background

P: Both quilts: polka-dot on yellow background

Q: Both quilts: brown on light background

R: Both quilts: pink on grey/purple background

S: Both quilts: white on red background

T: Both quilts: blue on white background

U: Both quilts: gray on white background

V: Both quilts: white on gray background

W: Both quilts: pink on white background

X: Both quilts: purple on light background

Y: Both quilts: yellow on light background

Z: Both quilts: navy or black

Boisson also noted that Banian's letters J, M, N, P, R, and W copied her unique way of making the shapes. The quilting was also the same, with both having diamond-shaped quilt motifs within the blocks and a wavy pattern in the plain white border that surrounded the blocks. All of the quilts were all edged with ⅜" green binding. Note how carefully the court compared the two quilts.

When you do the step-by-step analysis, it becomes clear that there was copying of the selection, arrangement, and coordination. The court writes, "We think defendants' quilts sufficiently similar to plaintiffs' design as to demonstrate illegal copying. In particular, the overwhelming similarities in color choices lean toward a finding of infringement. Although the icons chosen for each quilt are different and defendants added a green rectangular border around their rows of blocks, these differences are not sufficient to cause even the 'more discerning' observer to think the quilts are other than substantially similar in so far as the protectable elements of plaintiffs' quilts are concerned" And by not pirating all of it, it doesn't relieve Banian of infringement. The court found infringement.

In the second comparison, the court then turned to the comparison of Boisson's *School Days II* and Bannian's *ABC Green*. Here the court did not find they were substantially similar. The letters were arranged differently, the colors used were different, and the feel of "American patriotism" in Boisson's was not carried over to Banina's use of green as the predominant color.

The third comparison: Boisson's *School Days II* versus *ABC Navy*. In this case, the court **did not** find infringement. These were not the same color combination, the placement of the icons, the borders, and the quilting patterns was different, and the similarity of the lettering and the use of a blue edge were found to be trivial. So Banian's quilt was seen as different.

Boisson's Importance for Makers

Boisson, along with other infringement cases, help us to see how much (or how little) we have to change in order not to be infringing. In one quilt, Banian had taken too much. But in the other two instances, changing the color, placement, and quilting style was enough.

Aftermath of Boisson

The story doesn't end there. After the Second Circuit Court found that there was infringement for one of the quilts, the trial court was required to assess the request for damages, injunction, and attorney's fees and costs. Banian was no longer selling the infringing quilts, so the court did not find a need for an injunction to have him stop selling the quilts.

Damage Calculation

- **No statutory damages.** Boisson had elected statutory damages. Because she had registered her copyright, that was an option. The court did not find Banian willful or innocent. So, statutory damages would not be set at $150,000 per work. Statutory damages are not automatic, and left to the discretion of the court.

- **Actual damages.** Then the court turned to actual damages. The court looked at Boisson's profits, and did not see a reduction in the value because of Banian's version. Also, Banian did not mass market the quilts. Instead, he sold only 153 of them for a profit of $3,306. He also withdrew them from the market when he was faced with a lawsuit.

- **Saved expenses by using Bossion's design.** The court also looked to Banian's saved expenses by relying on Boisson's design. The court found that although Boisson claimed it took her a month to design, large portions of the design were in the public domain, and found no evidence that by borrowing Boisson's design that expenses were saved.

- **Materials used.** The court looked at the materials used to create the design—in this case Boisson used a pencil and tracing paper, along with labor.

The court decided to award $1,000 for labor and saved expenses by Banian. The court also looked at Banian's profits. The gross revenue on the 153 quilts was $7,150, with a profit of $3,306. The court seemed to consider actual profits, even though they could have awarded a greater amount. This goes to the character of the defendant. There was no evidence that Boisson lost revenue, and though Banian had already ceased selling the quilts, deterrence wasn't needed either, but the court did add $500 as a deterrent measure. **The total was $4,806 in statutory damages.**

The court found Banian reasonable in that he was just trying to sell quilts and the Second Circuit Court only found one infringing quilt. Boisson's settlement demands of $175,000 made it impossible for Banian to bring the case to an end. The court found no need for deterrence, as the defendant had stopped the behavior instantly and repeatedly tried to settle the case. So, no attorney's fees to Boisson.

The parties returned to court one more time in 2004 where both parties attempted to get an award for costs, including attorney's fees. Look at the amounts! Boisson submitted a bill of $44,88.60 for costs, and Banian submitted a bill of $8,889 plus attorneys' fees in the amount of $84,907. The court looks to Rule 54 of the Federal Code of Civil Procedure, which allows for cost by the prevailing party. First attorney's fees are not included in Rule 54. Both parties believed they were the prevailing party because one quilt was found infringing, while the others were not. The district court found Boisson the prevailing party, but did not award attorney's fees or find willful infringement.

But another rule, Rule 68 does allow for attorney's fees, but it gets more interesting. Banian had offered to settle early on in the case for $12,000, but Bossion refused, claiming that she was owed $175,000. In the end, the court found the damages awarded to Boisson in 2003 was for $4,886, much less than the original settlement offered by Banion in 1997.

The court also looked at plaintiff's lost revenues, defendant's profits, the value of the copyright and the deterrent effect of the award. Banion litigated in good faith, and when a settlement was proposed by Boisson, it was for $175,000, more than willful infringement statutory damages.

Boisson can recover costs under Rule 54, but only up until the point that the Rule 68 offer had been put on the table, which was July 10, 1998. As the Banian's Rule 68 motion to recover costs post-offer, the court denied the attorney's fees because these are covered by the Copyright Act of 1976, and were not rewarded as part of that. The costs, however, after July 10, 1998 are awarded to Banian after July 10, 1998. Banian's costs were $8,889.77.

What We Learned from Boisson

We think there are a lot of lessons to learn from Boisson, especially about the realities of litigation, without having to spend the money and learn the hard way. Before heading to court, remember what this case taught us.

1. Get a good expert. Banian's expert on whether the alphabet quilt structure was in the public domain did not convince the court. Make sure to have support.

2. The outward appearance. The court was looking to the colors and shapes—the total look and feel—if it is too close, infringement will be found, but it is easy to change some elements, at least with this court, to find no infringement.

3. Just because you win, doesn't mean you get a lot of money. And it is unlikely that you will get attorney's fees. So expect to pay the costs and attorney's fees, which can add up.

4. You can get penalized for not settling. It's a gamble.

5. The Court may not agree with you. Boisson won only one quilt, not the others. The others were deemed not infringing. She could have gotten more if she had settled for $12,000

6. The costs. We know that Banian had over $80,000 in attorney's fees. One would imagine so too did Boisson. But maybe the litigation deters others like Banian from using designs without permission. It's a high price for both.

Takeaways? In the end, why did Boisson continue to pursue the claim? Banian stopped. She kept going. She likely felt that she had the right to pursue the copyright claim, and that she would be compensated accordingly. We reached out to get a comment, but she didn't return our email.

A Fabric and Pattern Designer Sues

Thimbleberries was the brainchild of Lynette Jensen, who designed and sold quilt patterns and fabric designs beginning in 1988. A year into her business, Jensen created a Christmas wreath pattern, which she displayed at the industry trade show Quilt Market in Houston and in Denver. Her quilt design was also featured in *America's Best Quilt Projects* in 1993. Lynette, like so many pattern makers, saw a near identical copy of her pattern being mass-produced without her permission or a license. This is a pattern maker's worst nightmare. She saw it in a *Charles Keath* catalog in October, 2000. She contacted a lawyer, who sent a cease and desist letter to stop all sales through the catalog. Thimbleberries also sent a letter to C & F Enterprises requesting they stop production and sale of the allegedly infringing products. Both the manufacturer and the catalog refused to stop selling the table linens using the Christmas wreath pattern. So, Thimbleberries sued. *Thimbleberries, Inc. v. C & F Enterprises, Inc.,* 142 F. Supp. 2d 1132 (D. Minn. 2001).

Please Register Your Copyright in a Timely Manner We turn to the district court's decision relating to copyright. First, Thimbleberries waited more than five years from first publication to file for a copyright registration. So, there was no presumption that they held the copyright. That doesn't keep Thimbleberries from obtaining a registration, it just means that now the court will look into whether the work has the sufficient amount of originality and protectability, rather than presuming that if filed within the first five years after publication.

Lynette does not have a monopoly on the idea of shapes arranged into a wreath. "However, as Thimbleberries easily demonstrates, the pattern which it seeks to protect represents only one of many ways to express a quilted wreath design." Thimbleberries' counsel provided nine other wreath patterns that were an arrangement of squares, triangles, octagons, and rectangles that were different from Thimbleberries. The court found that with this evidence, Thimbleberries

had enough creativity to meet the minimum bar for copyright. "Moreover, the variety of patterns reveals that Thimbleberries's particular arrangement of public domain shapes is not at all compelled by the underlying idea." In other words, the court found that the merger doctrine did not apply (see Merger Doctrine and the Blank Forms Rule, page 36.)

The court did not think changes in the defendant's work were enough to be distinguishable: "To the contrary, the court finds that the subtle distinctions in color and fabric choice, background quilting stitches and border trim are irrelevant to the similarity determination because these features do not constitute the subject matter of the copyright." The court even notes that the list of differences only highlighted to the court how much they are the same.

"[T]he court concludes that the two works are so strikingly similar as to preclude the possibility that the defendant's designer independently arrived at the same result." In particular, the court believed the subtle changes looked as if the pattern maker was making deliberate changes to escape copyright infringement. With this, Thimbleberries could show a presumption of irreparable harm, and seek to obtain a preliminary injunction to stop manufacturing and selling the pattern until the case was resolved. Moreover, the court found that the economic hardship would fall to Thimbleberries if the pattern continued to be mass-produced without a license in place. The court issued a preliminary injunction for Thimbleberries.

Making Exact Copies: Some Common Scenarios

Not everything, in fact, most of the time, making copies does not rise to an infringement suit.

Making copies is a complicated fact-specific topic. But we see that this question arises quite often. When thinking about making copies, the first question to ask is whether by making the copy are you creating a market replacement for purchasing a copy of the work? Let's look at some common instances when people make copies and whether those circumstances equate to a market replacement.

Copying Family Photographs

When you make copies of family photos, you are not creating a market replacement. You are preserving the works, or using them for a creative purpose.

For example, let's say someone takes 5,000 family photographs and scans them into her computer. By doing this, she is making a copy. She is preserving the photographs. But, she also intends to make a mosaic quilt, where each photograph acts as part of a larger photograph. She alters the photos in Photoshop and then uploads the images to a program which helps her place them. When she is satisfied with the compiled image, she purchases a copy—of the selection, arrangement, and coordination of those photographs that she uploaded. She then uploaded the compilation to Spoonflower to print the mosaic on fabric but did not post the image for sale. There was lots of copying—the images scanned into her computer, the images uploaded to create the mosaic, the compilation to the fabric printer. But all of this has been done under personal use (not something legally acknowledged as a category but generally noted). Transformative use under fair use may also apply, and she is not planning to sell the work (although Spoonflower might!). She is not the author of the photos, or at least not all of them, so she has technically violated the copyright of the other photographers. So, the next question is who is going to object, and who is going to sue? If these are family photographs for a present, the threshold is fairly low. But, if you take professional wedding photos and make copies in violation of the agreement with the wedding photographer, that might be a problem.

The Pattern Requires Copying

Katja Marek is the author of *The New Hexagon*, and also *The New Hexagon 2*. These are books that each have 52 patterns for English Paper Piecing, and as part of the book, you have to make a copy of the pattern in order to complete the projects. She is giving you permission to copy. Now, how far can that copying go? You purchased the book. It's for your personal use. What if your friend wants to do the patterns? They can borrow the book, and make their own copies. That's First Sale Doctrine at work (see First Sale Doctrine, page 62). You can't make ten copies of a pattern for your sewing group. That would be a market replacement and uncool—you would be committing copyright infringement, and not supporting the quilting community. Katja worked hard on that book.

Copying a Pattern for Your Friends, a Guild, or Group

This gets tricky. Is the pattern a common block? If it is, you are likely good. Is the pattern something older than 1924? Good again. Is the pattern something first published in the United States before 1989 that does not have copyright notice (for example, a magazine where there is no ©)? This is likely also okay. You can see what we're getting at: Is the pattern in the public domain?

If the pattern is something you found out in the world published after 1989: that's under copyright. The selection, arrangement, and coordination of the pattern, the image, and the expression of the instructions are all protected. Ask permission. The patternmaker may give permission to use for groups. But mass producing copies as a market placement is infringement. Why you are using the pattern, for example charity knitting, doesn't absolve the crime. It's better than if you were selling it, but still don't make copies.

Making Binders of Patterns to Share

One of the most egregious examples of copyright infringement I've heard about is someone who suggested that as part of a retreat, everyone copy all the patterns they have, and they could make binders for each person of all of the patterns. No, you do not have the right to do that.

A Reminder About Digital Copies

Unlike paper copies and books, digital copies do not fall under the First Sale Doctrine. You can't borrow someone's digital copy and you can't sell your digital copy. You really can't do much, unless the copyright holder has given you permission. And yet, digital copies are the easiest to email to a friend, print, and share. It's the great irony of our times.

Other Rights and Infringement

We have spent a long time going through the right to reproduce. It gives you a feeling for how copyright infringement is analyzed. There are still other rights, with specific elements to discuss. In particular, let's take a look at the right to make derivative works and the right to distribute. These are two other key rights. When filing a lawsuit, these three are often included.

Right to Make Derivative Works

The right to make derivative works connects sometimes also to fair use. Is the work an unauthorized derivative work or does it fall under fair use? These cases involve the use of pre-existing work, see Making Derivative Works (page 32). We have to do the same kind of analysis of where the pre-existing underlying work comes from as we did with the right of reproduction. We look to independent creation and public domain as key elements, along with non-protectable elements and idea/expression.

Also, the derivative work does not have to be fixed to be infringing, which is weird, right? While to gain copyright protection, a work has to be fixed, to be infringing, it does not. An example is a dance based on an opera. The dance may not be fixed, but it still may be infringing.

> **COPYRIGHT INFRINGEMENT: HIRE AN ATTORNEY**
>
> If you are contemplating an infringement suit in any way, you should contact a lawyer, but if you are thinking about suing on an unfixed derivative work, you really need an attorney.

Obviously, the derivative work right overlaps or clashes with fair use, where someone is potentially making a derivative work, sometimes in this situation called a transformative work, but it is legal and not violating the Section 106 exclusive rights of copyright holders. It's messy. Is it an unauthorized derivative work or a transformative fair use? It really depends on whether it satisfies fair use. If it doesn't, then it is an unauthorized derivative work.

We also have the question of when something *becomes* a derivative work. We will be discussing derivative work and infringement more in How Far Can You Go? A Different Perspective on Enforcement (page 166).

Repurposing and Creating Derivative Works

So, we have a slightly weird problem. If you take something and repurpose it, like making bottle caps into earrings, is that allowed because of the First Sale Doctrine, or is that an unauthorized derivative work? Two different Circuits went a different way on this issue and the cases were about the same thing: images being mounted on tiles. In both instances there was no copying. A legitimate, purchased copy was used. There was only recasting, which is part of the derivative right.

But, we see that a lot of people do this, but there are not a lot of lawsuits about this. One example is Kita Harvey who repurposes Calico Critters into My Chemical Romance band members. People are doing this, and it all seems okay.

We have two cases about the A.R.T. Company, with completely opposite decisions. The Albuquerque A.R.T. Company purchased artwork prints or high quality books. They then glued the images onto ceramic tiles. Did that constitute creating a derivative work? The Ninth Circuit Court thought they had recast and transformed, violating the derivative right. *Mirage Editions, Inc. v. Albuquerque A.R.T. Company*, 856 F.2d 1341 (9th Cir. 1988). A decade later, the Seventh Circuit Court ruled the opposite, that this was not a derivative work though they were doing exactly the same thing. This is called a *circuit split*. To date, the U.S. Supreme Court has not taken up the case. *Lee v. A.R.T. Company*, 125 F.3d 580 (7th Cir. 1997). In many ways, the *Andy Warhol Foundation* case in 2023 seems to reserve the derivative work right for copyright holders, when it is created for the same purpose.

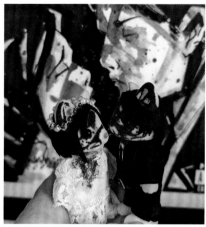

Kita Harvey's Emo Critters are an example of repurposing. These two critters, titled *Kitty Demo Lovers*, are based on the Demolition Lovers, two characters from the band My Chemical Romance's second studio album. Harvey is known as @emocritters on Instagram. •
Photo and artwork © Kita Harvey

The law is not certain. This relates to the right to distribute. So, before we do the final takeaway, let's look at the right to distribute.

Right to Distribute

Section 106 provides to the copyright holder the right to distribute the work. Once that distribution occurs, the copyright holder has no more control over the physical item. This is called first sale, or sometimes exhaustion.

The right of distribution is limited by the First Sale Doctrine, Section 109(a) of the Copyright Act of 1976. Let's take a look:

> Notwithstanding the provisions of section 106(3), **the owner of a particular copy** or phonorecord lawfully made under this title, or any person authorized by such owner, **is entitled, without the authority of the copyright owner**, to sell or otherwise dispose of the possession of that copy or phonorecord.

What does that mean exactly? Once you purchase a copy of a book, you do not pay the copyright holder a percentage if you sell it at a used book store. You can also lend it to someone, or even destroy it.

Secondary Infringement

So far we have been talking about direct infringement. Someone copies your work. But there is also something called secondary infringement. If you facilitate infringement or benefit from it, you could also be held liable. Secondary infringement can be either contributory or vicarious.

Contributory Infringement

You do not do the copying, but you benefit from the infringement. The two key elements are:

1. Knowledge of the infringing activity

2. Material contribution to the activity

Vicarious Infringement

You have the right and ability to supervise the infringing activity and you have a direct financial interest. A dance hall was held liable when an orchestra played unauthorized music, and the dance hall benefited from the performance financially. Vicarious liability requires:

1. The right and ability to supervise or control the infringing activity

2. A direct financial benefit from the activities. *Dreamland Ballroom, Inc. v. Shapiro*, Bernstein & Co, 36 F.2d 354 (7th Cir. 1929).

Inducement

One other kind of secondary liability is inducement. You don't do the infringing, but you encourage others to do. it. This was a U.S. Supreme Court Case, *MGM v. Grokster* (545 U.S. 913 (2005), where the court unanimously held that a peer-to-peer file sharing company had induced people to commit copyright infringement. When Napster, the most famous peer-to-peer file sharing company got closed down, other technologies and companies rose to try to capture the users. One of these was Grokster. So, don't have a website where you say, "Hey come post copyrighted patterns here." That's Grokster, and you might be found in court accused of inducement.

Criminal Liability

You can go to jail for copyright infringement. That is not a joke. You really can. Criminal infringement is covered under Section 506 of the Copyright Act of 1976. Criminal copyright infringement applies only to the reproduction right and the distribution right. Criminal infringement occurs when a person willfully infringes under one of the following circumstances.

- The infringement is for commercial advantage or private financial gain.

- The infringement is the reproduction or distribution during any 180-day period, one or more copies which have a total retail value of more than $1,000, OR

- Distributing the work to the public, when it was known, or should have been known, that it was intended for commercial distribution.

The penalty is a felony conviction, up to three years in prison, and a $250,000 fine. It can be increased to five years if the infringement was for commercial advantage or private financial gain. And repeat offenders can get between six and ten years in prison. If it is found to be a misdemeanor, the prison time is one year and a $100,000 fine. A misdemeanor is less serious than a felony (remember those cop shows?), with a misdemeanor carrying a shorter jail time, and you aren't considered a felon.

Criminal liability also includes fraudulent copyright notice (for example, putting your name on something where you are not the copyright holder), which carries a fine of not more than $2,500; fraudulently removing copyright notices, again with a fine of no more than $2,500; and false representation of a material fact in the application for copyright registration, again with a fine of no more than $2,500. Note: moral rights do not have criminal penalties. There is a five year statute of limitations for copyright crimes, but for civil disputes it is for three years of discovering the copyright violation.

So, who gets put in prison? Someone trafficking in bootleg videotapes of movies. *U.S. v. Larracuente*, 952 F.2d 672, (2d Cir. 1992). In 2021, three employees from Stamford Connecticut were convicted for installing unlicensed versions of software and then generating fake license keys. So, yes, there can be jail time for copyright infringement, but only for really bad copyright criminals, and those cases are related to piracy, not a misreading of fair use.

What About *Plagiarism*?

Plagiarism is not the same as copyright infringement. Copyright infringement is unauthorized copying. Plagiarism is falsely claiming the work as your own. Plagiarism is a separate, although related concept to copyright infringement. You can have both. Plagiarism can also be considered state causes of action like **fraud, misappropriation, and/or unfair competition**. You could be sued for both copyright infringement and these other state-specific causes of action.

What is Plagiarism?

The simplest definition is presenting someone else's ideas as your own. You did not get permission from the original author to do so, and you did not give attribution to the original author.

Plagiarism can come in similar forms to copyright infringement:

- Literal copying

- Paraphrasing too closely and not giving attribution

- Claiming someone else's work as your own, like hiring someone to write your paper

Interestingly, plagiarism can also include failure to acknowledge that someone assisted you with the work, especially in an academic context.

If you go to Amazon, there are dozens of books about how to avoid plagiarism. And we have software, including TurnItIn, to detect plagiarism. Universities and K–12 take great pains to enforce rules against plagiarism. In those settings, even submitting work you have already submitted to another class can be considered plagiarism. At the University level, you might even be brought up on Honor Code violations if you used previously created work in a class without alerting and getting permission from the instructor. And technology has caught up. Tools like TurnItIn, a plagiarism detection application, have become standard tools built into grading, which alerts both student and professor/teacher the percentage of plagiarized words and their likely origin point. Every paper turned in gets reviewed. The phrase the company uses is "Empower students to do their best, original work."

In 2023, the President of Harvard, Claudine Gay, had to step down following plagiarism accusations. In his article on the topic, Jonathan Bailey explains "Some of the examples, such as one involving a full paragraph of near-verbatim copying, definitely do point to significant issues. Others, however, involve either extremely short passages or longer ones that aren't as close of a match to one another as presented." (See Jonathan Bailey, *Understanding the Claudine Gay Plagiarism Scandal*, Plagiarism Today, December 12, 2023.) What's interesting is not the plagiarism, but the label of being a plagiarist. It can spiral fast. Especially for politicians, celebrities, and other high-profile people. During Ben Carson's presidential campaign run, he was accused of plagiarism in his book, *America the Beautiful* (2012).

Call-Out Videos: YouTube, Social Enforcement, and Plagiarism

Plagiarism has become a big topic on social media. Instagram accounts repost people's art and claim it as theirs. Tweets get stolen and passed off as original poetry. Plagiarism is more than a middle schooler ripping off someone else's paper. It's everywhere, and it's on your social media feeds.

And, more often than not, the way plagiarism is handled is through social enforcement, call-out culture, and a good bit of public shaming towards those who did the plagiarizing.

On December 2, 2023, popular YouTuber and video essayist Hbomberguy posted a nearly four-hour video titled, *Plagiarism and You(Tube)*. As of March 2024, it has over 18 million views. This video made plagiarism a trending topic in a major way at the end of 2023.

In his video, Hbomberguy carefully goes through and calls out four different creators for plagiarism, each more egregious than the last. He also contextualizes these modern acts of plagiarism in a larger context of pre-Internet plagiarism. It ultimately culminated in a lengthy discussion about video essayist James Somerton whose videos centered around queer media analysis. In one graphic, Hbomgerguy color codes a script of Somerton's to indicate where each sentence has been stolen from.

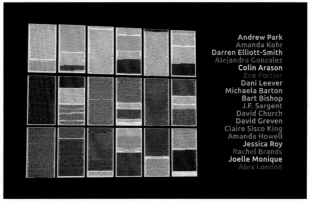

Hhomberguy, a queer man himself, goes through many of Somerton's videos, breaking down how and where the content was being stolen from with the underlying thesis looking at how Somerton is harming and stealing from the very community that makes up his audience. It effectively ended Somerton's YouTube career. It also put plagiarism into the current zeitgeist of the younger generations that consume video essay content.

Plagiarism is not something that is easy to, or is often, litigated. Social media and the Internet allow for a much more visible way to enforce and react to plagiarism, but it necessitates having to ask where your favorite content creators are sourcing their material and research.

PART 4: ENFORCING

What About Plagiarism?   **161**

Copyright *Claims* Board

On June 16, 2022, the U.S. Copyright Office started the Copyright Claims Board, an online alternative for copyright disputes.

Background

The CASE ACT of 2020 created the Copyright Claims Board (CCB), a dispute mechanism procedure at the U.S. Copyright Office that is voluntary and is meant to provide relief for small claims up to $30,000 total. The vision was that copyright holders could find someone infringing their work, and have recourse that was speedy and not too expensive.

The CCB, located at the U.S. Copyright Office, is entirely virtual. The office handles narrowly defined kinds of cases and are not precedent-setting. Three permanent officers who are expert copyright attorneys (not judges) preside, with a support staff of additional attorneys.

The anticipation of the CCB was fraught with anxiety. Will this work? How will a system that includes both non-lawyers (pro se) and sophisticated intellectual property lawyers work? How will this impact our current vision of copyright, with so many crevices for infringement that are not pursued? Will this positively add to the copyright system? Will we see something similar for trademarks? We have so many unanswered questions.

Basic Information

The CCB is designed for small claims, those under $15,000, but there is an even speedier option within the CCB available for those whose claims are even smaller, no more than $5,000.

Types of Works

The types of works eligible for consideration under the CCB are the same as we have seen throughout this book: literary, musical, dramatic, sound recordings, musical works, visual arts, audiovisual works, choreographic works, and even architectural works.

Requirement of Registration

To go to court in the United States you must have already registered your work with the U.S. Copyright Office. This does not apply if you are a foreign author, but if you don't register, you can't get statutory damages.

For the CCB, you can file your claim, whether you registered or not, but you will have to register your work along the way. This pauses the proceedings until registration occurs. If you have not filed for registration, you can file an expedited registration claim as part of the CCB process, which is much less expensive than if you did it separately.

Types of Relief

Monetary Damages

Unlike district court, where you can be awarded up to $150,000 in statutory damages per work, CCB damages are capped at $15,000 per work, and a claim can only have up to $30,000 in total damages. This is a big incentive for respondents (people responding to the allegation) to engage with the system; the potential monetary damage is much smaller.

There are two kinds of damages available:

Actual damages and profits. Actual damages is the amount you can prove was lost sales revenue. This can be hard to prove, and caps at $30,000. If you have had more than this amount in actual damages, you should be suing in federal district court.

Statutory damages. If you elect statutory damages, you don't have to prove actual damages or profits. The maximum is $15,000 per work, with a per claim maximum of $30,000, but we are not seeing these higher amounts awarded yet. And, if you do not register your work in a timely fashion (meaning registered within three months of first publication), the statutory damages are cut in half, to up to $7,500 per work, and a max of $15,000.

Stop Infringing Activity

The CCB can't issue an injunction like federal courts would issue. However, the CCB panel can issue a statement to stop engaging in wrongful activities, but both parties have to agree to do that. The allegedly infringing party doesn't have to admit guilt, but can agree to stop certain behavior before a final determination is made by the CCB. This could be beneficial to the respondent. If the CCB does find the respondent liable, it may reduce damages in the final determination because the respondent stopped their activities in good faith. This does not go to admitting the respondent is wrong. The decision is independent of that.

Let's look at a scenario to understand this concept. Sari accuses Lexi of copyright infringement, because Lexi used the same public domain image in creating tea towels for sale on Etsy. Lexi decides to halt her sales of that particular towel until the CCB proceedings go forward. The CCB panel finds that Lexi is not infringing on Sari's work using the public domain image, but that there was access and substantial similarity on how they both used the image. The CCB reduces the monetary award because Lexi had already taken steps to stop the behavior.

Attorney's Fees

Most of the time, no one is awarded attorney's fees or reimbursement for costs. However, if a party acts in bad faith, attorney's fees can be awarded. But the penalty is not great—up to $5,000 for those represented by an attorney, and costs up to $2,500 for those that are not represented by an attorney.

Types of Claims

Alleged Copyright Infringement

The CCB is designed to allow you to pursue a remedy if you think someone is violating your exclusive Section 106 rights (see Copyright Infringement, page 145).

Declaration That Specific Activities Do Not Infringe Copyright.

If you are accused of infringement you can file a claim in the hopes of receiving a ruling from the CCB that your actions are not infringing. This is like a declaratory judgment (where the person potentially in the wrong starts the lawsuit, instead of waiting for the copyright holder to instigate. You are trying to get out ahead of any potential controversy. So, if you receive a cease and desist letter, you can respond by filing a declaration claim at the CCB. When you do that, you are asking for a ruling that your actions do not infringe on the work of the cease and desist letter.

Claims Related to Takedown Notices on Social Media Platforms

If you start a notice and takedown on a social media platform or you are a victim of one. If there are *known misrepresentations* within this system, you can file a claim with the CCB. This usually is like the person filing the claim is not the actual owner. (See Notice and Takedown, page 140.)

SOCIAL MEDIA AND NOTICE AND TAKEDOWNS

Want to know more about the process? This is referred to as Section 512 of the U.S. Copyright Act. We'll discuss it further in this book in Notice and Takedown (page 140), but you can get more information at copyright.gov/512.

The Sticky Point of Opting Out

Respondents (the people accused of the problem) do not have to participate in CCB proceedings. If you file a claim and identify someone as infringing, the respondent can opt out of the proceedings. If they do so, the only choice you have is to sue in federal court. You would have to start again.

When the CCB was first available, people worried that most respondents would opt out. That's not been the case so far. There are some that do, but a surprising number stay in the system. They find the limited damages and quickness of the system a better alternative to litigation, where the average cost is $150,000 in costs and takes around 670 days.

You Have to Choose

If you are pursuing an action using the federal legal systems, you either file with the CCB or with a federal court. You can't do both. If you don't like the result of the CCB and think there was an error of fact or law that was material to the outcome, then you can seek reconsideration at the U.S. Copyright Office. You can ask the Register of Copyright to review whether the CCB abused their discretion; and sometimes, very rarely (and we don't think it has happened yet), you can request a federal court to review the determination.

Timing and Statute of Limitations

You have three years from the time of the alleged infringing activities to file a claim. Once you file the claim, the period is paused. If your claim doesn't move forward, the time it was paused doesn't count. You are measuring from the last act of infringement. If an image is on a website, for instance, the statute of limitations doesn't start until the image is removed.

Which Circuit?

The Circuit is where the infringement occurred, because that is where you would have to file in a federal court. If the company does business in a different place, you might be able to use that Circuit. The CCB is supposed to use the law of the Circuit in which the claim would have been brought. Jurisdiction and venue are a bit beyond the scope of this book. If you are thinking about suing, now is a good time to talk with a lawyer.

How Much Does it Cost?

The fee to start a claim is $40. If the claim goes forward, meaning neither party opts out, you pay a second payment of $60, for a total of $100 to file a claim. There are more costs. If you are a corporation, partnership, or unincorporated association, you pay $6 to designate a service agent. If you also have to expedite your registration, it is an extra $50 on top of whatever the registration costs are.

You must also officially make the respondent aware that you are filing a claim with the CCB. You've heard "You've been served!" on TV, that's what we are talking about here. This is called service of process, and usually costs around $25 to $100, depending on where you live. And there are also potential legal costs if you hire an attorney. To pursue the claim, you are looking at around $250. That's without a lawyer.

What If You Get a CCB Claim Notice as a Respondent?

If you are served notice that you are a respondent on a CCB claim, you have a choice whether or not to opt-out. But recognize that if you do, potentially higher damages and the possibility of going to federal court is a reality.

Also, if you ignore the notice, that's bad. We are seeing default judgments being made against respondents that do not respond. **Respond**. This means opening an eCCB account and doing all of the things you are asked to do. If you don't, you may find yourself with a hefty bill for ignoring the service of process and claim. In addition, there are many opportunities to tell your side of the story throughout the process, including responses to the claim and meetings with the U.S. Copyright Office. You could also apologize, and stop the infringing activity.

What About the Smaller Claims Option

You can file a smaller claim with the CCB. *Smaller claims* are those for monetary damages not more than $5,000. They involve one Copyright Claims Officer, instead of three, and have fewer procedures in place. They have the same impact as the full claims review. The ability to file for smaller claims is particularly awesome. If you know that your damages are less than $5,000, it is a way to streamline the process. The first final determination of the system was actually a smaller claim.

What We Know So Far

The CCB system is only a few years old, and there will be tinkering. We know that people are using it, and getting results. We have learned that the service of process (letting the respondent know you have filed a claim against them) and respondents' responding throughout the entire process have been the two main problems. The CCB staff help people when there are issues with a claim by producing a letter of noncompliance, and give them a couple of chances to fix it, providing written guidance on how to do so. All kinds of people and companies are using the system. It is an economical way to settle disputes. Copyright infringement cases in federal court can cost exponentially more. So far, the final determinations have been awarded around $1,000 to $3,300. That may change over time. Relating to unauthorized use of photographs, we are consistently seeing that the CCB is awarding three times the licensing fee, had the fee been paid originally.

How Far Can You Go? A Different *Perspective* on Enforcement

For a long time, as a society, in the age of the Internet and increased entrepreneurial activities, we didn't quite know what people legally could and couldn't do with someone else's copyrighted works. In particular, what fans (or people appealing to fans purchasing things) could do with a content owners' work. Make no mistake. People were doing all kinds of things. In the last few years, we are starting to get clarity. But before we begin there are some very important points to understand.

1. **Unless your use falls under fair use (or another permissible use like Section 108 library uses, or Section 110 classroom uses),** and the work is still under copyright, and you haven't obtained permission, **a copyright holder can object to your use.** The copyright holder has three years from the use to file with the Copyright Claims Board or initiate a lawsuit in federal court (see Timing and Statute of Limitations, page 164).

2. **Content owners** have started to provide information on their website about what fans can do.

3. **Copyright holders get to decide.** They may object to one use but not another and that might not seem fair. That's just the way it is. They get to decide. See Netflix Versus Bridgerton, page 168.

4. **If there is a copyright notice, you are not an innocent infringer.** If there is a copyright on the original work, you can't claim you didn't know.

5. **You may not hold a copyright in the work that you have created.** If the work is so dependent on the characters that you used without authorization (and doesn't fall under fair use), you do not get copyright on your work using those characters. See Beware of Section 103(a), page 105).

6. **Using photographs as a basis for fan portraits:** We learn in the *Three Stooges* case (see Creating Things Versus Copying Things—*The Three Stooges* Case, page 102) and also the recent *Andy Warhol* case (see First Factor: The Purpose and Character of the Use, page 78) that you can't take a photograph and merely create an illustration or painting. They are seen as the same use. If you are using an underlying photograph to create an illustration or painting, be careful. The more commercial your activity, the more likely you will have problems and may need a license for that underlying work. In reality, we see people doing this all of the time, and even making their living from it. It is not usually policed until it is commercially visible.

The rest of the chapter will help us better understand how far we can go creating fan works (or any work based on someone else's copyrighted work). Each of these cases tells the story of an original work and then someone using it to create something new, sometimes with permission, sometimes not. Let's see what we learn. **The question to keep in mind is how far can you go in creating a derivative work before someone sues for infringement?**

Pretty Far

First, we are going to head into a particular territory: fan musicals. These can serve as a means to help us understand many spaces. In the last few years, there has been a new trend: fan musicals on TikTok. These didn't start on TikTok, but they have grown as a web phenomenon. They started small, and they grew both in popularity and production value. They also help us understand where big content owners stand on fan creations.

Musical Parodies

We have had musical parodies before, and the courts have upheld them under fair use. A parody of *Grease*, called *Vape* was found to be fair use. Vape uses the same characters, story arc, and setting as *Grease* but using millennial slang, pop culture references, and exaggerated elements to comment on and critique the misogynistic and sexist elements of *Grease*. At the district court level, the court found that it was indeed a parody, which means we will have to see if it is appealed. It focuses on the female point of view to comment and criticize *Grease*. It was not considered a derivative or a sequel but is mocking the original. *Sketchworks Indus. Strength Comedy, Inc. v. Jacobs*, No. 19-CV-7470-LTS-VF, 2022 U.S. Dist. LEXIS 86331 (S.D.N.Y. May 12, 2022).

Others get licenses for their parodies and satires. Weird Al Yankovich famously got licenses for his parody/ satire songs. Here's what his FAQ includes: "Al does get permission from the original writers of the songs that he parodies. While the law supports his ability to parody without permission, he feels it's important to maintain the relationships that he's built with artists and writers over the years. Plus, Al wants to make sure that he gets his songwriter credit (as writer of new lyrics) as well as his rightful share of the royalties."

MUSICAL PARODIES

Want to see a list of musical parodies? We thought you might! Here is a list to get your started theatretrip.com/musical-parodies.

Musical Fan Adaptations: A New Trend, and What They Tell Us About Boundaries

We have a new trend—TikTok fan musicals of things that were not originally musicals. *Ratatouille the Musical* and *The Unofficial Bridgerton Musical* are two very well-known examples. Neither would qualify as parodies. They are fan-based homages to the original. They tell us about boundaries. They are important milestones that help us understand every area of creativity.

Ratatouille the Musical

Ratatouille the Musical started during the pandemic when Emily Jacobsen wrote a tribute song to Remy, the main character in *Ratatouille*, a Disney/Pixar film, and posted it on TikTok. Then, Daniel Mertzlufft did one too, and more followed until there was a full musical version. In 2020, Seaview Productions (which produces real Broadway shows), with director Lucy Moss (co-director of the musical *Six*), and a professional cast that included Broadway actors, put on a more polished version as a charity event for the Actors Fund, raising $2 million. A Disney Channel actor, Milo Manheim, performed one of the songs while at Walt Disney by the Ratatouille-theme ride. There was even an unauthorized, turned-authorized, *Playbill* designed for it. It's important to note that Seaview Productions contacted the creators, not the other way around.

Over 200,000 tickets priced between $5 and $100 were sold as donations. It is estimated that 350,000 people viewed the show. So, how did this occur? This is not a parody and does not fall under fair use. This is the full movie reimagined as a musical by fans on TikTok.

And Disney? They didn't shut it down. According to Vox reporter Rebecca Jennings, "Seaview Productions ... secured a green light from Disney to put on a one-time benefit concert." It was considered a one-time project to raise money for charity during the pandemic. The show was deemed Emmy-eligible, and according to Variety, TikTok took to campaigning hard and submitted it for ten categories. Unfortunately, it didn't receive any Emmy nominations.

The show itself is a combination of the original script, with new materials, and references to all kinds of things thrown in—the first number, for instance, "Anyone Can Cook" includes references to *A Chorus Line*, *Beauty and the Beast*, and *Cats*.

The other part is context. Both the original TikTok versions and the professional versions were made during the COVID-19 pandemic. Each person was in their own home. In some ways, it is an ode to the experience of the pandemic. In short, it is brilliant. It is a derivative work. And it was supported by the whole industry with the restriction that it was a one-time performance for the benefit of a charity.

But it also didn't cross a very important line: It didn't try to put up the show as a commercial theater production. Even though professionals were involved, the show only ran a few times for charity. And that seems to be key. Start a musical on TikTok. Watch all of Broadway get excited. Do a charity performance. Get someone big involved and get permission for a one-time charity performance. *The Unofficial Bridgerton Musical* would follow the same path, but then they crossed into the commercial lane, and Netflix sued.

The formula appears to be Limited Run + for Charity = Okay.

And maybe ... do it during a pandemic where you capture people's imagination, and big players come to you.

Netflix Versus Bridgerton

We can take another look at this same boundary with *The Unofficial Bridgerton Musical*.

This gives us legal insight into how far you can go with fan creations. It was settled, so there is no case. But the complaint helps us understand what we are intuitively seeing: You can go pretty far, at least with fan musicals, but the line drawn at commercial uses that are in direct conflict with the copyright holder's interest and plans.

In 2020, people fell in love with *Bridgerton*, a Netflix original series following a fictional high-society in early 1800s England. Within a year, over 82 million people watched. Two of the people that loved it were Abigail Barlow and Emily Bear, who started making their own unauthorized musical songs based on dialogue and situations in Bridgerton. They posted them on TikTok, where they went viral.

This is the first important element. "They were not the only fans celebrating *Bridgerton*." Netflix writes that in the complaint, "We love the idea of 'fans celebrating.'" The complaint explains "At the time, countless other fans were creating and posting *Bridgerton*-inspired works, dressing in costume, acting out scenes, and performing dances inspired by the hit series."

Fans can celebrate by doing all of these things and more, and Netflix is not suing them. They felt the same way about the initial TikTok posts by Barlow & Bear. The first post was so similar to the *Ratatouille the Musical*, asking what a *Bridgerton* musical version would look like, and then they started composing songs. The complaint notes that the two "repeatedly admitted" that they "intentionally based every single song on creative elements of the series." And Netflix is not suing them over this. This is really really important. They still see Barlow & Bear as **fans celebrating**.

Barlow & Bear were basing the songs they were writing on scenes and dialogue from the series, including using verbatim dialogue, characters, plot, pace, sequence, mood, setting, and themes. And Netflix still wasn't filing a lawsuit. They still saw Barlow & Bear as **fans celebrating**. (Netflix gives examples in Exhibit D of their complaint). There is no question as to whether they were infringing *Bridgerton* in their musical version. They were not authorized to use the work or create a derivative version. And they are not commenting or criticizing; they are fans celebrating.

Barlow & Bear continued to create their fan celebration of *Bridgerton*. Netflix saw this as a personal expression of their love for the series, and Netflix tweeted "Absolutely blown away by the Bridgerton musical playing out on TikTok." We have seen this before, with an unauthorized *Harry Potter* lexicon, which Warner Bros. Entertainment Inc. and J.K. Rowling loved, until they didn't, and then sued. The question is at which point did both of these content owners turn against the use of their works, and how do we understand that in a larger context for creatives making works with others' properties.

Netflix remained agnostic for quite a while. When Barlow & Bear requested Netflix's blessing to put

on a charity concert in the United Kingdom using their songs, the response was that Netflix did not approve or disapprove but Netflix described what they were doing as "fans' expression of their appreciation for the series,", and that because of this Netflix was "not standing in the way.'" The complaint also notes that "Barlow & Bear did not ask for, and Netflix never granted, ongoing authorization or any license." The performance didn't happen for other reasons.

Then, Barlow & Bear released an album to Spotify in September 2021. Netflix found out before its release, and "stressed to Barlow & Bear's representative that Netflix would not authorize and did not want to engage them to engage in any live performances or other derivative works that might **compete with Netflix's own planned live events**." Netflix was creating the Bridgerton experience. Barlow & Bear's representatives agreed no live events were planned.

The previously-planned charity event in the United Kingdom was rescheduled, and a discussion between Netflix and Barlow & Bear ensued about what would be included, that this would be a one-time event only, that other music by Barlow & Bear would be included, and that only a few songs from *The Unofficial Bridgerton Musical* would be included.

Six months later, Barlow & Bear were nominated for a Grammy for their album, *The Unofficial Bridgerton Musical*. Netflix still did not file a lawsuit. Still **fans celebrating**. And Barlow & Bear kept promising that they had only the United Kingdom charity event scheduled. From the complaint, Netflix's representatives write, "Netflix relied on these representations in deciding not to pursue any additional enforcement activity."

Barlow & Bear then won the Grammy for Best Musical Theatre Album for 2022. This was a big deal. Musical theater songs that originated on TikTok just took the Grammy. Their album had been up against Andrew Lloyd Webber's *Bad Cinderella*; Burt Bacharach and Steven Sater's *Some Lovers*; a staged concert version of *Les Miserables*; Steven Schwart's *Snapshots,* and *Girl from the North*

Country. For another context, all of the previous winners since 1959 were Broadway shows. This was a big moment. **Fans celebrating and creating fan content** had just won a Grammy.

Netflix still didn't file a lawsuit, but the ground did shift. Now Barlow & Bearwanted to perform a commercial, non-charity event of *The Unofficial Bridgerton Musical* in Washington D.C. for one night in addition to the United Kingdom. And here is where Netflix said no. Barlow & Bear still went ahead. The D.C. event looked like a live concert, a for-profit event, not a charity event.

Netflix filed a lawsuit. A Grammy-award winning album was commercially competing with the copyright holder, Netflix. However, they sued to stop the live performance. **That's what it took for Netflix to sue.** That's going pretty far.

Barlow & Bear admitted that they did not have a license to create a derivative work, but their attorney took the position that they did not need to get a license, because Netflix didn't object sooner. Netflix responded: "This is not how copyright law works. Netflix is not required to sue every infringer." And this is true. This is the law. The copyright holder gets to decide. And Netflix felt that the live concert "stretches 'fan fiction' well past its breaking point."

The lawsuit was settled and no live performances took place.

◈ ◆ ◈

Don't Raise a lot of Money and Compete with the Copyright Holder

Let's explore another example, this time the creation of a movie based on *Star Trek*. There's a character in *Star Trek* named Garth, and Axanar Productions, Inc. decided to make a twenty minute film based on the character to raise money for a $1 million full-length film. They were borrowing from *Star Trek* lore, but they did not get permission from the owners. CBS and Paramount sued.

The court found the work infringing but then turned to a fair use analysis. The court found that Axanar's use was not transformative because it served the **same purpose** as the original *Star Trek* works, making films. The use was also determined to be commercial, even though it was free because Axanar profited from the views and was also raising money. The third factor was hard to decide, said the court, but that the Axanar version had the "*Star Trek* feel." And the fourth factor weighed against fair use; this was a market replacement for *Star Trek* films. The fan film competed directly with the authorized films.

Later, CBS (the copyright holder) released parameters outlining how and when fans can use and create works. In summary, fan productions using *Star Trek* can only be fifteen minutes long; the subtitle has to include the phrase "A *Star Trek* Fan Production"; the content must be original; you must use official merchandise and not bootleg or imitation items; it must be a "fan" production with amateurs without compensation; it must be non-commercial (under $50,000 budget); it can only be shown for free an/or on streaming services without generating revenue; it cannot be distributed in a physical format; it cannot be used for advertising revenue (meaning no ad revenue on YouTube); no creation of merch related to the film; it must be family friendly; must include a disclaimer; creators can't register the works under copyright or trademark; and can't imply an association with CBS or Paramount Pictures. This is a summary of the terms used as an example, if you plan to make your own *Star Trek* fan fiction, read the full terms for yourself.

Those are a lot of restrictions. But at this point, that's what copyright holders can do—they can decide who and under what circumstances derivative works are made. Contrast that to fair use, where content owners have no say. The maker creating the derivative work can operate independently if fair use applies.

What is the lesson in all of this? Don't try to make things that compete with the original work. That's the space for copyright holders. For fans, you are supposed to stay in your lane of **fans celebrating**, and if you're making a fan work that is a larger project you plan to distribute, make money off of, etc. take a minute to search online to see if the Intellectual Property owner of your fandom has put out guidelines for that.

CELEBRATE
STAR TREK SAFELY

If you are a *Star Trek* fan and are planning to create a fanwork, jump on over to startrek.com/fan-films to see the full terms for yourself.

Don't Commercialize Your Cool Website

When we turn to book publishing examples we see the same patterns. **Don't commercialize your fan work in a way that competes with the original work.** The copyright holder may sue you. Up until that point, they may celebrate you.

Warner Bros. Entertainment v. RDR Books tells the tale of going from loved to being sued when creating an unauthorized derivative work. Steve Vander Ark, a fan of *Harry Potter*, decided to create a website, *The Harry Potter Lexicon,* which launched in 2000. (It is still up and live, hp-lexicon.org). He gathered every little bit of information about the *Harry Potter* series, and developed hyperlinks, cross-listing, and an index. People loved it, including J.K. Rowling, the author of the *Harry Potter* series. She posted: "This is such a great site that I have been known to sneak into an Internet cafe while out writing and check a fact rather than go into a bookshop and buy a copy of *Harry Potter* (which is embarrassing). A website for the dangerously obsessive; my natural home." (from case). Vander Ark was invited to Warner Brothers to visit the set of *The Order of the Phoenix*, where he was told that Warner Brothers uses the Lexicon every day. So, all was good, right? Then Vander Ark published *The Lexicon*, without getting permission. Remember, Vander Ark did not have permission to create the website. But publishing *The Lexicon* was different, and Warner Brothers sued. *Warner Bros. Entertainment v. RDR Books*, 575 F.Supp 2d 513 (S.D.N.Y. 2008).

That's the commercial divide again. It's real, and Vander Ark lost. He had taken too much from the originals. He had infringed. He had made an unauthorized derivative work. The court looked carefully and found unauthorized copying. And, what's worse, they applied Section 103(a), which does not give copyright protection to the non-infringing original parts.

In case you are curious, you can still get a used copy on Amazon.

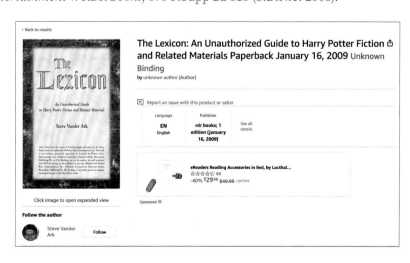

Don't Mess with Dr. Seuss

We have not one, but two cases where people used Dr. Seuss for satire without a license.

When Alan Katz and Chris Winn decided to create a book about O.J. Simpson using *The Cat in the Hat* and other Dr. Seuss stories, they probably thought it would be seen as a parody and funny. The court did not find it funny and labeled it a **satire**. The court felt like the authors used the Dr. Seuss structure and artwork style to "get attention" or maybe even "to avoid the drudgery in working up something fresh". The court did not find it transformative. For the last twenty-five years, this case has been used as an example of using an original work when you are just not creative enough to think of things on your own. *Dr. Seuss Enters., L.P. v. Penguin Books USA, Inc.,* 109 F.3d 1394 (9th Cir. 1997).

And, in the stupidest move ever, someone did it again, this time with *Star Trek*.

So, we have at least two instances where people used Dr. Seuss, the estate of Theodor Seuss Geisel sued, and in both cases, fair use was not found. One we've already discussed—the use of *Cat in the Hat* to describe the O.J. Simpson murder. It was seen as satire, not parody.

In 2020, there was a Ninth Circuit Court decision about the use of a Dr. Seuss story, *Oh, the Places You'll Go* mash up with *Star Trek* into a *Star Trek* primer titled *Oh, the Places You'll Boldly Go!*

Oh, the Places You'll Go! has been licensed a lot, but a license was not obtained for the *Star Trek* version. They planned to commercially sell the primer and the authors started a crowdfunding campaign on Kickstarter to raise money for publication. The Geisel Estate sent a cease and desist letter when they found out, and sent a takedown notice to Kickstarter as well, which Kickstarter obliged.

The authors admitted copying and trying to make their version nearly identical to the original. They believed their use fell under Section 107, fair use. Regarding the first factor of the test, the Court found that the use was **not transformative** and that it was intended as a commercial use. They also found that it was **not a parody** and was not trying to comment or criticize the original. The court cited the O.J. Simpson book (which was a satire) as suffering from the same problem. It was merely a retelling using Dr. Seuss's work. Considering the second factor, Dr. Seuss's work is creative. The third factor fares no better. They took a substantial amount of the original—14 out of 24 of the original pages, close to 60 percent of the book. They also took from *How the Grinch Stole Christmas!* and *The Sneetches and Other Stories*. They replicated the images and dropped *Star Trek* figures in the exact compositions.

And finally, the fourth factor—the Estate licensed Dr. Seuss materials. "The bottom line is that ComicMix created, without seeking permission or a license, a non-transformative commercial work that targets and usurps Go!'s potential market." For a refresher on the test see Four-Factor Test (page 77).

The point? You can license your use from Dr. Seuss. We were walking through Whole Foods and saw an authorized version, *The Cat on the Mat*, a story using Cat in the Hat for yoga for children. Just ask. Get permission. At least from Dr. Seuss.

Don't Use Others' Work Without Permission As a Commercial

The Beastie Boys created the song "Girls" in 1987. It wasn't a good depiction of women. Some of the lyrics were "(Girls!) To do the dishes/ (Girls!) To clean up my room/(Girls!) And in the bathroom/(Girls) That's all I really want is girls … " So, not the best.

Flash forward to 2014 when GoldieBlox created a video *Girls* that used the same song but new lyriccs, reminiscent of 2 Live Crew's *Pretty Woman* parody. Some of the lyrics were "(Girls!) To build a spaceship/ (Girls!) To code a new app/To grow up knowing/That they can engineer that" Brilliant. An anthem in our house. And it would have been held up as the parody of our times, except they ended with the advertisement of their toys. A commercial? No! Fair use failed. Everyone was in uproar. And everyone was talking about this new toy company for girls. Brilliant marketing or a copyright misstep? We're not really sure what the lesson is from this.

Just Get Permission and License, but Fanwors Are Often Okay

The musical *Hamilton* obtained tons of permissions for all kinds of things, including the underlying biography. There is no shame in getting permission or paying a licensing fee. It spreads around the wealth. It's a good thing. And a kind thing. For the musical *Hamilton*, it is reported that Lin Manuel Miranda, the sole writer, received a 7 percent royalty from the Broadway musical. He was said to pay the underlying rights owner, Ron Chernow, author of the *Hamilton* biography, from his share of the royalties. Miranda also got permissions for the works that were sampled, known as preliminary permission.

On the other hand, *Hamilton* has been generous with its fans, even highlighting fan art. And many fans have created animatics (a partially animated storyboard) for songs. They stay up on YouTube. They do not harm the market. And they actually promote the show and fans celebrating the work. On the *Hamilton* musical Facebook page, they highlight fan art. Here are some examples:

And then what happened when a church created an unauthorized and altered lyrics version of *Hamilton*? The *Hamilton* legal team shut it down. The Door Christian Fellowship McAllen Church apologized, had to pay damages, and destroy their performance recordings. You probably figured that would have happened. That's the core of the commercial market for *Hamilton*, and doing that harms the brand in more ways than one.

A Word of Warning: Copyright Claims Board and Photographers

We've seen a lot of copyright holders being very generous with their copyrighted works. That is *not always true*. We see that photographers are going after people who use their images online as part of their website. But again, this makes sense. What they have is the photograph; that's their only way to make money. So, be careful. Make sure you understand the economic interests of the copyright holder before you use their work without permission.

Respect the Little Guy

Throughout this chapter, we've looked at some pretty big players, and we've seen that you can go pretty far in your unauthorized derivative works so long as you aren't a commercial competitor to the original work. You can't become a market replacement or endanger the original author's revenue streams. (And if you're a parody, like the GoldieBlox girls, advertising takes you out of being fair use.)

These cases and examples of bigger entities and unauthorized works can help us understand similar principles for the little guys.

Fans want to make and sell fan creations. It's just part of our world. And fandoms come in all sizes. It's not just *Star Wars* and DC Comics and Mattel. Smaller creative works and entities can have huge fan bases as well.

It's really hard to become a market replacement for Pokemon. It's not as hard to become a market replacement for merchandise of a small scripted series that a TikToker makes.

So, how far can you go in making and selling derivative works of smaller creators? Often, not as far, but it's a case-by-case basis, and different creators have very different feelings about what they are okay and not okay with fans doing. Sometimes they'll have set guidelines. Sometimes they won't.

We're going to look at two different approaches to this. First, we're returning to some of our favorite YouTube artists, Drawfee, and then we'll be looking at what the scripted queer horror podcast *Welcome to Night Vale* has to say about selling fan works.

On their website, Drawfee has a section in their FAQ titled "Fan Merch Guide" which outlines what they are and aren't cool with in regards to fans selling merch based on Drawfee videos and characters:

Fan Merch Guide

Looking to sell fan merch or see fan merch in the wild but don't know what's okay? We got you. Here is our handy guide for Drawfee items!

THE OVERALL OKAYS:

Making and selling limited numbers (under 100) of hand-made items inspired by our show is very cool! Just make sure it's clear that it's **unofficial**. Otherwise, you don't need our permission!

THE OVERALL DON'TS:

- Don't make large batch items for selling (anything over 100 units of an item)
- Don't use drawfee logo, Drawfee assets (images created on the show, photos of our faces)
- Don't make it anything offensive, racist, sexist, defamatory.
- Don't sell items very similar to items we sell in our DFTBA merch store.
- Don't sell on large distribution websites like RedBubble, Society6, Amazon, etc.

- Don't sell art that you didn't make.
- No NFTs or cryptocurrencies involving Drawfee IP.

NON-COMMERCIAL:

- Making a small batch of a Drawfee thing for a small personal event is fine! If you aren't selling it and just using it for person, you're fine.

GAMES:

- Games based on Drawfee properties can be listed for free on itch as long as they follow the general do's and don'ts..

ALSO:

- We reserve the right to ask you to remove any works at any time.

It ends with reminding the reader that they reserve the right to ask people to take fan merch down at any time, but they are incredibly open to fans making and selling fanworks of the show so long as it is done in small batches. Why is this? We can't say for sure, but we think there are two factors to consider: 1.) Their primary revenue isn't through merchandising. It's through their YouTube videos, Patreon, and Twitch. They have their own merch, but it is a fairly small pool of options and is secondary to their main focus, and 2.) A lot of what Drawfee does and what the four artists on the channel do as part of their art practice is making fan art of other IPs. It's not surprising that they are willing to let people make and sell small batches of fan art of their work.

Another example, *Welcome to Night Vale*, a long-running and groundbreaking podcast with a cult following of Zillenials, takes a very different approach. On their website, their FAQ also gives some insight into how they feel about fan works:

I DESIGNED MY OWN NIGHT VALE T-SHIRT/PHONE CASE/POSTER/ETC. CAN I SELL IT?

Please don't.

I HAVE AN IDEA FOR A FAN PROJECT WHERE I _____.

Non-commercial fan projects are fine by us. Please keep it free and let us know how it goes!

I WANT TO HOST A LISTENING PARTY AT MY HOME/MY LIBRARY/MY BAR/MY STORE/ETC.

Non-commercial listening parties are fine by us. We ask that you please do not sell tickets to or otherwise sell food/drink/merchandise at a listening party. This is a free podcast.

It's clear that they don't want fans selling their own fan merch, but at the same time, they seem very encouraging of noncommercial fan works.

Why is this? Well, *Night Vale* as a brand relies on their merchandising. They have an extensive online store full of pins, tarot cards, T-shirts, plushies, and posters. They make custom posters for each of their live show tours, and they have a professionally published series of novels and script books. They care about not having a market replacement for their own merch.

Of course, fans still do sell fan art of *Night Vale*. There are *Night Vale* earrings and crochet dolls on Etsy. You still have a half-decent shot at finding a fan-made *Night Vale* poster at a Comic-Con. But it changes one's thought process on the risk assessment equation, and what one feels personally okay with.

Every creator is going to have their own opinions and feelings about others selling derivative works. You might be in that position, too. Think about what you would be okay with fans doing with your work.

And if you're selling fan art of a smaller creator/creation, take a moment to see what their guidelines are and also what matters to them. Sometimes content owners have posted the requirements for a non-exclusive license. Sometimes they don't. Additionally, remember that you can always ask for permission to use works for a fee.

Large Lessons from Crochet and Knitting

In the end, we see that the divide between commercial use (less likely fair use, more likely trouble if you don't ask permission) and noncommercial use (less likely anyone legally cares) is both simple and complicated. But it is when the copyright holder thinks you have crossed a line, morally or economically, that there is a problem. The copyright holder is not always right, of course. And not everything we make is necessarily protectable, even if it becomes famous and in demand.

We do get some additional guidance from three knitting and crochet situations that occurred fairly recently.

Commercial Use of a Copyrighted Property: Crocheted Baby Yodas on Etsy

On November 12, 2019, Disney released a new *Star Wars* series, the *Mandalorian,* and with it a new, adorable, unexpected character, Din Grogu, otherwise known as Baby Yoda. Disney had purposely kept Grogu a secret, and fans went crazy. The trouble was that there was no merchandise with Baby Yoda out in the world because Disney wanted it to be a surprise. Enter the crocheters.

It was Christmas, and people wanted their Baby Yodas. Disney recognized this was the tradeoff. But, they likely didn't realize the market void would be filled by Etsy sellers. People started making and selling unofficial Baby Yoda crocheted dolls, and they were incredible. The craze was real. At the height of the craze, there were over 12,000 search results for unauthorized Baby Yoda merchandise on Etsy. One Esty shop reported having 200 orders for Baby Yoda dolls. And there were so many people making them—for fans—for commercial sale.

By January, 2020, Disney had their legal team on the case, to put a stop to this, or sort of. The large producers were taken down on Etsy, but you can still find Baby Yoda crocheted dolls on the site. You can use the search term "Baby Yoda," or the alternative "Baby Alien," which was adopted by many in the community. You still get unauthorized Baby Yodas. Why? Because Disney, in reality, can't take them all down. And also, as a brand, that wouldn't be good PR. But they got the message out, and went after big producers, and you can be sure that if there was a seller that was commercially producing them rather than hand stitching them, Disney would be shutting that down by having their listings or shops shut down. But it seems that Disney isn't stopping the smallest players.

That Photograph of Bernie Set off a Mitten Craze

On January 20, 2021, at President-elect Joe Biden's inauguration, Senator Bernie Sanders arrived with a mask, warm coat, and large, distinctive, knitted mittens made for him by Vermont school teacher Jen Ellis. Photographer Brendan Smialowski took a photo as Bernie sat in a folding chair with his hands on his knees. The photograph went viral and instantly became a meme.

Photo by BRENDAN SMIALOWSKI/AFP via Getty Images

The Meme

Like most memes, these spread fast. What's a photographer to do? Enjoy the ride. Smialowski noted that he didn't feel like it was his best photograph, and didn't know why the craze had happened.

The Mittens

Ellis received thousands of requests for mittens. Too many requests. She did make three pairs to auction off to help with her kid's college fund. But once again, the Etsy crowd filled the gap; and did they. And of course, makers also made crochet dolls based on the photograph, which even got picked up by *Newsweek* as a story when one version was auctioned off for $20,000 to benefit Meals on Wheels America.

The mitten pattern was also for sale. It could conceivably be protected by copyright—the pattern on the mittens, but not likely. And we don't know if the original mitten maker had made her own pattern. But even so, she didn't seem to stop others from making them. It was out in the world, and the world was loving them.

The Response

Traditionally, we might have seen the photographer, or in this case, the photographer's employer, threatening lawsuits for the unauthorized use of the photograph. But no. Neither the copyright holder nor the photographer seemed upset that people were making and selling dolls. And What about the subject of the photograph, Bernie Sanders? Bernie's organization ended up having merchandise made with the photograph, too! Sweatshirts, T-shirts, and mugs. In fact, they were able to raise over $1.8 million for charitable organizations in Vermont.

The Photographer and Getty

But if you think the photographer got left out of the story, do not fear. First, he works for the news agency Agence France-Presse, so he might not even be the copyright holder, depending on his employment situation. You can license the image from Getty Images and the credit reads: "Photo by BRENDAN SMIALOWSKI/AFP via Getty Images." Regardless, Getty agreed to donate the proceeds of the licensing sales to Meals on Wheels America during the height of the craze.

Everyone Wants to Wear Harry Styles's Knitted Cardigan

Harry Styles is one of the biggest musicians in the world. Originally from the boy band, One Direction, he is known for his colorful and crazy fashion. Amidst a tour, he wore a knitted patchwork cardigan while performing on *The Today Show*. And then it went viral on TikTok. Everyone wanted to make it. People learned to knit just to make this cardigan. It was everywhere.

Photo by NBC/NBCUniversal via Getty Images

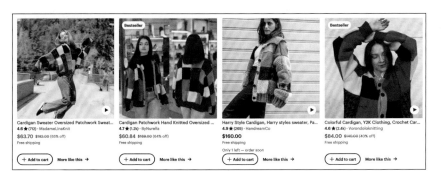

The cardigan was designed by a British fashion label JW Anderson, and it originally sold for £1,250. What did the designer do when everyone wanted to make his pattern?

"I am so impressed and incredibly humbled by this trend and everyone knitting the cardigan. I really wanted to show our appreciation so we are sharing the pattern with everyone. Keep it up!" wrote designer Jonathan Anderson, who then even shared the knitted pattern himself on his website!

So, here is a situation again where the copyright holder embraces the viral trend, and even offers the pattern for free. It's how our world works. The publicity of the pattern and the company is more important. Locking up culture behind a paywall is not always the answer in our Internet-filled, engaged world. We want to make that cardigan we saw on the *The Today Show*, and the designer, in this case, understood.

WANT TO MAKE THIS?

Have a yearning to make the Harry Styles cardigan? The pattern is available for free on the designer's website! jwanderson.com/gb/cardigan-pattern

The Reality of Copyright Today

If you have learned anything from this chapter, and this book, is that the reality of copyright is fun, messy, unpredictable, and very creative. There are the rules that we get from the law, copyright holders respond, and then there is the unpredictability of our crazy, amazing, Internet-driven world. There is room for everyone to play. We all just have to make sure we understand that sometimes what we want to do is just fine, and then sometimes, we've gone too far in the copyright holder's eyes. As you make your way in the world, know copyright law, and keep an eye on cultural trends. At the moment, it seems like we are all living in a place where there is space for us all.

Conclusion

We hope you are more confident in your copyright knowledge, and that it helps in your creative practice. We see all kinds of choices. Remember, if you are *not commercializing* your work, you really have a lot of freedom, but respecting each other's creative work is also part of the system.

Copyright can be scary. It can also be fun! We hope you feel that way, too. And so, we thought we would end with Teddie Bernard's lovely gang, and a new friend, who has lost his (red) shirt.

BAD PARABLE

Resources

We've provided a few key resources for you!

The U.S. Copyright Office offers several resources for the general public.

Copyright Office Main Page

copyright.gov
On the home page, you will find numerous resources, including basic information about copyright, tools to search the U.S. Copyright Office records, the system to register your works online, how to record transfers of copyright, the law itself, and fees for services. They also have a news section about the U.S. Copyright Office, and new developments in legislation. This is also how you reach the Copyright Claims Board to file a small copyright claim.

Compendium III

copyright.gov/comp3
We have cited the Compendium throughout the text. This is the manual created by the U.S. Copyright Office and used by its employees during the registration process. It provides great insight into issues that might arise.

Circulars

copyright.gov/circs
The U.S. Copyright Office also produced a series of short explanations of copyright in their circulars. They are always a great place to start in understanding basic concepts and procedures at the U.S. Copyright Office.

Fair Use Index

copyright.gov/fair-use
This is a database of summaries of fair use cases, and it is very useful.

Registering Your Copyright

copyright.gov/registration
The U.S. Copyright Office walks you through the steps of registration, with directions and online forms.

U.S. Copyright Law

We have spent a lot of time discussing copyright law. For your convenience, we have included key parts of the law. For the full law, go to copyright.gov/title17.

Section 101: Definitions

copyright.gov/title17 > Chapter 1 >

While these official definitions are key to understanding copyright, we have not duplicated them here, but we do encourage you to visit the official circular by the copyright office and read them for yourself. It is a very long section, but very useful.

Section 102: Subject Matter of Copyright, In General

copyright.gov/title17 > Chapter 1 > 102. Subject matter of copyright: In general

(a) Copyright protection subsists, in accordance with this title, in original works of authorship fixed in any tangible medium of expression, now known or later developed, from which they can be perceived, reproduced, or otherwise communicated, either directly or with the aid of a machine or device. Works of authorship include the following categories:

(1) literary works;

(2) musical works, including any accompanying words;

(3) dramatic works, including any accompanying music;

(4) pantomimes and choreographic works;

(5) pictorial, graphic, and sculptural works;

(6) motion pictures and other audiovisual works;

(7) sound recordings; and

(8) architectural works.

(b) In no case does copyright protection for an original work of authorship extend to any idea, procedure, process, system, method of operation, concept, principle, or discovery, regardless of the form in which it is described, explained, illustrated, or embodied in such work.

Section 103: Subject Matter of Copyright: Compilations and Derivative Works

copyright.gov/title17 > Chapter 1 > 103. Subject matter of copyright: Compilations and derivative works

(a) The subject matter of copyright as specified by section 102 includes compilations and derivative works, but protection for a work employing preexisting material in which copyright subsists does not extend to any part of the work in which such material has been used unlawfully.

(b) The copyright in a compilation or derivative work extends only to the material contributed by the author of such work, as distinguished from the preexisting material employed in the work, and does not imply any exclusive right in the preexisting material. The copyright in such work is independent of, and does not affect or enlarge the scope, duration, ownership, or subsistence of, any copyright protection in the preexisting material.

Section 106: Exclusive Rights in Copyrighted Works

copyright.gov/title17 > Chapter 1 > 106. Exclusive rights in copyrighted works

Subject to sections 107 through 122, the owner of copyright under this title has the exclusive rights to do and to authorize any of the following:

(1) to reproduce the copyrighted work in copies or phonorecords;

(2) to prepare derivative works based upon the copyrighted work;

(3) to distribute copies or phonorecords of the copyrighted work to the public by sale or other transfer of ownership, or by rental, lease, or lending;

(4) in the case of literary, musical, dramatic, and choreographic works, pantomimes, and motion pictures and other audiovisual works, to perform the copyrighted work publicly;

(5) in the case of literary, musical, dramatic, and choreographic works, pantomimes, and pictorial, graphic, or sculptural works, including the individual images of a motion picture or other audiovisual work, to display the copyrighted work publicly; and

(6) in the case of sound recordings, to perform the copyrighted work publicly by means of a digital audio transmission.

Note: Section 106A concerns moral rights, which is covered in detail in Moral Rights (page 127).

Section 107. Limitations on Exclusive Rights: Fair Use

copyright.gov/title17 > Chapter 1 > 107. Limitations on exclusive rights: Fair use

Notwithstanding the provisions of sections 106 and 106A, the fair use of a copyrighted work, including such use by reproduction in copies or phonorecords or by any other means specified by that section, for purposes such as criticism, comment, news reporting, teaching (including multiple copies for classroom use), scholarship, or research, is not an infringement of copyright. In determining whether the use made of a work in any particular case is a fair use the factors to be considered shall include—

(1) the purpose and character of the use, including whether such use is of a commercial nature or is for nonprofit educational purposes;

(2) the nature of the copyrighted work;

(3) the amount and substantiality of the portion used in relation to the copyrighted work as a whole; and

(4) the effect of the use upon the potential market for or value of the copyrighted work.

The fact that a work is unpublished shall not itself bar a finding of fair use if such finding is made upon consideration of all the above factors.

Section 108: Limitations on Exclusive Rights: Reproduction by libraries and archives.

copyright.gov/title17 > Chapter 1 > 108. Limitations on exclusive rights: Reproduction by libraries and archives

Section 108 is lengthy and complicated, and is designed for libraries to make preservation copies, engage in interlibrary loan, and limits liability when patrons make copies. Note: this does not apply to the patrons making the copies. That would fall under either fair use or the works were in the public domain.

Section 109. Limitations on Exclusive Rights: Effect of Transfer of Particular Copy or Phonorecord

copyright.gov/title17 > Chapter 1 > 109. Limitations on exclusive rights: Effect of transfer of particular copy or phonorecord

(a) Notwithstanding the provisions of section 106(3), the owner of a particular copy or phonorecord lawfully made under this title, or any person authorized by such owner, is entitled, without the authority of the copyright owner, to sell or otherwise dispose of the possession of that copy or phonorecord. ...

Section 120. Scope of Exclusive Rights in Architectural Works

copyright.gov/title17 > Chapter 1 > 120. Scope of exclusive rights in architectural works

(a) Pictorial Representations Permitted.—The copyright in an architectural work that has been constructed does not include the right to prevent the making, distributing, or public display of pictures, paintings, photographs, or other pictorial representations of the work, if the building in which the work is embodied is located in or ordinarily visible from a public place.

(b) Alterations to and Destruction of Buildings.—Notwithstanding the provisions of section 106(2), the owners of a building embodying an architectural work may, without the consent of the author or copyright owner of the architectural work, make or authorize the making of alterations to such building, and destroy or authorize the destruction of such building.

Section 201. Ownership of Copyright

copyright.gov/title17 > Chapter 2 > 201. Ownership of copyright

Note: Section 101 also contains definitions related to work for hire.

(a) Initial Ownership.—Copyright in a work protected under this title vests initially in the author or authors of the work. The authors of a joint work are coowners of copyright in the work.

(b) Works Made for Hire.—In the case of a work made for hire, the employer or other person for whom the work was prepared is considered the author for purposes of this title, and, unless the parties have expressly agreed otherwise in a written instrument signed by them, owns all of the rights comprised in the copyright.

(c) Contributions to Collective Works.—Copyright in each separate contribution to a collective work is distinct from copyright in the collective work as a whole, and vests initially in the author of the contribution. In the absence of an express transfer of the copyright or of any rights under it, the owner of copyright in the collective work is presumed to have acquired only the privilege of reproducing and distributing the contribution as part of that particular collective work, any revision of that collective work, and any later collective work in the same series.

(d) Transfer of Ownership.—(1) The ownership of a copyright may be transferred in whole or in part by any means of conveyance or by operation of law, and may be bequeathed by will or pass as personal property by the applicable laws of intestate succession.

(2) Any of the exclusive rights comprised in a copyright, including any subdivision of any of the rights specified by section 106, may be transferred as provided by clause (1) and owned separately. The owner of any particular exclusive right is entitled, to the extent of that right, to all of the protection and remedies accorded to the copyright owner by this title.

(e) Involuntary Transfer.—When an individual author's ownership of a copyright, or of any of the exclusive rights under a copyright, has not previously been transferred voluntarily by that individual author, no action by any governmental body or other official or organization purporting to seize, expropriate, transfer, or exercise rights of ownership with respect to the copyright, or any of the exclusive rights under a copyright, shall be given effect under this title, except as provided under title.

Section 202. Ownership of Copyright As Distinct from Ownership of Material Object

copyright.gov/title17 > Chapter 2 > 202. Ownership of copyright as distinct from ownership of material object

Ownership of a copyright, or of any of the exclusive rights under a copyright, is distinct from ownership of any material object in which the work is embodied. Transfer of ownership of any material object, including the copy or phonorecord in which the work is first fixed, does not of itself convey any rights in the copyrighted work embodied in the object; nor, in the absence of an agreement, does transfer of ownership of a copyright or of any exclusive rights under a copyright convey property rights in any material object.

Section 401. Notice of Copyright: Visually Perceptible Copies

copyright.gov/title17 > Chapter 4 > 401. Notice of copyright: Visually perceptible copies

(a) General Provisions.—Whenever a work protected under this title is published in the United States or elsewhere by authority of the copyright owner, a notice of copyright as provided by this section may be placed on publicly distributed copies from which the work can be visually perceived, either directly or with the aid of a machine or device.

(b) Form of Notice.—If a notice appears on the copies, it shall consist of the following three elements:

(1) the symbol © (the letter C in a circle), or the word "Copyright", or the abbreviation "Copr."; and

(2) the year of first publication of the work; in the case of compilations or derivative works incorporating previously published material, the year date of first publication of the compilation or derivative work is sufficient. The year date may be omitted where a pictorial, graphic, or sculptural work, with accompanying text matter, if any, is reproduced in or on greeting cards, postcards, stationery, jewelry, dolls, toys, or any useful articles; and

(3) the name of the owner of copyright in the work, or an abbreviation by which the name can be recognized, or a generally known alternative designation of the owner.

(c) Position of Notice.—The notice shall be affixed to the copies in such manner and location as to give reasonable notice of the claim of copyright. The Register of Copyrights shall prescribe by regulation, as examples, specific methods of affixation and positions of the notice on various types of works that will satisfy this requirement, but these specifications shall not be considered exhaustive.

(d) Evidentiary Weight of Notice.—If a notice of copyright in the form and position specified by this section appears on the published copy or copies to which a defendant in a copyright infringement suit had access, then no weight shall be given to such a defendant's interposition of a defense based on innocent infringement in mitigation of actual or statutory damages, except as provided in the last sentence of section 504(2).

Section 411. Registration and Civil Infringement Actions

copyright.gov/title17 > Chapter 4 > 411. Registration and civil infringement actions

(a) Except for an action brought for a violation of the rights of the author under section 106A(a), and subject to the provisions of subsection (b), no civil action for infringement of the copyright in any United States work shall be instituted until preregistration or registration of the copyright claim has been made in accordance with this title. In any case, however, where the deposit, application, and fee required for registration have been delivered to the Copyright Office in proper form and registration has been refused, the applicant is entitled to institute a civil action for infringement if notice thereof, with a copy of the complaint, is served on the Register of Copyrights. The Register may, at his or her option, become a party to the action with respect to the issue of registrability of the copyright claim by entering an appearance within sixty days after such service, but the Register's failure to become a party shall not deprive the court of jurisdiction to determine that issue.

(b)

(1) A certificate of registration satisfies the requirements of this section and section 412, regardless of whether the certificate contains any inaccurate information, unless—(A) the inaccurate information was included on the application for copyright registration with knowledge that it was inaccurate; and

(B) the inaccuracy of the information, if known, would have caused the Register of Copyrights to refuse registration.

(2) In any case in which inaccurate information described under paragraph (1) is alleged, the court shall request the Register of Copyrights to advise the court whether the inaccurate information, if known, would have caused the Register of Copyrights to refuse registration.

(3) Nothing in this subsection shall affect any rights, obligations, or requirements of a person related to information contained in a registration certificate, except for the institution of and remedies in infringement actions under this section and section 412.

Section 412. Registration as prerequisite to certain remedies for infringement

copyright.gov/title17 > Chapter 4 > 412. Registration as prerequisite to certain remedies for infringement

In any action under this title, other than an action brought for a violation of the rights of the author under section 106A(a), an action for infringement of the copyright of a work that has been preregistered under section 408(f) before the commencement of the infringement and that has an effective date of registration not later than the earlier of 3 months after the first publication of the work or 1 month after the copyright owner has learned of the infringement, or an action instituted under section 411(c), no award of statutory damages or of attorney's fees, as provided by sections 504 and 505, shall be made for—(1) any infringement of copyright in an unpublished work commenced before the effective date of its registration; or

(2) any infringement of copyright commenced after first publication of the work and before the effective date of its registration, unless such registration is made within three months after the first publication of the work.

Section 501. Infringement of Copyright

copyright.gov/title17 > Chapter 5 > 501. Infringement of copyright

(a) Anyone who violates any of the exclusive rights of the copyright owner as provided by sections 106 through 122 or of the author as provided in section 106A(a), or who imports copies or phonorecords into the United States in violation of section 602, is an infringer of the copyright or right of the author, as the case may be. For purposes of this chapter (other than section 506), any reference to copyright shall be deemed to include the rights conferred by section 106A(a). As used in this subsection, the term "anyone" includes any State, any instrumentality of a State, and any officer or employee of a State or instrumentality of a State acting in his or her official capacity. Any State, and any such instrumentality, officer, or employee, shall be subject to the provisions of this title in the same manner and to the same extent as any nongovernmental entity.

Section 1202. Integrity of copyright management information

copyright.gov/title17 > Chapter 12 > 1202. Integrity of copyright management information

(a) False Copyright Management Information.—No person shall knowingly and with the intent to induce, enable, facilitate, or conceal infringement—(1) provide copyright management information that is false, or

(2) distribute or import for distribution copyright management information that is false.

(b) Removal or Alteration of Copyright Management Information.—No person shall, without the authority of the copyright owner or the law—(1) intentionally remove or alter any copyright management information,

(2) distribute or import for distribution copyright management information knowing that the copyright management information has been removed or altered without authority of the copyright owner or the law, or

(3) distribute, import for distribution, or publicly perform works, copies of works, or phonorecords, knowing that copyright management information has been removed or altered without authority of the copyright owner or the law, knowing, or, with respect to civil remedies under section 1203, having reasonable grounds to know, that it will induce, enable, facilitate, or conceal an infringement of any right under this title.

(c) Definition.—As used in this section, the term "copyright management information" means any of the following information conveyed in connection with copies or phonorecords of a work or performances or displays of a work, including in digital form, except that such term does not include any personally identifying information about a user of a work or of a copy, phonorecord, performance, or display of a work:

(1) The title and other information identifying the work, including the information set forth on a notice of copyright.

(2) The name of, and other identifying information about, the author of a work.

(3) The name of, and other identifying information about, the copyright owner of the work, including the information set forth in a notice of copyright.

(4) With the exception of public performances of works by radio and television broadcast stations, the name of, and other identifying information about, a performer whose performance is fixed in a work other than an audiovisual work.

(5) With the exception of public performances of works by radio and television broadcast stations, in the case of an audiovisual work, the name of, and other identifying information about, a writer, performer, or director who is credited in the audiovisual work.

(6) Terms and conditions for use of the work.

(7) Identifying numbers or symbols referring to such information or links to such information.

(8) Such other information as the Register of Copyrights may prescribe by regulation, except that the Register of Copyrights may not require the provision of any information concerning the user of a copyrighted work.

Index

#

2 Live Crew "Oh, Pretty Woman" four-factor fair use analysis.................................... 80–82

10% change rule for copyrighted material 97–100

A

access controls 58

aesthetic non-discrimination 30

aesthetic separability 15

Agreement on Guidelines for Classroom Copying In Not-For-Profit Educational Institutions With Respect to Books and Periodicals 97

AI (artificial intelligence) 21

AI-generated art 54

American Idol 26

analytics writing, fair use best practices.......88

anonymous works 54

Ao3 (Archive of Our Own) 103

Aqua "Barbie Girl" 93

art. *See also* photographs

    collage art 86

    commercial setting 87

    craft, and quilt exhibitions 128

    First Sale Doctrine..................................87

    Koons, Jeff...86–87

A.R.T. Company, ...158

art creation, fair use best practices 89

art instruction, fair use best practices 88

artist reference photographs 56–57

artistic challenges 28

artistic value, copyright and 30

artistic works

    audiovisual works 125

    cartoons 124

    comic strips/books 124

    copyright notice 116

    installation art 124

    maps 125

    motion pictures 125

    photographs 125

    registering copyright...............................124

artwork 72

    open access through museums 73

Astaire, Fred 92

Attribution license (CC BY) 120

Attribution NonCommercial license (CC BY-NC)..120

Attribution NonCommercial Share Alike license (CC BY-NC-SA)................................120

attribution rights...21

Attribution Share Alike license (CC BY-SA).. 120

Attribution-No Derivatives license (CC BY-ND) 120

Attribution-Noncommercial-No Derivatives license (CC BY-NC-ND) 120

audiovisual works..125

    copyright notice 116

authorship

    AI-generated 54

    collective works 48

    copyright term 111–112

    death, copyrights and.............................. 112

    derivative works 48

    individual authors 47

    joint authorship.......................................48

    photographs 55

    tenants on common 48

    work for hire 50–53

B

Bad Parable (Bernard) 9

"Barbie Girl" song 93

Barney, Andi, and Dear Jane quilt 31

Bentham, Jeremy..22

Bernard, Teddie...9

Best Practices in Fair Use for the Visual Arts 88–89

Big Trademark Application List 37

Blank Forms Rule 36

book designs..43

borrowing 15, 105

C

Cambell Soup Cans (Warhol) 78–79

Cambridge University Press course packets case 98–99

Canada, copyright terms 113

cartoons 124

CASE ACT of 2020.......................................162

The Cat in the Hat parody of O.J. Simpson story..82

CC BY (Attribution license) 120

CC BY-NC (Attribution NonCommercial license)..120

CC BY-NC-ND (Attribution-Noncommercial-No Derivatives license) 120

CC BY-NC-SA (Attribution NonCommercial Share Alike license) 120

CC BY-ND (Attribution-No Derivatives license)..120

CC BY-SA (Attribution Share Alike license) .. 120

CC (Creative Commons) license 119–120

CC0 (Public Domain Dedication license) 120

CCB (Copyright Claims Board) 162–165

    claim types...163–164

    photographers..174

    relief, types 163

    statute of limitations 164

CCC (Copyright Clearance Center) 98

CCE (Catalog of Copyright Entries)................69

cease and desist letters 142–143

characters 45

    Sunbonnet Sue 46

choreography 42

classrooms

    course packets.....................................98–99

    permissible uses......................................63

clothing patterns 36

Code of Best Practices for Visual Arts 88–89

collage art 86

    fair use and 83

collective works...32

    copyright notice 116

colorization 44

comic strips/books 124

commenting, fair use and 80–82

commercial copies 84

    copyright term 111

commercial use 22

    fair use...78

commercialization of fanwork....................171

commissioned works 52–53

Compendium of U.S. Copyright Office Practices .18

compilation of facts 32

conceptual separability 37

concerts 58

cons (fan conventions) 105

contracts 27

contributory infringement 159

copies

    10% change rule 97–98

    classroom use..97

    versus creating..102

    fair use and 83

    family photographs 156

    infringement and 64, 145

    patterns 156–157

    subconscious......................................147–148

    substantial similarity 145–146, 149–154

Copyright Act of 1976 .... 16, 68, 77

Copyright Claims Board............................144

copyright law reference 181–187

Copyright Life Cycle Worksheet...... 10, 106–109

copyright notice 13, 68, 114

    advantages 117

    components 115–116

    location 116–117

    public domain 68

    publication....................................114–115

    renewal 69

    Stanford Copyright Renewal Database........69

Copyright Term Extension Act 66

copyright treaties 18–19

copyrighted works

    independent creation 32

    metadata and 134

    modicum of creativity 29

    originality standard 29

    public domain works 29, 32–33

copyright.gov pages...................................181

copyrights 13
  10% change rule 97–100
  AI (artificial intelligence) 21
  always under copyright 68
  artwork 72
  Berne Convention 113
  bundle of rights 16
  Canada 113
  CCE (Catalog of Copyright Entries) ... 69
  derivative works rights 118
  description 13–14
  distribution rights 118
  economics and 21
  enforcing 13
  existence 13–14
  foreign works 70
  history 20–21
  holder's death 112
  moral rights 21, 133
  MUD system 75
  object and 33
  orphan works 74
  other countries 113
  public display rights 118
  public performance rights 118
  published works before 1978 ... 69
  registering (See registering copyrights)
  reproduction rights 118
  right of attribution 21
  rights statements 114, 119
  sound recordings before 1972 ... 71–72
  technology and 20–21
  term of, authorship 111–112
  termination of transfer 112
  versus trademarks 95
  transfer 112
  unpublished works before 1978 ... 70
course packets, Cambridge University
Press case 98–99
court case citations 17
  creativity 30
Creative Commons (CC) license 119–120, 127
creative labor 23, 31
  tangible items 24
creator size 175–176
criminal liability 159
criticism, fair use and 80–82
crochet, granny squares 41

D

dance moves 42
de minimis copying 141, 146–147
death of author 112
derivative works 48, 118
  exceptions 33
  exclusive right to make 33
  first sale doctrine and 63
  licensing 57

MUD system 75
  originality standard 32
  registering 122
  repurposing 157
  right to make 157
  Sanders Sides 100
  Super Mario characters 99–100
descriptive fair use 96
diaries 123
digital copies, first sale doctrine ... 62
dilution, trademarks 91
distribution rights 118
documentation 27
dog toys, VIP company 94
domestic works, public domain and ... 68
Dr. Seuss cases 172–173
Drawfee videos 28
droit moral 127

E

enforcement
  Baby Yoda dolls 177
  Bernie Sanders mittens 177–178
  cardigan, Harry Styles 179
  commercialization of fanwork ... 171
  commercials 173
  competition with copyright holder ... 170–171
  creator size 175–176
  crochet 177–179
  Dr. Seuss cases 172–173
  fans celebrating 61, 169–170
  knitting 177–179
  musical fan adaptations 167–170
  musical parodies 167
events, photograph 58
expression of ideas 25–26

F

F Newsmagazine 9
fabric designs 45
  copyright notice 116–117
facts
  fictional facts 38
  government documents 39
  medical documents 39–40
fair use 15, 64
  art and 86–89
  celebrity social media photos ... 85
  collage work 83
  commenting and 80–82
  commercial context 85
  commercial copies 84
  copies and 83
  Copyright Act of 1976 and 77
  criticism and 80–82
  descriptive (classic) 96
  Emmy Statuette 85
  eyewear in advertisements 85

  four factors 77–80
  infringement and 140
  karaoke 84
  museum exhibits 83
  novels, condensing and sanitizing ... 84
  parody and 80–82
  preamble 77
  quotes in artwork 83
  scholarship 83
  teacher's work 84
  website 181
  website images 87
fan art, intellectual property and ... 103–104
fan conventions (cons) 105
fandoms 101
fanfiction, intellectual property and ... 103–104
fans celebrating 61, 169–170
fanworks 101
  borrowing grey area 105
  commercialization 171
  musical adaptations 167–170
fictional facts 38
fine art, photographs 55
first sale doctrine 62–63
  infringement and 140
First Sale Doctrine, art 87
fonts 43
Ford, Gerald 80
foreign works 70
  public domain and 68
four factors of fair use
  commercial 78
  effects of use 80
  nature of copyrighted work 79
  non-profit 78
  "Oh, Pretty Woman" 80–82
  qualitative and quantitative quantities ... 79
  transformative 78
functionality 15

G

games 46
Gay, Claudine 160
Getty Images 57, 178
"Girls" Beastie Boys 173
goodwill, trademarks 91
government documents 39
graffiti artists and moral rights ... 132–133
granny squares 41
Greenaway, Catherine "Kate" 46

H

Hamilton 173–174
Hbomberguy on plagiarism 161
heart of the work 79
HIPPA (Health Insurance Portability and Accountability) laws 39
how-to instructions 36

I

idea contracts 26–27
ideas
   as artistic challenges 28
   documenting 27
   encouraged 27
   protecting 15, 27
   solicited 27
   tangible medium of expression 25–26
   unsolicited 27
independent contractors 50–52
   commissioned work and 53
independent creation 32, 147
infringement 16, 139
   cease and desist letters 142–143
   copying 64, 145, 155–157
      subconscious 147–148
      substantial similarity 145–146, 149–154
   Copyright Claims Board 144
   criminal liability 159
   derivative work 157–159
   enforcers 140
   fabric designer 154–155
   independent creation 147
   innocent infringers 144
   nature 149
   notice and takedown system 140–142
   Online Copyright Infringement
   Liability Limitation Act 140–141
   pattern designer 154–155
   public domain 148–149
   results 143–144
   right of reproduction and 145–146
   right to distribute 158
   secondary 159
   social pressure 143
   substantial similarity 64
installation art 124
intellectual property
   copyrights 19
   fan art 103–104
   fan writing 103–104
   iPhone 20
   patents 19
   rights of publicity 19
   trade dress 19
   trade secrets 19
   trademark 19
   interviews 124

J

Jack Daniel's case 94
Jensen, Lynette 154–155
jewelry 45
Just Wanna for Makers series 9
Just Wanna Quilt podcast 9

K

karaoke 84
known representations 164
Koons, Jeff 86–87

L

Lapacek, Kim 28
legal assistance 74
letters (alphabet) 41
letters (correspondence) 123
library use 64
licensing 135–137
   derivative works 57
   first sale doctrine and 63
   infringement and 140
   permissions and 61–62
literary works
   computer programs/apps 123
   copyright notice 116
   copyright registration 122–124
   correspondence, private 123
   diaries 123
   interviews 124
   letters 123
Locke, John 23
Lockean Labor Theory 23
logos 42

M

maps 125
Marek, Katja 156
medical documents 39–40
merger doctrine 36
metadata 127
   copyright management and 134
Mickey Mouse in public domain 67
model releases, photographs 56
modicum of creativity 29–31
moral rights 21, 127–134
   art, craft, and quilt exhibitions 128
   copyright relationship 133
   Creative Commons (CC) license 127
   credit 128
   droit moral 127
   duration 130
   graffiti artists 132–133
   metadata 127
   photographs 55
   qualified items 129
   right against destruction of works by
   authors of recognized stature 130
   right of attribution 130
   right of integrity 130
   VARA (Visual Artists Rights Act) 127
   visual art 129
   waivers 131
motion pictures 125
MUD (main, underlying, derivative) system .. 75

museums
   fair use and 83
   fair use best practices 89
   open access to artwork 73
musical fan adaptations 167
musical parodies 167
musical works, copyright notice 116

N

nature 43, 149
NDA (non-disclosure agreement) 27
nominative use, trademarks 95–96
non copyrightable items 35–37
noncommercial use 22
non-profit educational use 78
non-protectable elements 15, 34
notice and takedown system 140–141
novels, condensing and sanitizing 84
numbers 41

O

"Oh, Pretty Woman" four-factor fair use
analysis 80–82
Online Copyright Infringement Liability
Limitation Act 140–141
open access to artwork 73
original work
   independent creation 32
   modicum of creativity 30–31
   originality standard 29
originality standard 29–32
orphan works 74
ownership, tenants in common 48

P

Paper Pieces 40
parody 80–82
patents 19
patterns 36, 156–157
   clothing 36
   infringement and 154–155
   sewing 36
performing arts, registering copyright 124
permissible uses 61
   classrooms 63
   fair use 64
   first sale doctrine 62–63
   library uses 64
   licenses 61–62
   permission, requesting 61–62
permissions 15
personhood theory 23
photographs 125
   access controls 58
   author 55
   Bernie Sanders 178
   CCB (Copyright Claims Board) 174
   covers 58
   derivative works 57

documentation for registration..................55
events 58
as fine art 55
model releases................................56
moral rights 55
public areas..56
as reference for artists........................ 56–57
registering 58
right of publicity 56
slavish copies 55
stock images......................................57
Unsplash..57
phrases 41
pitching ideas 27
plagiarism 160–161
Popeye and Super Mario characters 99–100
Prince's symbol 105
Project QUILTING..................................28
pseudonymous works 54
public display rights 118
public domain 15, 29
before 1923 66
copyright notice 68
domestic works 68
foreign works 68
infringement and 148–149
Mickey Mouse 67
Public Domain Day...............................65
published *versus* unpublished 68
published works 65–66
time period 66, 68
unpublished works 68
using works 76
Winnie-the-Pooh 67
Public Domain Dedication license (CC0) 120
public performance rights.........................118
publicity, right of publicity in photographs ...56
published works
commissioned works....................52
pre-1978 69
public domain 66
versus unpublished works 68
puppets 46

Q

QR code 11, 106
quotes in artwork, fair use and 83

R

Ratatouille the Musical....................167–168
reference art, photographs 56–57
registering copyrights 114, 121–122
applications 125–126
artistic works 124–125
CCB (Copyright Claims Board) and 162
compilations 122
derivative works....................................122
literary works................................ 122–124

necessity 126
performing arts.....................................124
website 181
relationships, copyrights 16
renewal records..69
Rent 49
reproduction rights 118
resources
copyright law 181–187
copyright.gov pages 181
Rice, Anne 103
right of attribution 21, 127, 128
right of integrity 128
right of publicity...56
Three Stooges case 102
right of reproduction 145–146
right to distribute 158
rights, copyright protection and 16
rights of publicity 19
rights statements................................114, 119
All Rights Reserved 119
No Rights Reserved 119
Some Rights Reserved 119
Rocky IV..105
Rogers, Ginger..92
Rogers test for trademarks............................92
Jack Daniel's case 94
University of Alabama.......................94–95

S

Sanders Sides... 100
scène à faire 45
scenes 45
scholarship, fair use and.............................83
secondary infringement 159
Section 103(a) 105
Section 303(a) of Copyright Law 70
separability 15
sewing patterns 36
shapes 40–41
short phrases...41
shtetl scenery 83
slavish copies 55
social dances 42
solicited ideas.......................................27
Sonny Bono Copyright Term Extension Act ...66
sound recordings
before 1972..71–72
copyright notice 116
source identifiers, trademarks.....................91
Stanford Copyright Renewal Database..........69
stencils...36
stock image photographs 57
stuffed animals 46
substantial similarity 145–146, 149–154
The Sunbonnet Babies Book 46
Sunbonnet Babies Primer 46

Sunbonnet Sue character 46
Super Mario characters 99–100
sweat of the brow.......................................31

T

tangible medium of expression...............25–26
tarnishment, trademarks 91
technology, copyrights and.....................20–21
templates..36
tenants on common 48
termination of transfer 112
theories of creating 22–24
Thimbleberries 154–155
Three Stooges case 102
titles..41
tolerated uses 61
toys 46
trade dress 19
trade secrets 19
trademarks..19
artistic relevance 92
blurring 91
classic fair use 96
versus copyrights 95
derivative works..................................99–100
descriptive fair use 96
dilution 91
expressive use 91, 93
function 90
goodwill..91
incidental use 96
Jack Daniel's case 94
likelihood of confusion............................91
nominative use..................................95–96
Rogers test..92
source identifiers 91
tarnishment 91
Three Stooges case 102
transferring copyright
assignment.................................... 135–136
licensing 136
reason for.. 136–137
transformativeness, fair use and 78
tropes..45
typeface 43

U

underlying work 113
The Unofficial Bridgerton Musical 168–170
unpublished works 68
pre-1978 70
unsolicited ideas.......................................27
Unsplash images 57
upcycling, first sale doctrine and.................63
U.S. appellate court citations 17
U.S. Copyright Office...................................18
Circular 33 34

Compendium of U.S. Copyright Office Practices..................18, 34
  non-protectable elements..........................34
U.S. district court citations...........................17
U.S. Supreme Court citations.......................17
USPTO (United States Patent and Trademark Office)...19, 20
  images..20
utilitarianism..22

V

VARA (Visual Artists Rights Act)............55, 127
  right of attribution..................................128
  right of integrity.....................................128
vicarious infringement.............................159

VIP dog toys...94
visual art
  Best Practices in Fair Use for the Visual Arts..88–89
  Code of Best Practices for Visual Arts........88–89
  moral rights...129

W–Z

Warhol, Andy...78–79
websites, images..87
Welcome to Night Vale...............................176
Winnie-the-Pooh in public domain..............67
Wolkoff, Gerald.................................132–133
words...41

work for hire
  commissioned works............................52–53
  copyright term..111
  employees vs independent contractors . 50–52
  independent contractors......................50–53
World Intellectual Property Organization.....19
writing, fair use best practices.....................88

About the *Authors*

Photos by Azueree Wiitalae © 2023

Sidne K. Gard (they/them) is the Managing Editor of *F Newsmagazine*, and is completing their BFA with an emphasis in Writing at the School of the Art Institute of Chicago in 2025.

Elizabeth Townsend Gard (she/her) is the John E. Koerner Endowed Professor of Law at Tulane University Law School, specializing in copyright, trademark, and entrepreneurship.

Visit Sidne online and follow on social media:

Website
sidnekgard.com

Visit Elizabeth online at:

Website
law.tulane.edu/faculty/full-time/
elizabeth-townsend-gard

Visit Just Wanna Quilt (where this project began)

Website
justwannaquilt.com

Podcast
Just Wanna Quilt

Facebook
Just Wanna Quilt